An Introduction to the New Testament for Catholics

Joseph F. Kelly

A Michael Glazier Book

LITURGICAL PRESS

Collegeville, Minnesota

www.litpress.org

4   5   6   7   8   9

Library of Congress Cataloging-in-Publication Data

Kelly, Joseph F. (Joseph Francis), 1945–
    An introduction to the New Testament for Catholics / Joseph F. Kelly.
      p. cm.
    ISBN 13: 978-0-8146-5216-9
    ISBN 10: 0-8146-5216-6
    1. Bible. N.T.—Introductions. I. Title.

    BS2330.3.K45 2006
    225.6'1—dc22   2005029712

To my brother Robert,
who deserves far more from me
than a book dedication

Contents

Acknowledgments

Mark Twomey, now retired from Liturgical Press, first asked me to do this book, and I thank Mark for his confidence and support. The LP publisher, Peter Dwyer, supported the project as has Mark's successor as editor at LP, Susan Hogan/Albach, and I am grateful to them both. Thanks also to Colleen Stiller for supervising the printing.

At John Carroll University, the former dean of the college, Dr. Nick Baumgarter, supported my request for a reduced load to work on this as did his successor, interim dean Dr. Sally Wertheim; my thanks to them both and to Dr. David LaGuardia, JCU academic vice-president who gave final approval to the load reductions.

My colleague, Dr. Sheila McGinn, has taught me a lot about the New Testament over the years, and I could not have written this book without all that she imparted to me. Much credit also goes to my graduate assistant, Mrs. Kathleen Philipps, who searched out information for me and who read this entire book more than once and at several stages; this is a better book because of her.

My sincerest gratitude, as always, goes to my wife Ellen who took time from her own busy schedule to make myriad sacrifices, large and small, so that I would have the time to write.

This book is dedicated to my older brother, Robert Donald Kelly, who greatly influenced me for the good when I was young and who, in 1962, introduced me to a wider world via a trip that changed my life. This book is a tangible sign of my gratitude to him.

Introduction

The first thing most readers see about a book is its title, and the title of this book may be a bit puzzling—a *Catholic* introduction to the New Testament? The New Testament belongs to all Christians, and the modern study of the New Testament has benefited from the enormous contributions by scholars of all Christian denominations as well as those by Jewish scholars who have provided ecumenical and appreciative studies of their ancient brother Jesus. Surely no one needs a Catholic introduction in the twenty-first century.

While I would not basically dispute these views, I still have found, as a classroom teacher and as a lecturer to religious education programs in the Diocese of Cleveland, Ohio, that there are problems and issues with the New Testament (NT) that are specific to Catholics. Like all Christians, we grew up in a certain tradition. We believe our Church to be faithful to the witness of the first disciples, yet we know that on some matters, such as the real presence of Christ in the Eucharist, we differ from some other Christians, who in turn often differ from one another. Specifically Catholic issues like this impact our approach to the Scriptures. Occasionally they can even be disturbing because some Catholics expect to find all the Church's current teachings and organization laid out in the Bible, and they become upset when, instead of bishops and priests, they read (even in modern Catholic translations) about "overseers" and "elders." And why doesn't the New Testament use the words we expect to find there, like "sacrament," or "Trinity"?

These may not be problems for scholars, but they are for students and people in the pew. Most modern NT introductions do not deal with these problems, considering them concerns for later generations and thus not belonging in a book on the NT. Such an approach can leave many readers confused, thus weakening their appreciation of Scripture.

What we will do here is concentrate primarily on the NT books and attempt to comprehend them within the communities that produced them. We will never understand what role the NT can play in modern Catholic life if we do not understand what it meant to the earliest Christians; we cannot understand what it means for us if we do not understand what it meant for them. But in our journey back to NT times we will also consider issues that may concern modern Catholics. We will not take a negative approach and try to prove our view is right while those of Orthodox and Protestant Christians are wrong. That is unscholarly, unecumenical, and contradicts Catholic teaching that Scripture is God's gift to all God's children, regardless of our differences. Rather, we will simply explain how Catholics have traditionally interpreted some biblical passages, accepting that there are some points on which all Christians do not now agree and hoping that ecumenical dialogue will someday bridge that gap.

This book has been kept concise in order to make it more useful for group work. It will give you a start by helping you to understand what modern scholars say about the individual books, and there will be an outline for every book to help you to grasp its structure. But you should keep a New Testament handy when reading this book, and nothing could be better than for you to read the New Testament on your own— to become familiar with its contents, to get a sense of each author's style (for example, Mark's popular-level writing differs considerably from Luke's refined prose), and to explore books that are not usually read during liturgies, such as the Third Letter of John.

Because of the foundational importance of the New Testament for Christian life, generations of scholars have proposed various theories for its interpretation, theories ranging from the shockingly radical to the disappointingly retrograde. We will walk a middle line, using the methods of modern study but staying within the general consensus of scholars. We will also look at some newer approaches.

Since the book is intended for students and the general reader, it will play down the technical terminology, but some is inevitable. The terms will be defined at their first appearance in the text, and in general we will use brief working definitions rather than long, elaborate ones. The emphasis throughout will be on clarity.

When using this book you will need a good modern Bible translation. Some older translations contain wonderful English phrases and images, but they are often inadequate. Many Catholic publishers offer reliable, reasonably priced complete Bibles or New Testaments. It would be better to have a complete Bible because the NT makes endless references to the Old Testament (OT), but it is possible to use this book with just a New Testament and to put off checking OT passages to another time.

Please try to get in the habit of citing the Bible by book, chapter, and verse. If you're part of a group and everyone is using the same edition, it is all right to say, "Please turn to page 173," but it is better to say, "Please turn to the Gospel of Luke, chapter 16, verse 4." That way people who have different versions or even the same version but in different editions will be able to find the passage under discussion.

You will notice that a disproportionate amount of the book focuses on the gospels. That is because these are the NT books most familiar to Catholics from liturgical readings and, of course, because they are the most important books since they deal with Jesus himself. This does not mean that questions about Paul or Peter or other NT figures are not important, but questions about Jesus carry far more weight for all believers. Furthermore, this is an introductory book that cannot go into depth. I had to make some choices and decided that the gospels should get the most attention.

This book introduces the topics; it cannot cover them in much detail. There are literally tens of thousands of books and articles on the New Testament. Scholars have written entire books on one verse. In 1974 a scholar wrote a two-volume, *849-page* book about the letter to the Ephesians, which runs to *seven* pages in a standard New Testament, for an average of 121 pages of commentary for every one page of text! So you can see that you will have no difficulty getting information about the NT.

Besides books like these, there are many books on specific topics, such as Jesus' birth, his crucifixion, his resurrection, Paul's life, the theology of particular books or writers, explanations of the symbols in Revelation, Palestinian geography (so that you know the country where Jesus lived), and even things like animals and plants in the Bible. So while I hope you will find this book handy, it can only get you started. At the end of the book, I will discuss some tools for further study.

And, of course, you must read the Scriptures themselves. As you will see many times in this book, nothing—not a book, a movie, not an educational video—substitutes for reading the Bible itself. All these others may help, but you will know the Scriptures best by reading them.

A final suggestion: enjoy yourself. Because of the mountain of scholarship on the Bible and its use for the most elaborate theological and dogmatic formulations, people can often be intimidated if not actually scared off from reading it. No way. The New Testament was produced by the first generations of Christians, our sisters and brothers in the communion of saints, and it was read by unsophisticated believers or, more often, read *to* illiterate believers. It was accessible then, and it is accessible now, not least because it is often a great read. It tells the story of the most remarkable person who ever lived and of how his disciples tried to work out the significance of his life, death, and resurrection for themselves, both individually and as members of communities. It includes some of the most famous narratives in the world, such as the birth of Jesus at Bethlehem; some of the most memorable tales, such as the Good Samaritan; some of the most immortal words, such as the Lord's Prayer; some of the most striking images, such as the pearly gates and streets of gold. It introduces us to great people who moved history, such as the apostle Paul, who brought Christianity from its Jewish birthplace into the heart of the Roman world. It also tells of the now anonymous people who took the difficult step of leaving the religions of their ancestors and families to become Christians.

Very encouragingly for us modern believers, the NT also shows the first Christians as fallible, weak, and sinful. Some of the Twelve squabble over who will get the highest place in heaven; Paul loses his temper and actually calls his converts in Galatia "fools"; in the Third Letter of John we read of a man named Diotrephes who enjoys being the head of the local church and bossing others around. We see the same people we see in the church today, and, who knows, we may occasionally even be looking in a mirror! But we always see real people, communicating with us, sharing their beliefs, their fears, and their hopes, and our shared humanity bridges any gap.

Distant yet familiar, challenging yet comprehensible, the New Testament is a precious heritage, and one we must make our own.

Abbreviations

NJBC	*New Jerome Biblical Commentary*
NT	New Testament
OT	Old Testament

Biblical Books

Old Testament (selected)

Gen	Genesis
Exod	Exodus
Lev	Leviticus
1 Kgs	1 Kings
1 Chr	1 Chronicles
Dan	Daniel
Isa	Isaiah
Nah	Nahum
Zeph	Zephaniah

New Testament

Matt	Matthew
Mk	Mark
Lk	Luke
Jn	John
Acts	Acts of the Apostles
Rom	Romans
1 Cor	1 Corinthians
2 Cor	2 Corinthians

Gal	Galatians
Phil	Philippians
Phm	Philemon
1 Thess	1 Thessalonians
2 Thess	2 Thessalonians
Col	Colossians
Eph	Ephesians
1 Tim	1 Timothy
2 Tim	2 Timothy
Tit	Titus
Heb	Hebrews
1 Pet	1 Peter
2 Pet	2 Peter
1 Jn	1 John
2 Jn	2 John
3 Jn	3 John
Jas	James
Jd	Jude
Rev	Revelation

Chapter One

Approaching the New Testament

The Bible has an odd distinction. Many people have not read it a great deal, yet they still know much of what is in it because they have heard it read at liturgies or seen movies or television programs about it. But reading the Bible itself can be a real surprise. For example, in 1 Corinthians 7:21-22, St. Paul says, "Were you a slave when called (to Christianity)? Do not be concerned about it. Even if you can gain your freedom, make use of your present condition now more than ever. For whoever was called in the Lord as a slave is a freed person belonging to the Lord, just as whoever was free when called is a slave of Christ." We can see the point the apostle wants to make, that being a Christian transcends all human conditions, but it disturbs us that he can say to someone who is owned by another human being, "Do not be concerned about it." In the Letter to Titus (2:9) we read, "Tell slaves to be submissive to their masters." These instances could be multiplied, and they reflect a very old biblical tradition: for example, in the book of Genesis, Abraham owns slaves. No matter how offensive this may be to modern Catholics, the Bible simply does not condemn slavery. We will take up this topic when we get to the Pauline Letters. I mention it here just to illustrate the point that the Bible can often contain surprises for those approaching it for the first time.

Yet many of us Catholics think that we know the Bible well because we have heard so many Scripture readings at Mass. The value of that cannot be overlooked, but there are two big drawbacks to learning the Bible this way. First, the liturgy's focus is the whole liturgy, not just the readings, and so when liturgists prepare the readings, they choose them for their liturgical value and effectiveness, and not primarily as ways to

1

teach about Scripture. This means that many parts of the Bible simply do not get read at Masses because they would not be liturgically effective. To use a common example, the Old Testament is filled with genealogies. That is because in the ancient world it was essential to know your family's roots. The First Book of Chronicles starts off with *nine full chapters of genealogies with more than 1,000 names.* You will never hear that at a liturgy for the obvious reason that it would be unbelievably boring. How can people at Mass be expected to pay attention to dozens of names being rattled off with the formula "and he begot a son, and his son begot his son . . ."? (A bishop friend of mine once said that just because the Bible is always inspired does not mean that it is always inspiring.) So no liturgist would use a genealogy as one of the readings, but this in turn means that people who know the Bible only through the liturgy have no sense of how important genealogies were to the ancient Israelites. The same could be said of many passages in the New Testament.

A second drawback to relying primarily on the liturgy to learn about the Bible is that the liturgy must use only excerpts. For example, we all know the story of the Good Samaritan from Luke's Gospel, but it does not stand alone. Luke put it where he did in the gospel because he wanted it to be read after one passage and before another one; he wanted his readers to see it in a particular context. Would any of us understand a modern book if we read only portions of it? We would know a lot about what was in the book, but we certainly would not understand it very well.

The best way to approach the New Testament is to read the different books in their entirety, although not necessarily in one sitting, and, eventually, the entire New Testament. This does not mean that there is no value to reading only parts of the books, as long as we remember that the authors hoped and expected their readers to read them as whole works. Furthermore, every part of the book contains God's word, and we should try to grasp all of that word.

Development of Doctrine

A problem for many Catholics is reading the contemporary church back into the New Testament. That can lead to some real surprises, such as when the First Letter to Timothy (3:2) says that a bishop should not be married more than once! (One of my Jesuit professors at Boston College said this was the least-preached-upon passage in the entire Bible.) The gospels of Matthew (8:4), Mark (1:30), and Luke (4:38) all tell us that St. Peter had a mother-in-law. There is only one way to get a mother-in-law. What's going on here? The answer is very simple. In the early church not all ministers were celibate. In the Middle Ages the popes decided that celibacy should be a requirement for ordination, as it is today, but we should not be surprised to find that the earliest church did not have every practice the contemporary church does.

So the earliest church had different views on slavery and celibacy, and these views have now changed, but what about doctrine? Many of us think that although some things may change, doctrine never has and never will. But this view must be understood more clearly. Let me give the classic example.

We cannot imagine the church without the New Testament, but the NT could not exist until all its books had been written. Scholars date the earliest book, Paul's First Letter to the Thessalonians, about the year 50 and the last book, the Second Letter of Peter, around 125. For the first two decades of its existence the church had no NT books, and it did not have all of them until 125. But just because the books existed, does that mean there was a New Testament, that is, a fixed collection of books considered to be inspired? No, because no one used the term "New Testament" to mean a collection of books until ca. 200. In fact, the first time any Christian said "These are the books of the New Testament," and listed the twenty-seven that we accept, was in 367. Does that mean the church was not "really" the church until 367? Of course not. It was the church before any books were written, and it was the church before all the books were written, and it was the church before someone decided on the current twenty-seven books. The church of the fourth century had changed from the church of the earliest believers by accepting a New Testament, a significant doctrinal change because the NT contains inspired teaching that has formed the basis for innumerable doctrines: for example, about the sacraments, the church, and, most obviously, Jesus.

No one can deny that changes occurred, but doesn't change compromise Catholic teaching? After all, how could the church have taught something that could change?

Catholic theologians contend that doctrine does not change in the sense of turning upside down what had previously been believed. Instead they say that doctrine develops: that is, the theologians look at a particular doctrine and draw out from it some points that had not previously been understood. Sometimes this development arises from purely theological work; other times it arises from new knowledge, often from outside theology. For example, when geologists and biologists showed that the creation account in Genesis 1–3 did not fit into what modern science tells us about the physical beginning of the world, Catholic scholars began to reconsider the Genesis creation account in theological and symbolic terms.

To use an example of purely theological development, we can consider the beliefs of Catholics in the Trinity, the three divine persons, truly individual yet united by their participation in the one divine substance. But the word "Trinity" does not appear in the NT, nor is there any statement about the divine persons and the divine substance. And even though Father, Son, and Spirit are frequently mentioned individually, they appear in only one biblical scene, the baptism of Jesus (the voice of the Father, the Incarnate Son, and the Spirit in the form of a dove). The three persons are also united verbally in a post-resurrection scene when Jesus urges his disciples to baptize "in the name of the Father and of the Son and of the Holy Spirit" (Matt 28:19).

For many conservative Protestants, this settles the matter. No word "Trinity" in the Bible means no Trinity, period. But, like Catholics today, many early Christians believed that the Holy Spirit, who inspired the people of Israel and the first Christians, remains active in the community. They believed that the community continues to be a source of God's revelation and presence in the world. The Church must be faithful to what the Scripture teaches but can also use Scripture as the basis to look deeper into particular questions. The Bible may not use the word "Trinity," but it refers to God the Father frequently; the Gospel of John emphasized the divinity of the Son; several New Testament books treat the Holy Spirit as divine. Many early Christians understandably backed away from an obvious conclusion—there were three gods—because that would make Christianity no different from polytheistic paganism. But other Christians wondered if there were some way to preserve the unity of God while still understanding Father, Son, and Spirit to be divine.

By the end of the second century Christian intellectuals spoke of a tri-unity or Trinity. In the third century many believed all the persons of the Trinity to be divine but in a subordinationist way, that is, the Father was the most important member of the Trinity but the Son was inferior or "subordinate" to him. (For some reason the third-century thinkers did not focus on the Spirit.) But in the fourth century an Egyptian priest named Arius drew the logical conclusions of subordinationism. If the

Son were inferior to the Father he could not really be divine. Arius thus insisted that the Son could be no more than a created being, the most wonderful creature that ever existed but a creature nonetheless. His potent arguments forced other Christians to refine their thinking about the Trinity. At two ecumenical councils, Nicea I in 325 and Constantinople I in 381, the church at large defined the Trinity in the way now so familiar to us from the Nicene Creed.

This exemplifies development of doctrine at its best. The ancient theologians did not violate the biblical teaching but sought to develop its implications. The Bible may not use the word "Trinity," but trinitarian theology does not go against the Bible. On the contrary, Catholics believe that trinitarianism has carefully developed a biblical teaching for later generations. This is a sensible approach because there was no way the writers of the New Testament could anticipate what questions would come up in the next 2,000 years. (Can any of us predict what Catholics will be asking about in the 41st century?)

These are ancient examples and general Christian ones. Is there a particularly Catholic modern one? Absolutely. Theologians routinely note that the approach of the First Vatican Council (1869–70) to the understanding of the church was juridical, hierarchical, and scholastic in its theology, whereas Vatican II (1962–65) was pastoral, collegial, and scriptural. It is the same church. No one has denied the teaching of Vatican I; on the contrary, it is an essential part of Catholic ecclesiology (theology of the church). But in the approximate century between the two councils, Catholic ecclesiology developed, and those developments manifested themselves at Vatican II. And whenever there is a Vatican III we will see yet more ecclesiological development.

So Catholics speak of "development of doctrine," a technical term meaning the process by which the church draws upon the revelation in Scripture and the lived experience of the Christian people to understand God's revelation more deeply in every age. The notion of development of doctrine can be applied to many other basic Catholic teachings that do not appear explicitly in the Bible, such as the real presence of Christ in the sacrament of the Eucharist (the NT does not use the word "sacrament" or the phrase "real presence"). It is crucially important for Catholics to grasp this notion of development because problems always arise when people take an ahistorical approach to the Bible and then get upset when the first church does not mirror the church of today.

An example of unacceptable change? Mark's Gospel announces in its first verse, "This is the good news of Jesus Christ, the Son of God."

The church simply could not say that Jesus Christ is not the Son of God because this would directly contradict the Scriptures. Admittedly this is a radical example, but it illustrates the distinction between change as development and change as turning doctrine upside down.

Miracles and Devils

Another problem that faces many modern educated Catholics is the apparently unscientific nature of so much of the Bible. We live in an era when science reigns supreme, and we instinctively look for scientific answers for almost every question. To many people, to disagree with science is to disagree with THE TRUTH. To make things worse for believers, the media often haul out the Bible as a symbol of obscurantism or backward thinking, such as when fundamentalists use the Bible to oppose the teaching of evolution in schools. To many modern people miracles contradict science, and evil spirits are relics of a superstitious age, yet the Bible speaks constantly of miracles and evil spirits.

Miracles do not contradict true science because true science cannot deal with the supernatural, only the natural. A miracle is not a magic trick like pulling a rabbit out of an empty hat. A miracle requires faith: faith in a good God who chooses to intervene in human affairs for purposes of God's own. Many people, including most scientists, do not believe in God, and thus for them there can be no miracles because there is no one to effect them. These people are *secularists*, that is, they accept the existence only of this world. This is not a viewpoint that Catholics share. We believe in a God who acts in the world through the church, through the Scriptures, through the sacraments, and through us, and we believe that God can also act in a way that seems to contradict the laws of nature, such as when a deadly, unstoppable cancer suddenly goes into remission after relatives and friends of the sick person have been praying for divine help. Skeptics could say that some natural force we do not yet understand caused the cancer to remit, and this is why we say that a miracle requires faith. We believe that God acts in the world and, for the sick person's family and friends, that in this case God did. (For example, if it was an unknown natural force, why did it suddenly work in this particular case?) Believing in miracles is not easy in a scientific era, but Jesus made it clear that faith is not supposed to be easy in any age.

Well, this sounds fine in theory, but in practice belief in miracles is often embarrassing. We have all seen on local television news stories about people seeing apparitions in their backyards or rushing off to venerate a bleeding statue. In Ohio, where I live, there was a recent case of "Jesus" appearing on the side of a soybean tank in a rural town. The "miracle" ceased when the owner of the soybean tank had it repainted! And why does the Church never seem to criticize this apparent superstition?

We must always remember that the Catholic Church has more than one billion members, and diversity of belief and practice must be expected. Maybe bankers and lawyers and surgeons are not rushing out to see the miraculous soybean tank, but if other people want to, they have the right to do so. As for the Church's attitude, bishops carefully avoid making statements about these phenomena, not wishing to endorse them but simultaneously not wanting to patronize the faith of those who believe in them. This is the appropriate pastoral step to take. We must also remember that *no one is more skeptical of "miracles" than the Church officials responsible for investigating them.*

Modern Catholics have to walk a middle line between secularist skepticism and superstitious credulity, acknowledging that God can act miraculously in this world but being very careful not to use the word "miracle" in an indiscriminate way. A good place to start understanding miracles is the New Testament, which treats miracles differently from what many people believe.

"Jesus wanted people to believe in him, so he performed miracles so that they would have to believe that he was the Son of God, right?" Plausible, but completely wrong. The gospels repeatedly make it clear that Jesus performed miracles not to give people faith but because they already had it. He tells the woman with the hemorrhage, "Daughter, your faith has made you well" (Luke 8:50). Notice: not "my power" but "your faith." He says the same thing to the blind beggar Bartimaeus (Mark 10:52), and he cures a paralytic because of his faith and that of his friends (Matt 9:2). So strong is this notion in the gospels that Mark says that when Jesus' neighbors in Nazareth had no faith in him, *"he could do no deed of power there . . . and he was amazed at their unbelief"* (Mark 6:5-6). Mark does not mean that Jesus did not have the actual power to do miracles, but that the people's lack of faith meant that they would not recognize his deed as the work of God.

In the New Testament miracles demonstrate that the world has not been handed over to the forces of evil. When Jesus calms the sea we hear echoes of the people of Israel passing safely through the raging waters, and Jesus' feeding the multitudes with loaves and fishes reminds Christians that he continues to feed them in the eucharistic meal. Jesus' resurrection triumphs over death, the most potent natural evil.

So when we read the Bible we should recognize that the biblical miracles are not challenges to science or flashy displays of divine power but rather the products of faith—faith in a God who constantly acts in the world, sometimes miraculously, for the benefit of those made in the divine image and likeness.

Miracles are one thing, but evil spirits? Hasn't science, especially psychology, proved that they don't exist? Good point. There is a real difference between believing that God acts in the world and believing in evil spirits. In fact, the devil plays little role in Catholic theology today, and the most obvious example of this is moral theology. When moralists deal with questions of right and wrong behavior, they simply do not refer to any evil spirit tempting people to do wrong, instead taking more subtle theological and often psychological approaches. And it is not just the moral theologians who feel this way. If you knew someone who said the devil was appearing to her or him, would you urge that person to see an exorcist or a psychiatrist? Remember also that, as with miracles, no one is more skeptical of demonic apparitions than church officials who investigate them and who often urge the afflicted person to seek psychiatric help.

But modern skepticism about the devil does not prove that evil spirits do not exist.

What to do? As we did with miracles, we should look at what the New Testament says. First, it is clear that ancient people believed in evil spirits. Some modern believers put that on the same level as the ancient belief in alchemy or a geocentric cosmos, but we will not understand the first Christians by treating their ideas with skepticism. Second, the Bible presents evil spirits not just as actual beings but also as symbols of evil's domination of the world before the coming of Christ. In Luke's temptation scene the devil tells Jesus that "all the kingdoms of the world" are in his power, a claim Jesus does not deny (4:5-8). When Jesus encounters demoniacs, that is, people possessed by evil spirits, they are people who have lost the image and likeness of God, a sign of the dominance of evil in the world. Whatever science says about the devil, evil is an inescapable fact, and the New Testament makes it clear that Jesus has come to liberate the world from evil, no matter what form it takes. One of those forms was an evil spirit known as Satan.

We could probably multiply the number of issues that might separate modern Catholics from the first Christians, but we will stop with a general principle: the church has changed constantly since the first century. It started in the Middle East, became a European religion, and now a majority of Catholics live in the "Third World" of Africa, Asia, and Latin America. It started with a handful of disciples huddled together after Jesus' death, and it now numbers more than one billion faithful. Change is a constant. When we bear this in mind we will not be surprised or, worse, disappointed to find that the first church was not an ancient, miniature version of our own, although we recognize that the potential for growth and development was there from the first.

But if we are separated from the first Christians we are also united with them in faith. The contours of belief have changed, but the basics have not: belief in one God, in Jesus Christ his Son who came to redeem the world from evil, and in the community that, under the guidance of the Holy Spirit, continues Jesus' work. Every reader can add to this list. I mention just these three to remind us all that while we must never overlook the gaps, we should also never overlook the bridges.

Faith does more than just unite us with the first believers. It also enables the New Testament to speak more fully to us. Christianity has played a significant role in world history, and every educated person should know something about it. This means that many people who have read and studied and even written about the New Testament have no personal relationship with it. To them it is work of historical and cultural importance. This is a valid viewpoint, and some scholars of the New Testament share it. But for Catholics this misses the point. To people of faith Jesus is not just an important historical figure but the Son of God who redeemed the world. The church is not just a historical force but the witnessing community that continues Christ's work. We should bear this in mind as we read the New Testament.

Exegesis

Exegesis means the interpretation of the Bible, and *hermeneutics* means the methods of interpretation. Since this is an introductory book we will concentrate on the standard methods of understanding the biblical text, although with a brief look at an important new type of exegesis.

Textual Criticism

One of the first things an exegete has to know is what exactly the Bible says. This may seem a bit obvious, but it actually involves an important discipline called *textual criticism*. Scholars call ancient books *manuscripts*, books written by hand (from the Latin words *scribo*, to write, and *manus*, hand). The author's original manuscript, for example the original of Luke's Gospel, is called the *autograph*, but no autograph of any biblical book, Old or New Testament, survives, so when scholars want to know what the biblical text says they have to prepare an edition from the surviving manuscripts, all of which are copies. This can sound a bit unnerving to believers, but *all* ancient literature, such as Greek and Roman works, derives from later manuscripts. So many biblical manuscripts survive that textual critics consider the biblical text to be most reliable of all ancient literature.

Textual critics take the oldest and most trustworthy manuscripts and compare them to see what is the most reliable reading. Let's say that one group of manuscripts has "Jesus said to *the* disciples" and another group has "Jesus said to *his* disciples." Scholars would have to determine whether the correct reading should be "his" or "the." They would have to do this for *every* biblical verse where ancient manuscripts did not agree. This is painstaking but obviously necessary work. Even when the text has been *established*, scholars still like to check manuscript references, just to be sure. If you use a Bible with notes, every so often you will see at the base of the page, "Other ancient authorities have . . . ." The *other ancient authorities* are manuscripts that have different readings from the commonly accepted text.

Linguistic Analysis

Once the exegete has a reliable text of the Bible, she/he then has to read it in the original language, which for the New Testament means Greek. This involves more than just learning to read ancient Greek. It also involves knowing how that language changed and developed over time and in different places.

The English word "bishop" comes from the Latin word *episcopus*, which in turn comes from the Greek *epískopos*. Although some more traditional versions still translate the word as "bishop," modern translations recognize that the office of bishop took decades to develop and that *epískopos* did not immediately have that meaning. So what exactly did it mean? The New Testament does not provide much help because the word appears there only five times, so scholars turned to the use of the word in non-biblical Greek. They found that it meant "overseer" or "superintendent," someone who had charge of a particular project or who held a supervisory office. In one text it meant the boss of a chain gang of prisoners! On the safe assumption that the first Christians did not mean the word in that sense, scholars concluded that the word meant one who guided the community and represented it to other communities, and the word could have different meanings in different contexts. Bearing this in mind, the translators of *The Jerusalem Bible*, a well-known and widely-used Catholic version, translated *epískopos* in 1 Peter 2:25 as "guardian" since the verse calls Christ the *epískopos* of our souls, while for 1 Timothy 3:2 and Titus 1:7 they used "president," that is, "one who presides" over the community. These *Catholic* translators used two different English words for the same Greek one, and *in neither case* did they use the word "bishop."

Sometimes scholars have to determine not just what the word meant when it was used, but also where it was used. Let me use an English analogy. If a Briton has a flat, she or he has an apartment; if an American has a flat, it means an automobile tire with no air in it. (Recall George Bernard Shaw's remark that Britain and America are united by an ocean but separated by a common language.) When we throw into the mix English as it is spoken in Jamaica, Canada, India, Australia, Ireland, and Scotland, we would find even more regional differences. In understanding the NT, scholars have to recognize the impact of local dialects on biblical Greek because within the time the NT book came into being, Christianity had spread from Judea to Syria, Asia Minor, Greece, Italy, and Egypt. The Greek text also includes occasional Semitic words, such as Jesus' saying *Talitha kum* when he cured a little girl (Mark 5:41).

Literary Criticism

Now that scholars have a reliable text and are able to read it, they have to recognize that the NT books are works of literature whose authors used literary devices. Sometimes literary analysis focuses on a verse or two, sometimes on an entire work. Let's start with entire works.

Anyone looking at a list of the NT books would be struck by how many have "Letter/Epistle to" or "Letter/Epistle of" in their titles. Since these books reflect the life of the earliest church when particular problems arose and communities wanted advice on what to do, it is natural that much of the literature would consist of letters to communities or individuals to answer these problems, for example when Paul writes to the congregation at Corinth. But these are not the first letters to be written in the ancient world, and just as scholars looked at non-biblical literature to understand the use of the word *epískopos*, so they look at ancient letters, both personal and public, to see how writers constructed them, for example, in a very general way, with the formal salutation, development of the body of the text, and then the valedictory at the end. Particular letters exhibited other qualities besides these general ones. This research also helped to prove that some books often called epistles, or letters, in fact are not. The "epistles" 1 John and Hebrews are sermons, while the letter of James is more of a treatise on morality.

Literary analysis has also helped scholars to understand the book of Revelation or Apocalypse (*apokálypsis* is the Greek word for "revelation"). No biblical book has caused more confusion than this one, largely because so many Christians have given it a literal interpretation and looked for signs of the end of the world, most recently as the year 2000 approached. This genuinely sad situation could be resolved by a little research.

We will look at Revelation in more detail later but will note here that apocalyptic literature was an ancient Jewish literary genre, widely used in periods of struggle, especially against outsiders such as the Greeks and Romans. Apocalyptic literature contained visions and riddles that could only be interpreted by the religious elite, and maybe not even by them. Dozens of apocalypses, both Jewish and Christian, survive, and the biblical book of Revelation must be understood as one example of this type of literature, although a very important one since it is in the Bible. Just as scholars read ancient letters to understand the biblical letters, so they read the ancient apocalypses to make sense of the biblical one. (Having read all the ancient ones, I can tell you that the end of the world becomes pretty boring by the tenth apocalypse.) If the people who keep looking to Revelation for signs of the imminent end knew this, fewer would be troubled by false concerns.

Literary analysis also helps us to understand individual verses or groups of verses. Picture someone who finally decides to read the New Testament and starts right at the beginning with Matthew's Gospel, only to run headlong into a genealogy. In fact, scholars can learn a lot from this genealogy, but the average reader finds it boring, and understandably so. But it was an essential literary device to Matthew's readers, many of whom were converted Jews, because the Old Testament provided genealogies for most important people. No conscientious Jewish writer would fail to include a genealogy.

As long as we're at the beginning of Matthew's Gospel, we can see an example of *metonymy,* the literary device of using one person to represent a group. After Herod's slaughter of the Holy Innocents, Matthew uses the image of "Rachel weeping for her children," the one woman Rachel symbolizing the women of Bethlehem. In Luke 13:16 Jesus refers to the woman bent over with infirmity as "a daughter of Abraham," meaning that she is a good Jewish woman, using Abraham as a metonymy for the Jewish people.

Sometimes the biblical writers use literary devices openly. In Galatians 4:24 Paul says that the two wives of Abraham, Sarah the mother of Isaac and Hagar the slave woman and mother of Ishmael, are *allegories* of the two covenants, the covenant of the Law and the covenant of promise brought by Christ. An allegory is a story told on one level, often literal, with its true meaning on a higher, spiritual level.

Virtually every literature uses *symbolism,* and so does the NT. Jesus' cursing of the fig tree (Matt 21:19-22) symbolizes the fate of those who do not listen to his words. The Gospel of John uses the symbols of light and darkness in the Prologue (1:1-18) when the light shines in the darkness, and then in the conversation with Nicodemus (3:1-21) who comes to Jesus at night and whom Jesus brings to the light with his words.

Although the phrase "the simple teachings of the Gospel" sounds okay, we must recognize that many New Testament writers were skilled craftspersons who created sophisticated literature. Their works will repay careful reading.

Historical Criticism

The historical difference between the New Testament era and our own is probably the most important point for us in understanding the Bible. We have already seen some examples of this, such as the need to understand what the word *epískopos* meant in the first century and why Matthew opened his gospel with a genealogy. We will look at it in more detail here, and this historical approach will appear throughout the book.

Basically historical criticism can fall into two categories. The first is the attempt to understand what the biblical writer meant when he wrote the book: what were his life circumstances? what were the concerns of his community? of what did he hope to convince his readers? what was the situation of his audience? why was he writing to this group or individual? how would they have responded to his writing?

These are not easy questions, and sometimes they cannot be answered, but it is essential to establish, as much as possible, what the author *meant* because only in that way can we know what the book *means* to us. Since we will be studying each of the twenty-seven NT books individually we will skip examples of this method for now and save them for the specific books.

The second broad category of historical criticism is understanding the background. The authors of the NT books take much about their readers for granted. In some cases this can be a specific event in their readers' community. For example, the elder who wrote 3 John commends someone named Demetrius and says that this man "has been approved by everyone," but we don't know who this Demetrius was or what he did to earn communal approval. But much else of what they take for granted is accessible to us. In Acts 11:28 Luke speaks of a famine that occurred during the reign of the emperor Claudius. That is the only mention of Claudius in the NT, but we know from Roman historians that Claudius reigned from 41 to 54, succeeded the assassinated emperor Caligula (37–41), married four times, initiated the Roman conquest of Britain, and was poisoned by his wife Agrippina so that Nero, her son by a previous marriage, could become emperor (later showing his ingratitude by having her murdered). The average reader does not have to know a lot of details about Claudius but must know that Christianity grew up in the Roman empire. In fact, we also know that famine swept through the eastern Mediterranean (where this chapter of Acts is set) from 46 to 48, so we are able to situate this event chronologically.

Claudius is but one example. Non-biblical sources tell us about Herod and his descendants, about Augustus during whose reign Christ was born, Tiberius during whose reign Christ lived, and Pontius Pilate, the Roman governor who sentenced him to death. We also know much about the Jewish history of this period. This historical background situates the biblical figures in time and space, thus giving them an immediacy they would lack if we knew nothing about the framework in which the biblical events occurred.

But understanding the historical setting of the NT involves more than situating people and events in time and space. We must also learn that the ancients lived in a different mental and psychological world from us. In general they lived shorter lives. Death was close to them; the infant mortality rate demanded that a woman become pregnant six or seven times just to ensure that she would have two or three children survive to adulthood. Rudimentary medical skills could not counteract contagious diseases, and people feared an unstoppable plague. People acknowledged slavery as a normal part of economic and social life, and they accepted monarchy as a normal form of government. There was no "separation of church and state." People accepted that religion and politics went together; it was not uncommon for pagan kings to claim that they were gods on earth. No one considered ethnic or racial prejudice to be wrong; on the contrary, the Jews believed that God had chosen them as his special people, something the Romans considered ridiculous because their world empire proved that the gods favored them, an idea that never impressed the Greeks who considered virtually all non-Greeks to be barbarians. The world, indeed all of creation, was small. Few people traveled, and scientists believed that the planets, which included the sun and the moon, traveled around the earth in concentric circles in a cosmos of limited size. Most people were illiterate. Finally, ancient society thought nothing of consigning half of the human race to the status of inferior beings. The Greek philosopher Aristotle was just one of many thinkers who "proved" that women were weak, emotional, and less intelligent than men, and therefore should be kept in a permanently subordinate state of life.

This catalogue could go on a while longer, but even these references warn us that we should not think of ancient people as being exactly like us but living in a distant age. They certainly shared many of our views—they wanted to be happy, to love and be loved, to succeed at their professions—but in many other ways they lived in a world we cannot fully comprehend, just as they could not fully comprehend a world of travel, advanced medical care, democracy, and equality.

Feminist Exegesis

In recent decades several specialized forms of exegesis have emerged, including feminist exegesis, which some people fear is a radical plot to reinterpret the Bible. But, like all scholars, feminist exegetes must adhere to the biblical text, understand the meaning of the Greek words, look for literary devices, and see the Bible against its historical background. The real achievement of feminist exegesis has been to call attention to biblical passages that point to an active role for women in the first church, passages previously overlooked by male exegetes.

Several years ago I assigned to a group of graduate students an article on women in the Gospel of John, an article that argued for a strong role for women in that gospel (and was written by a Catholic priest-exegete, the late Father Raymond Brown). I asked a provocative question. If this gospel really does portray an active role for women, why didn't anyone notice it for the last two thousand years? The women students all knew the answer: because no one was looking.

When we look carefully at the NT we find a significant role for women. In *all four* gospels the first witnesses of appearances by the risen Christ are women—a significant fact because in the ancient world women could not give witness in court unless men verified their testimony. Obviously the gospel accounts of the women at the tomb were historically true, because the evangelists would certainly have mentioned male witnesses if any were there. All Catholics know the story of Jesus' apostles congregating together after his ascension, but Luke mentions that among those praying in the upper room were "some women, *including Mary the mother of Jesus . . .*" (Acts 1:14); few Catholics realize that Mary was still active in her son's movement after the resurrection. When Paul writes to the community in Rome (Rom 16:1-16) he mentions numerous women, such as the *deacon* Phoebe, his fellow-worker Prisca, the *apostle* Junia, and several other women who were part of his mission. Prisca is also mentioned in Acts, where she is a *teacher* (18:26), an office later denied to women (1 Tim 2:12).

The earliest Christians did not have churches, but rather met in the houses of wealthy people because they needed large houses. In the letter to Philemon, Paul greets Philemon and his wife Apphia and "the church that meets in *your* house" (vv. 1-2). In Greek the word for "your" is in the plural, something not evident in English, so the local church met in the house of the husband and wife.

This brief look at feminist exegesis does not exhaust the topic nor does it mean that all scholars necessarily agree with all the conclusions of feminist exegetes. But it does illustrate how valuable it is to look at the Bible with a different eye. Are their other different eyes in the field? Definitely. For the most part European and North American scholars have dominated exegesis. We are just now beginning to listen to Latin American and African exegetes, who ask what the Bible says to the impoverished Christians of the Third World. Spurred on by the events of September 11, 2001, many Christians now realize that they must know more about Islam and its scriptures and that they must invite Muslims to dialogue with them. Who can say how our understanding of the Bible will change as we interact with our Muslim sisters and brothers for whom the Bible is a sacred book and Jesus is a sacred figure, although less important than the Qu'ran and the prophet Mohammed?

Exegesis continuously changes, continuously reacts to new situations, and continuously reveals the meaning of the Bible in new and sometimes significant ways.

Chapter Two

The Historical Background

To understand the world in which Jesus grew up we have to go back, at least briefly, to the fourth century B.C.E. and the career of Macedonian king Alexander the Great (356–323 B.C.E.). Having conquered the Greek city states, in 334 he led an army against the Persian empire, and most of the Near East fell under his rule, including a small Persian province known as Judah. Alexander personally had little effect on the Jews, but he brought them into a world that looked to the West rather than the Near East.

After his death his generals divided up his empire, becoming kings of Egypt and Syria. To establish their rule they introduced Greek language and culture into non-Greek societies, a process called Hellenization. This explains something that often surprises the reader of the New Testament—why a collection of books written almost entirely by Jewish writers is written in Greek. In the Eastern Mediterranean world Greek was the language of government, business, and learning, and as the Christians moved into that world they had to speak its language.

The two Macedonian dynasties in Syria and Egypt often warred with one another, with much of the fighting occurring in Judah, which was left impoverished. Many Jews left their homeland for new opportunities, thus significantly increasing the size of the *Diaspora*, a Greek word meaning "dispersion," still used today to refer to Jews living outside the land of Israel. The Diaspora had started centuries before the Hellenistic age, but now Jews settled in many Greek-speaking areas, such as Antioch in Syria and Alexandria in Egypt, which would become major centers of early Christianity.

By the mid-third century B.C.E. the Alexandrian Jews used Greek so much that community leaders decided that the Torah, the first five books of the Old Testament, should be translated into Greek. The translation became popular in the Diaspora and eventually included all the biblical books. Tradition claimed that seventy translators had done the work, and this Greek version became known as the *Septuagint* or the "Work of the Seventy." The writers of the NT cited the OT hundreds of times, and they almost always used the Greek version even when they were translating citations made by Jesus, who obviously did not speak Greek to Galilean peasants. Scholars abbreviate the Septuagint with LXX.

LXX also helps to answer a criticism that often arises about Matthew's Gospel. At 1:23, Matthew quotes Isaiah 7:14 as "a virgin will conceive," the reference being to Jesus' mother Mary. Yet some critics point out, correctly, that the Hebrew text does not say "virgin" but rather "young woman." They then go on to accuse Matthew of changing the wording to support the Christian belief in the virginal conception of Jesus. But the Septuagint version of Isaiah says "virgin." Matthew did not change the text; instead, he quoted a Greek translation of the passage *made by Jews.*

A Greek dynasty ruled the Jews until the second century B.C.E. when the Jews revolted and won independence in 164. In 63 B.C.E. the Jewish kingdom passed under Roman rule. The Jews were part of a state that was not only in the West but stretched all the way to Spain. Jesus, all his disciples, and all of the first missionaries lived in the Roman world, and that explains Christianity's expansion primarily to the West.

The existence of an independent state remained in the hearts of the Jews, but the Romans ruled efficiently. They tolerated religious diversity and often showed considerable understanding of Jewish traditions. They just wanted peace and taxes. The Romans worked with local leaders as long as they remained loyal. In Judea they chose a half-Jew named Herod (37–4 B.C.E.), a violent, ruthless man. After his death Rome worked with his descendants, the Herodian dynasty, several of whom appear in the gospels and the Acts of the Apostles. Sometimes the Romans dispensed with local rulers, as in 6 C.E. when they deposed one of Herod's sons and put Judea under the overall rule of the Roman governor of Syria. Galilee, where Jesus grew up, was ruled by Herod Antipas (4 B.C.E.–39 C.E.), a son of Herod; when Jesus went to Judea he encountered the Roman governor, Pontius Pilatus (26–36 C.E.).

Although the Romans ruled no more harshly than native monarchs would have, many Jews resented these foreigners, and several revolts broke out. In 6 C.E., when Jesus was a boy, one of his countrymen,

Judas the Galilean, led a revolt against Rome. Other revolutionaries also arose, claiming to be kings. The Roman fear of a "king of the Jews" was real, and this contributed to Pilate's suspicions about Jesus, especially since the gospels tell us that one of Jesus' contemporaries, Barabbas, was a revolutionary. More than nationalism inspired the revolts. Often social, political, and economic grievances lay behind them. Many revolutionaries were peasants who had lost their land and their livelihood and saw overthrowing the existing system as their only hope.

In spite of underlying tension, no major revolt broke out during Jesus' public career. In 41 a grandson of Herod, Herod Agrippa I, became king of Judea, although subject to the Roman governor of Syria. But he died in 44, and Roman governors again ruled, now with increasing inefficiency and corruption. In 52 Herod Agrippa II, a son of Herod Agrippa I educated in Rome, assumed rule in some parts of the old kingdom such as Galilee, but the Romans continued to rule Judea directly. Both Herods appear in the Acts of the Apostles.

Jewish tolerance of Roman rule came to an end in 66 C.E., and the Jews revolted. In 70 the city of Jerusalem fell, and the revolt was effectively over. A second revolt broke out in 132 and lasted until 135, but the Romans and later the Byzantines ruled Judea until the Muslim conquest in the seventh century.

Thanks to the efforts of Paul and other now anonymous missionaries, by the year 70 C.E. Christianity had moved largely into Gentile territories. The history of Judea after 70 had little direct impact on the books of the New Testament, and neither did the history of Rome. Although Rome is always in the background, the Christians seem to have lived their own lives independent of the larger events in the empire. This should not surprise us. The average pagan Roman also was little affected by the scandals of the imperial court, the succession of emperors, or the foreign wars. Even Nero's notorious persecution of the Christians for supposedly having started the great fire of 64 does not appear directly in the New Testament, although if, as Christian tradition claims, the persecution claimed the lives of Peter and Paul, it certainly affected the New Testament. Of all the NT books, only Revelation focuses directly on Rome.

Let us now move from political history to a look at the world in which Jesus and his disciples lived.

The Temple Mount at Jerusalem

The World of Jesus

Too many Christians of all churches often overlook that Jesus, his family, and all his first disciples were Jewish, and as we shall see when we get to the Acts of the Apostles, after the resurrection most disciples did not want to break with Judaism but actually continued to worship in the Jerusalem Temple. Differences soon surfaced and a break between Christianity and Judaism resulted, but there is nothing in the life of the early church to provide any justification at all for anti-Jewish sentiments on the part of Christians. Pope John Paul II emphasized this on his visit to Israel in 2000.

Reconstructing the Judaism of Jesus' day has proved surprisingly difficult. Most writings, especially those of the rabbis, date well after the New Testament. In some cases scholars feel comfortable reading some of the later elements back to the first century, but in general they use the later material cautiously. Yet there is one invaluable source for first-century Judaism.

The Jewish writer Josephus (37–*ca.* 100 C.E.) came from a priestly noble family. When the revolt broke out, he joined the Jews as an officer, but after being captured by the Romans in 67 he went over to their side. After the war he lived in Rome and wrote about Jewish history and culture. Although reviled in Jewish tradition as a traitor, he provides invaluable information about Judea at the time of the NT. His description of Jewish customs also helps us to understand the Judaism of Jesus' day.

The obvious question would be: does he say anything about Jesus? This is disputed. One manuscript of his works includes references to Jesus but openly calls him the Messiah (see below) and speaks of his resurrection, hardly the sentiments of a believing Jew. Most scholars believe that a later Christian editor added the passage. Josephus does, however, mention John the Baptist as a preacher of righteousness whom the Roman puppet king Herod Antipas arrested and executed.

There are many places in which Josephus helps us to understand the New Testament. Let me cite a famous one. All Catholics know the story (Mark 6:17-29; Matt 14:3-12) of how John the Baptist criticized Herod Antipas for marrying Herodias, the estranged wife of his brother. She encouraged her daughter Salome to dance sensuously in front of the king, who impetuously said he would give her whatever she wanted. Prompted by Herodias, Salome asked for and received the head of John the Baptist on a platter. But the gospels *nowhere* mention the name of

Herodias' daughter. Josephus, who does not mention the dancing incident, tells us that the girl's name was Salome.

First-century Judaism had many features that figure into our understanding of the NT, such as ritual washings and religious fasting. We will consider just four important points: the Jerusalem Temple, the Law, the Messiah, and Apocalypticism/Eschatology.

The Jerusalem Temple

King Solomon built the first Temple in Jerusalem in the tenth century B.C.E., and the conquering Babylonians destroyed it in the sixth century B.C.E. When the Jews who had been exiled to Babylon returned in the late sixth century they rebuilt the Temple, but not to the glory of the earlier edifice. Solomon's Temple had been a royal structure, but without a king from David's line the Temple became the province of the high priests. The Temple Jesus visited was built by the notorious Herod, partly as self-glorification, partly to pacify the Jews who loathed him, and partly to show his Roman overlords the splendor of his kingdom. He began the work about 20 B.C.E.; it was not finished until 62 C.E., just four years before the revolt against Rome and eight years before the new building's destruction.

Detailed descriptions and archaeological remains make this building well known. It was enormous, about two hundred yards long and eighty yards wide, with many specific sections, such as the Holy of Holies, the innermost shrine, surrounded by the Priests' Court, beyond which was the Court of Israel, open to all male Jews, and beyond that the Women's Court, open to all Jews but beyond which women could not go. The priests, usually from aristocratic families, offered daily sacrifices there, mostly of animals but often of grains. Many Jews gave gifts to the Temple, and its beauty and wealth were widely famous in the Roman empire. Jesus' disciples (Luke 21:5) were not the only small-town visitors to look at it in amazement.

The Law

The Law has always posed problems for Christians, largely because of the difficulties it posed for the apostle Paul. A fervent Jew, Paul believed that God had given the Law to Israel, but he also believed that the life of Jesus had given a new meaning to the Law (as we shall see when we get to Paul's letters). Furthermore, the Law presented him and other missionaries with a serious pastoral problem since many Gentile (non-Jewish) converts did not wish to embrace all the demands of the Law. Christian interpretations of the Law in later centuries, especially the Middle Ages, made things worse as one verse in Paul, "the letter kills but the spirit gives life" (2 Cor 3:6), was widely believed to condemn the Law in contrast to the spiritual salvation brought by Jesus. All that did was further the view of Jews as hopeless legalists, which overlooked that Jesus and his parents obeyed the Law (Luke 2:21-38) and that in Matthew's Gospel (5:17-18) Jesus said that he had not come to abolish the Law but to fulfill it and that the Law would persist till heaven and earth pass away—a very strong endorsement of the Law's value. If Jesus thought that way, should we think otherwise? Modern ecumenical Catholics must look openly and sympathetically at this remarkable gift from God to the Jewish people.

"The Law" is the usual English translation for the word *Torah*, but the Hebrew word means "teaching" or "instruction." God gave the Jews *Torah* in the first five books of the Bible (Genesis, Exodus, Leviticus, Numbers, Deuteronomy), believed by the Jews, including Jesus (Matt 19:8), to have been written by Moses. The Torah contained the will of God for his people, and pious Jews could be sure that if they lived by the Torah, they would please God. Living by the Torah did not mean just fulfilling legal obligations. Many of us Catholics have the notion that, until Jesus came along, the Jews focused only on the letter of the Law, but we must remember that as early as the eighth century B.C.E. the great prophet Isaiah warned: "What to me is a multitude of your sacrifices, says the Lord . . . . Trample my courts no more; bringing offerings is futile . . . remove the evil of your doings from before my eyes; . . . seek justice, rescue the oppressed, defend the orphan, plead for the widow" (Isa 1:11-17). The prophet makes it clear that external legal observations and trappings mean nothing if there is not concern in our hearts for those in need. Some ancient Jews did think that following regulations was all that God wanted from them, but people like that exist in every age and society (and church). Most Jews wanted to follow the requirements of the Law, but to do so with the right attitude.

Jewish scholars pored over the biblical text and wrote commentaries on it. Inevitably some commentators interpreted the Law very strictly while others took a more open approach; their give-and-take enabled them to understand more deeply the ramifications of the Law and to make it more meaningful in the lives of the people.

The Law represented more than just a guide to living. It guaranteed that the Jews would remain God's chosen people if they observed it. Fidelity to the Law represented fidelity to God. No evidence survives that the average Jew considered the Law an impossible burden to carry. We must remember this when we read in the gospels about Jesus' constant run-ins with legalistic Pharisees. His opponents did not represent the whole Jewish people.

The Messiah

The word "Messiah" usually has the connotation of "redeemer," but the word originally meant someone who was anointed, often a king of David's line but also a priest (Lev 4:3-5). The name "Christ" is from the Greek *christós* or "anointed one." (It is not, as I was once asked, Jesus' last name.) But in the centuries just before Jesus' birth, when the Jews came under foreign rule, the meaning of the term changed more and more to mean a deliverer, one who would rid Israel of foreign tyrants. Belief divided into two types of messiahs, a royal one and a priestly one, and some people believed in both or in someone who would combine the two. Some Jewish texts refer to a heavenly messiah, such as the Son of Man in the Book of Daniel, a second-century B.C.E. work. But most sources saw the Messiah in political terms.

Christians routinely think of Jesus as the Messiah, but in the gospels he consistently avoids using that term for himself, and in the first part of Mark's Gospel he silences those, such as demons, who use it of him. Jesus feared that any use of the term would cause people to misunderstand his mission, which was to redeem people from sin, not to drive the Romans from Palestine. He was right to worry. His references to the kingdom of God or the kingdom of heaven were misunderstood by his disciples. In Mark's Gospel, Jesus was willing to accept the term Messiah only after he had told the disciples that he must suffer and die and that he would redeem not by power but by suffering. Yet the title died out when Christianity moved outside Judea. It does not appear in the epistles, most of which were written to Gentile converts for whom the term could be even more confusing than to the Jewish disciples. Although Jesus tried to convince people of a new idea of the messiah as one who would redeem by suffering, the notion of political messiah was so ingrained that some of Jesus' Jewish opponents as well as suspicious Romans did not make much distinction between popular belief and what Jesus had to say.

Apocalypticism and Eschatology

These two concepts are often linked. *Eschatology* is a set of beliefs about the "last things," the ultimate destiny of individuals and the whole created order. *Apocalypticism* is a belief in the imminent end of things, and is frequently expressed in apocalyptic ("revelatory") literature describing the end, when God will appear to set things right. God's appearance is marked by the heavens opening and/or signs in the sky and/or a cosmic battle between the forces of good and evil. The word comes from the Greek word *apokálypsis,* which means "revelation." We can easily see how eschatology and apocalypticism could be linked, but we must be careful in saying anything definite about either of them. They do not tell us about actual events. No one could accurately predict the end of the age nor could anyone be sure in what form God could come upon the world.

Most scholars believe that these two, and especially apocalypticism, arose from a puzzlement on the part of the ancient Jews as to why they, the Chosen People, continually found themselves under the thumb of foreign conquerors, such as the Persians, Macedonians, and Romans. The prophets had provided one answer, that this is how God punished the Jews for their unfaithfulness, an idea that later caught on among Christians. It has a distinct psychological appeal. We are not really being oppressed; we are doing this to ourselves. In other words, we are still in control. We must assert our goodness to redeem ourselves.

In the second century B.C.E. some Jews provided a new explanation for the people's suffering: that it was caused by demons. The most familiar demon, Satan, plays a small role in the OT; he is mentioned by name only three times. But in the second century the Jews adopted a dualist explanation of the cosmos. On the one side God led the forces of good; on the other Satan led the demonic forces. We suffer because the demonic forces oppress us. Linking up with eschatology, apocalypticism taught that at the end of the age the heavenly forces would descend upon the earth and defeat the forces of evil, vindicating God's rule and saving God's people. Not surprisingly, apocalyptically-minded Jews linked their oppressors (the Romans in Jesus' era) with the demonic forces.

Many Jews wrote apocalyptically oriented books that did not get into the OT and are thus unknown to larger audiences. The apostle Paul knew of apocalyptic literature and held apocalyptic ideas, although in less elaborate form than the author of the book of Revelation. Many

Jews linked these views to the Messiah, who would work with God to defeat the demons at the end of the age. Scholars debate how strongly Jesus accepted these views. Although we can never be sure how strongly Jesus or most of his followers held apocalyptic and eschatological views, we must consider them as part of the background of their lives.

Jewish Groups of Jesus' Day

Ancient Judaism was not monolithic, and four Jewish groups played prominent if very different roles in the life of the people. One group, the *Zealots*, was composed of dissident Jews, often landless peasants, who favored the violent overthrow of the Romans and their Jewish supporters such as the Herodian dynasty. Some Zealots acted like modern terrorists, assassinating individual Romans, often noncombatants, with no warning. The Romans called them *sicarii* or "dagger carriers." In the year 66 the Zealots' moment arrived when they raised a revolt against Rome, and found, to their surprise, large segments of the population, even some priests and aristocrats, joining them in the doomed cause.

Simon the Zealot, one of the Twelve (Luke 6:15; Acts 1:13), had no apparent influence on Jesus or his other disciples, nor does the NT provide any evidence for Zealot influence on the Christians after Jesus' life. The Jewish revolt impacted the Christians in Judea, and some Jewish Christians left their homeland because they could not in conscience join a political revolutionary movement. But we can trace no Christian teaching or institutional development directly to the Zealots. They mostly help us understand some of the popular reaction to Jesus' preaching and life.

The *Essenes* formed a second group in first-century Judaism. Jewish writers describe them as belonging to a philosophic community and withdrawing from the world in order to practice virtue. In the late 1940s and early 1950s scholars discovered and deciphered the Dead Sea Scrolls, a name given to a collection of documents (scrolls) found in caves at a site called Qumran on the northwest shore of the Dead Sea. The scrolls describe a community of pious Jews who had withdrawn from Jerusalem in order to live a ritually pure life, which they did until 68 C.E. when the invading Romans destroyed the community, causing the Jews to hide the scrolls in nearby caves where they lay undiscovered until the mid-twentieth century. Most scholars now believe the Qumran community was indeed Essene.

The impact of the Essenes on Jesus and the Christian movement has always been the subject of debate. Some writers initially thought that the scrolls had effectively explained away Christianity as a movement that simply borrowed Essene ideas, a view no one holds today. Now scholars value the scrolls for telling us a great deal about the Judaism in which Jesus grew up. It is easy to find similarities between Christianity and the Qumran community but virtually impossible to find a definite one-to-one relationship. Like the Christians, the Essenes believed themselves to be a group chosen by God; they believed in an apocalyptic end of the world; they interpreted the books of the OT in a way that applied directly to themselves. But many Jews had apocalyptic leanings, and more than one group found biblical support for its views. And while the Christians may have considered themselves a special group chosen by God, they did not reject Jewish society and move into the desert. On the contrary, they stayed in Jerusalem and brought the message to the very Jews the Qumran community had shunned. There are also many dissimilar elements, most notably that while the Qumran community had no use for the Jewish monarchy or the Romans, the Christians emphasized their acceptance of the political order ("Render unto Caesar that which is Caesar's," Matt 22:21; "Fear God; honor the emperor," 1 Pet 2:17), even to the point of acknowledging the Herodian dynasty as Paul is portrayed as doing in Acts (25:13-27). The Christians decided to work in the world rather than flee from it.

The Essenes may have wielded direct influence on Jesus or his disciples, but to date no one has discovered in earliest Christianity any Essene elements that could not also have come through mainstream Judaism or other groups.

The *Sadducees* are much better known than the first two groups, but they actually play a rather small role in the New Testament. They only appear in three of the gospels (John does not mention them) and in the Acts of the Apostles, which mentions them more often than the gospels of Mark and Luke combined. They came from the ruling class, although not all aristocrats were Sadducees, and they had little to do with the mass of the people. Their name probably derives from Zadok, a priest in the reign of David (1000-961 B.C.E.). Like most aristocrats, they lived well and had no real interest in changing the status quo. They had little to do politically under the Romans and the Herods, and they put their efforts into Temple service and interpreting the Law, which they did very conservatively; for example, they denied the notion of resurrection as a new idea not found in the Torah (Acts 23:6-10). They were not fond of prophets or others who might stir things up, but, significantly, they ignored Jesus while he was preaching in Galilee. Only when he went to Jerusalem, the home of the Temple, did they oppose him. Matthew has passages that join the Sadducees with the Pharisees as opponents of Jesus, suggesting that their opposition to Jesus (or his followers) may have been deeper than the few gospel references suggest. Both the Sadducees and the Pharisees employed *scribes* to keep records for them, which is why they often appear in the gospels.

The *Pharisees* stand out in the New Testament as opponents of Jesus, something for which Christian history did not forgive them. The English word "pharisaic" means "self-righteous" and "hypocritical." The word is rarely used today, but it appears frequently in unecumenical ages, a testimony to how this group's reputation has suffered. Yet much of their unfortunate reputation is undeserved. The apostle Paul was a Pharisee (Phil 3:5). He did not repudiate his earlier career, but even boasted of it to the Jewish king Herod Agrippa II (Acts 26:5). Luke, who often treats the Pharisees harshly, still tells us (Luke 7:36-50) that Simon the Pharisee invited Jesus to dinner, an invitation he accepted, and in the Acts of the Apostles Luke shows the Pharisee Gamaliel convincing other members of the Jerusalem council to free the apostles who had been arrested (Acts 6:34-42). Some Pharisees even became Christians (Acts 15:5).

The word "Pharisees" most likely means "the separated ones," suggesting that the Pharisees, who first appear in the late second century B.C.E., separated themselves from other Jews not physically but by their observance of the Law. They lived a simple life and interpreted the Law accurately, says the historian Josephus, and were thus popular with the people. They did not renounce the Temple, but they formed a lay movement that had its power base in the *synagogue* or meeting house. This was a logical development because the Jerusalem Temple was a distant icon, and many pious Jews wanted to study and discuss the Law in their own villages. The Pharisees' popularity made them a political power.

The Pharisees survived the Roman conquest and continued to influence the people. They were less conservative than the Sadducees, accepting the resurrection of the dead and adding their own interpretations to the Law. Sometimes they protected the Law by making their own requirements more stringent on the theory that if a pious Jew did not violate the stricter Pharisaic injunction, that person could not possibly violate the Law. In fact, many of their debates with Jesus about the Law dealt not just with the Torah but also with their interpretations.

We know the Pharisees primarily as opponents of Jesus, which some of them were. But we must be fair to them. Some Pharisees misunderstood

Jesus, fearing that his teaching might undermine the Law, for example on the issue of picking grain on the Sabbath (Mark 2:23-28). Later Christians, like the gospel writers, were not from Palestine and did not understand them well. Some Pharisees were legalists who cared more about the letter of their law than the new message Jesus was bringing, and the gospel writers emphasize this as well as the hypocrisy of those who were ready to stoop to anything to stop him. It is understandable that the gospel writers would paint the worst picture of those who opposed Jesus, yet the evangelists also show Jesus willing to debate them and to take their views seriously.

So while we can lament the shortsightedness and legalistic attitude of some of the Pharisees who opposed Jesus, we must also realize that most Pharisees were good, sincere people who feared that this Galilean preacher might mislead their fellow Jews. We, of course, think very differently of Jesus, but his message was difficult to comprehend and radical in its newness, so we can understand the Pharisees' inability to recognize the Jesus in whom we believe.

Finally, we should recall that most Jews of Jesus' day were solid, hard-working women and men who did not belong to any specific group, but who faithfully worshiped the God of their ancestors by observing Torah. In fact, this would be a perfect description of Jesus' own family.

Let us close by showing how historical background can help us to understand the NT. We always wonder why the gospels constantly picture tax collectors as sinners. Few people like to pay taxes, but we don't consider tax collectors to be sinners; they are civil servants who are just doing their jobs. Why are they such villains in the gospels?

In Jesus' day Jewish tax collectors worked for the Roman empire, which made them resented agents of the occupying power. Furthermore, the system assumed that they would extort from the taxpayers in order to get money for themselves. Such sleazy behavior extended upwards as well. The great Roman orator Cicero once acidly remarked that the only honest Roman governor was one who came back from the provinces less prosperous than when he went there. In Luke's Gospel Zaccheus was the chief tax collector in Jericho, who, after his meeting with Jesus, offers to repay fourfold anyone whom he has cheated. So when Jesus says that his opponents accuse him of being "a friend of tax collectors and sinners" (Matt 11:19), he does not have to explain that reference to his hearers. They all knew too well what he meant.

Chapter Three

Paul and the Risen Christ

Because the letters of the apostle Paul come first chronologically, most introductions to the NT deal with those before turning to the gospels, as we shall. We will presume most readers are familiar with the basic gospel accounts, so we can see how Paul, by being the first great Christian theologian and an inspired writer, put an indelible stamp on how Christians came to understand their savior and their church.

Paul knows quite a bit about the historical Jesus. He says that Jesus is a descendant of Abraham (Gal 3:16) and of the house of David (Rom 1:3). He had brothers (1 Cor 9:5), particularly one named James (Gal 1:19). He had disciples, one of whom was named Cephas (Peter), and twelve special disciples (1 Cor 15:5), one of whom betrayed him (1 Cor 11:23). He instituted the Lord's Supper (1 Cor 11:17-27). He was crucified (1 Cor 1:23; Gal 3:1), died, was buried, and rose from the dead (1 Cor 15:4). Yet in spite of these biographical references Paul focuses not on the historical Jesus but rather on the Risen Christ whom Paul experienced personally. We will see how Paul understands Christ when we get to his letters; for now let us see what we know about the great apostle.

A Brief Account of Paul's Life

Paul was the first great interpreter of the life and mission of Jesus, that is, the first Christian theologian, and all subsequent Christian doctrine and theology depend in some way on him. His ideas impacted some major churches, including those at Ephesus, Corinth, Rome, Antioch, and even Jerusalem, and we can hear his voice, strong or faint, in many of the other NT books. By the mid-second century most Christians recognized Paul's genius and believed his letters to be inspired. That guaranteed his major role in the church's teachings, but the nineteenth century increased that role to new heights. As we shall see later, scholars in that century proved that the gospels of Matthew and John were not written by eyewitnesses to Jesus' public career, which in turn meant that the Pauline writings represent the earliest witness to the early church's understanding of Jesus as well as to its life, beliefs, and practices.

Aside from Jesus, Paul is the NT figure we know the most about, primarily through his seven authentic letters—First Thessalonians, Galatians, First and Second Corinthians, Philippians, Romans, and Philemon. Other letters claim Pauline authorship, but scholars generally credit only these seven with authenticity—a topic we will discuss as we look at those letters individually. Just because Paul did not write the other letters does not mean they tell us nothing about him. The letter to the Colossians shows that Paul had an impact on that community, while those to Titus and Timothy confirm the importance of these two disciples in Paul's work since the *pseudonymous* (falsely named) author thought letters supposedly written to them would sound Pauline. But these details do not help us to construct a life of Paul.

The Acts of the Apostles, written in the 80s by the same author who wrote the Gospel of Luke, plays a different role, making Paul the central figure of more than half the book. Acts, not the letters, tells us of Paul's three missionary journeys as well as such famous accounts as Paul's watching over the cloaks of those who stoned the Christian protomartyr Stephen (Acts 7:59) and his conversion by being knocked from his horse on the road to Damascus (Acts 9:3-12). Yet scholars use Acts very carefully as a source for Paul's life because of discrepancies between some Acts accounts and the authentic letters. (Most problematically, Acts never mentions that Paul wrote letters.) To cite one well-known example, Acts 17:10-15 says that when Paul left Beroea in Greece and traveled to Athens he left behind two of his coworkers, Silas and Timothy, telling them to join him later. But Silas and Timothy never made it to Athens and instead joined Paul in Corinth (Acts 18:5). Yet in his letter to the Thessalonians, Paul says, "we decided it would be best to be left without a companion in Athens, and so we sent our brother Timothy, who is God's helper in spreading the gospel of Christ, to keep you [the Thessalonians] firm and encourage you about your faith" (1 Thess 3:1-2). Paul says that Timothy was with him in Athens, while Acts says he was not. Obviously Paul knew what had happened, so Acts has the wrong information.

But does that mean that Acts contains no reliable information about Paul? Some scholars say "Yes" and will not use Acts at all. Most scholars—and we follow this path—believe that Acts can be used for information about Paul, but only when that book agrees with or at least does not contradict the authentic letters. For example, Acts says that Paul converted a dye merchant named Lydia in the town of Philippi. Paul mentions nothing about this, but we know (1 Thess 2:2) that Paul evangelized in Philippi and thus there is no reason to doubt the Acts account that he converted someone named Lydia there. Paul could not possibly have included everything he did in his life in his letters, and accounts of the famous missionary would have circulated in the early church.

As for Paul's life, Acts tells us (21:39) that he was born in Tarsus of Cilicia, in modern southeastern Turkey, thus making him a Diaspora Jew. The quality of Paul's Greek and his knowledge of the eastern Mediterranean provinces support this idea. Furthermore, Tarsus had a sizable Jewish community, and Paul visited Cilicia shortly after his conversion (Gal 1:21). He was a Roman citizen (Acts 16:37-39; 22:25-29), which means that he had certain political rights that others did not. Since Paul could read and write and traveled quite a bit, he came from a family of some income, probably one that had earned or purchased Roman citizenship before Paul's birth because Acts says he was born with citizenship (22:28). A Diaspora background would also explain Paul's knowledge of Gentile ways and his recognition that what worked for the Christians of Judea would not necessarily work in the Gentile world.

Diaspora Jews often used two names, one Semitic and one Hellenized. Acts says that Paul was called "Saul" in Judea (7:59) but "Paul" in Gentile territory. Saul was the name of the first king of Israel, who came from the tribe of Benjamin (1 Sam 9:1-2), a claim Paul proudly made for himself (Rom 11:1; Phil 3:5), so Saul was indeed his Jewish name.

Paul also points with pride to his Pharisaic background (Phil 3:5). Pharisaic activity was concentrated inside Judea, which supports Acts' claim that Paul studied in Jerusalem with the famous teacher Gamaliel (22:3). Acts says that Paul began his persecution of Christians in Jerusalem (8:3), and Paul knew about a persecution there (1 Thess 2:14).

Sometime after he began to persecute Christians, Paul received "a revelation of Jesus Christ" (Gal 1:13). Why? ". . . so that I should preach him to the Gentiles" (1:16). Luke tells the famous story of Paul's being knocked from his horse by a bright light and hearing the words, "Saul, Saul, why do you persecute me?" (Acts 9:4), although Paul himself says nothing of that. This revelation changed Paul's life. It proved to him that the disciples told the truth when they said Jesus had risen from the dead. It also affected Paul's understanding of Jesus. He never played down the significance of Jesus' earthly life, but his own experience and his understanding of Jesus were of the Risen Christ. This put Paul in communication with modern Catholics in a way the Twelve could not be because we, too, have experienced only the Risen Christ.

After the revelation he went to Damascus, then controlled for Rome by Aretas, king of a local Arab tribe. Then he went to "Arabia," presumably some place east of Damascus and within the territory of Aretas, and "I came back to Damascus. Only after three years did I go up to Jerusalem . . ." (Gal 1:17-18). He had some adventures during those three years. Aretas had attacked the kingdom of Herod Antipas *ca.* 36 but soon backed off in order not to antagonize the Romans. In 2 Corinthians 11:32-33 Paul gives a picturesque account: "When I was in Damascus, the governor who was under King Aretas put guards round Damascus to catch me, and I was let down in a basket through a window in the wall, and that was how I escaped from his hands." What did Aretas have against Paul? Most likely the anti-Jewish Aretas objected to his being a Jew.

Can we put any dates to these events? We know that the emperor Caligula gave control of Damascus to Aretas in 37, so Paul was in that city some time after that date. The book of Acts has Paul in Jerusalem within a few years of Jesus' death, so most scholars favor a timeline of:

- Paul converted to Christianity about 36.
- He went to Damascus in that year or shortly after.
- His three-year stay lasted until about 39, after which he went to Jerusalem.

Paul had received a revelation of Jesus, but how much did he know about his savior? During a fifteen-day stay in Jerusalem Paul met with Cephas (Peter) and "James, the Lord's brother" (Gal 1:19). Clearly those two knew far more about Jesus than the people who had previously instructed Paul. Probably he learned much about Jesus and also about how Jesus was preached in the Jerusalem community. In a letter to the disorderly Corinthians he stresses the importance of preserving traditions (1 Cor 11:2, 23) and specifically mentions a tradition "which I had myself received" (15:3). What better source of traditions about Jesus than the Jerusalem community, which included the leader of the Twelve and the brother of the Lord?

But there was work to do. Paul left Jerusalem and "went to places in Syria and Cilicia" (Gal 1:21), not returning to Jerusalem for another fourteen years (2:10), by which time he had come to share the mission with Barnabas and Titus. Luke says that Paul went to Antioch, the largest city in Syria and one of the most important cities in the Roman eastern Mediterranean.

Luke speaks of a missionary journey Paul took from Antioch to Cyprus and Asia Minor with Barnabas and his nephew John Mark as fellow missionaries (Acts 13:3–14:28). Paul does not mention such a specific mission, yet he did preach to Gentiles (Gal 2:1-3) before his return to Jerusalem. Furthermore, his list of sufferings in 1 Corinthians (11:25) includes being stoned, which Luke says happened to him in the Asian town of Lystra (Acts 14:19). Although generally successful, this first mission demonstrated to Paul how difficult spreading the Faith would be. It also proved his own determination to stay the course no matter what.

Around the year 50 Paul went to Jerusalem for a conference with James. This was less than fourteen years after his first meeting, and scholars believe that "fourteen years" of Galatians 2:1 refers to the time from his conversion. By now Paul had become a seasoned missionary with his own associates, and he claimed a revelation as the inspiration for his visit. He approached the leaders of the Jerusalem church as an equal. Paul wanted their recognition of his mission to the Gentiles. He insisted that this implied no division of the message, just a recognition that God had different plans for different apostles: ". . . once they saw that the gospel for the uncircumcised (Gentiles) had been entrusted to me, just as to Peter the gospel for the circumcised (Jews)—for he who empowered Peter's apostolate to the circumcised also empowered mine to the Gentiles—and when they acknowledged the grace that had been given to me, then James and Cephas (Peter) and John, who were the ones recognized as pillars, offered their right hands to Barnabas and to me as a sign of partnership" (Gal 2:7-9).

This represented a major breakthrough for Paul on both the theological and practical levels. The Jewish notion of a chosen people, if interpreted narrowly, marginalized Gentiles, but Paul insisted on their equality because "there is no favoritism with God" (Gal 2:6). To accept this was quite a concession for the Jerusalem church leaders, and they deserve credit for making it. Neither they nor Paul abandoned the

notion of a chosen people, but Paul would reinterpret the notion not as superiority but as a greater responsibility and obligation. On the practical level Paul did not have to tell potential Gentile converts that they had to obey all the Jewish laws, as some Jewish Christians thought they should. This lessening of obligations made the Christian message more attractive.

But change can be difficult, and not everyone can live up to their good intentions. After the Jerusalem meeting Paul was at Antioch with Peter and Barnabas. Some visitors from Jerusalem arrived, representatives of James. Strongly conservative, they refused to share table fellowship with the Gentile converts. Disappointingly, Peter and Barnabas did likewise. The infuriated Paul reproached Peter to his face and did so in front of everyone there (Gal 2:11-14); he does not say how he handled Barnabas' defection. We don't know what if anything Peter said back. After this Paul halts the biographical material in Galatians, and scholars have to pick up threads from his letters, supplemented carefully from Acts.

Luke (Acts 15:40–18:22) speaks of a second missionary journey that took Paul back to Asia Minor and then into Europe, specifically Macedonia and Greece, where he came to Philippi, Thessalonica, Beroea, Athens, and Corinth. The first two and the last became recipients of Pauline letters. The Corinthian stay has proved most important in following Paul's life. He was in that city for eighteen months (Acts 18:11) and encountered the Roman proconsul of the city, Gallio. We know from Roman sources that Gallio was in Corinth in 52, so Paul's meeting with him provides the first firm date of the NT era. Since Acts indicates that Paul had been working in Corinth for some time before meeting Gallio, he probably arrived there in 51. While there he met Prisca and Aquila, two Roman Jews who probably had to flee the capital when the emperor Claudius expelled Jews from the city in 49. While we cannot say what they did after leaving Rome and how long it took them to get to Corinth, their arrival there fits the period of 50–51. So we can say that Paul was evangelizing in Greece in 51–52, sometimes successfully and sometimes to fierce resistance, but overall he brought the faith to those areas. During this period Paul wrote his first letter, 1 Thessalonians.

Paul returned to Judea, going via Ephesus in Asia Minor and then landing at the port city of Caesarea. After that he "went up to greet the church" (Acts 18:22), probably the church at Jerusalem, and then he went back to Antioch in Syria. Luke has no information about what he did during this time; instead Luke gets him back on the road, going through

The Theater at the city of Miletus visited by Paul

Asia Minor to the major city of Ephesus on the Aegean Sea. He stayed there for three years (Acts 20:31), probably from 54 to 57. Luke portrays his stay as simultaneously effective and tumultuous. Literarily it was productive. Scholars believe that while he was in Ephesus, Paul wrote Galatians, 1 Corinthians, Philippians, and Philemon. He left Ephesus and headed north along the Aegean coast, stopping in Troas to greet his disciple Titus and probably to write 2 Corinthians. Around 58 he returned to Corinth; from there he wrote his letter to the Romans, in which he says he hoped to take the faith to Spain (15:23), something a later Roman tradition says that he did, although modern scholars do not accept that.

According to Luke, around 58 Paul returned to Judea where he met with James of Jerusalem, who insisted that Paul follow Jewish customs while he was in the city. But some Diaspora Jews accused him of being the troublemaker who had spread new and dangerous ideas in Asia Minor, and so a riot broke out against him in the Temple court. The Romans arrested him, kept him in prison for two years (Acts 24:27), and finally put him on trial, probably in 62. Paul appealed his case to Caesar (at the time, Nero) and was sent in chains to Rome, where an already existing community of Christians greeted him. Luke finishes Acts by saying that Paul stayed in Rome for two years in rented lodgings, but he does not say what eventually happened to Paul. Roman tradition says he died in Nero's persecution of the Roman Christians after the Great Fire of Rome in 64; it is also possible that he lost his legal appeal and was executed. All we know is that after 64 he was no longer alive.

Paul was a remarkable person, faithful, courageous, temperamental, brilliant, adventurous, aggressive, and intolerant of those who, he felt, threatened his mission, even if those people were the leader of the Twelve and the head of the Jerusalem community. Never having known the earthly Jesus, he made the Risen Jesus the center of his faith and that of those he evangelized. A firm Jew, he believed that the Christian message also included the Gentiles, and he worked tirelessly to bring that message to them. He did not write much about the universal church but rather about the local churches, especially those he founded. Unlike many theologians who work in colleges, universities, or seminaries, Paul had the practical experience of mission and ministry, and he wrote almost on the run, dealing with a crisis in a practical way while simultaneously bringing Christian teaching and principles to bear on the most immediate situation.

This remarkable organizer and thinker took Christianity into the West, thus determining its historical and geographical orientation for two millennia. The language of his communities, Greek, became the language of the NT and of the church as whole for two centuries and of a major part of Christianity ever since. His views inspired many great Christian thinkers, and all Christian doctrine and theology must take his writings into account. He certainly had his faults. He insulted the Galatians (Gal 3:1), criticized the Corinthians on the basis of second-hand information (1 Cor 1:11), and, instead of calling him aside privately, embarrassingly rebuked Peter in front of others (Gal 1:14). Yet this should cause no lasting concern. Everyone in the church has something in common: we are all sinners, and that includes saints. But Paul's strengths far transcended his shortcomings, and we cannot conceive of the church without him.

Now let's take a look at his earliest writing, the First Letter to the Thessalonians.

Chapter Four

Paul's Shorter Letters

The First Letter to the Thessalonians

    I. Greeting (1:1)

    II. Thanksgiving for the faith of the Thessalonians (1:2-10)

    III. Paul as the model apostle (2:1-12)

    IV. Thanksgiving again (2:13-16)

    V. Account of Paul's activities and plans (2:17–3:8)

    VI. Second thanksgiving and moral exhortations (3:9–4:12)

    VII. Resurrection and Second Coming (4:13–5:11)

    VIII. Exhortations, prayer, and greeting (5:12-28)

This is the earliest surviving letter of Paul and thus the earliest surviving piece of Christian literature of any kind, which gives it great historical status.

Read: Since 1 Thessalonians is both important and brief, please read all of it.

Thessalonica was a city in Macedonia that Paul evangelized about the year 50 during what Acts portrays as his secondary missionary journey. It served as the capital of Roman provincial government. Thessalonica was his second stop after Philippi, where he received "rough treatment and insults" (1 Thess 2:2). Although the Thessalonians treated him better, conflicts with the local Jewish community forced Paul to leave, literally to sneak away at night and apparently at the wish of the local

Christians (Acts 17:10). Paul naturally worried about the fledgling community, so when he got to Athens he sent his coworker Timothy to check up on things (1 Thess 3:1-13). Assured by Timothy that the community was doing well although a few problems had surfaced, Paul decided to write to the Thessalonians, although he courteously did so in the names of Silvanus and Timothy as well as himself (1:1). When Paul had to write to reprove a community (Galatians, 1 Corinthians), he wrote in his own name, taking full responsibility for what had to be said.

Paul starts on a positive note, complimenting his readers on how God loves them (1:4), how the Gospel came to them in the Holy Spirit (1:5), and how they took the Lord as their model (1:6). Since we spoke about the development of doctrine and that modern Catholics should not expect to find current teaching all laid out in the Bible, we should point out that although the word "Trinity" is not actually used here, the first six verses of Christian literature refer to the Father, Son, and Holy Spirit. The seeds were sown very early.

After some more compliments, Paul gets to the point of his letter. Events at Thessalonica are fresh in his mind (2:17), and he feels a need to justify his hurried departure. Paul stresses his affection for the community and theirs for him. He addresses them as "brothers"—as Raymond E. Brown points out (*Introduction to the New Testament*, 459), this should be understood as "brothers and sisters"—fourteen times in a short letter. He also credits them for turning to the truth. The missionaries started the work, but the Thessalonians abandoned their false gods. He next reminds them of how hard he had worked among them, "slaving day and night so as not to be a burden on any of you" (2:9), and he uses parental imagery (2:7, 11) to characterize his care for them.

The Thessalonians repaid Paul's work, accepting the Word but also enduring a persecution of some sort. Whether this was a formal one instituted by the government or just some local people abusing the converts, Paul does not say, although the latter is more likely. Acts tells us that the local Jews moved some pagans against Paul. Probably both groups contributed to the difficulties the converts faced, since Paul makes a point of comparing (2:14-15) the Thessalonians' suffering to those of the Jewish Christians in Judea and even to the death of Jesus (the only reference in this letter to the earthly life of Jesus). But the crisis in Thessalonica has apparently now passed.

Paul had wanted to visit the community, but Satan prevented him (2:18). He does not explain this. It probably means difficulties he encountered in Athens, which he attributed to demonic causes. He expected that Satan might do the same to the converts, so he sent Timothy to them. "Timothy has just now come to us from you, and has brought us the good news of your faith and love . . . . How can we thank God enough for you in return for all the joy that we feel before our God?" (3:6, 9).

Confident of the community's security and even its ability to spread the Gospel beyond its borders (1:8), Paul turns to specific issues. Like most Jews, Paul had a very low view of pagan moral norms, and so he urges the Thessalonians to ethical behavior, warning about sexual immorality and shady financial dealings and then going on to encourage mutual love (4:1-12).

Next he turns to a very specific problem. The Thessalonians do not understand why some members of the community have died. They all expected to be alive when Jesus returned at the Second Coming (or *parousia* in Greek), a view the apostle shares. Paul makes it clear that most Christians will be alive "[at] the archangel's call and the . . . sound of God's trumpet" (4:16) when Jesus returns. Then "the dead in Christ will rise first. Then we who are alive, who are left, will be caught up in the clouds together with them to meet the Lord in the air" (4:17). If this sounds familiar, it is the so-called Rapture, a firm belief of very conservative evangelical Christians and the subject of many books, including novels. Like most first-generation Christians, Paul did indeed believe in an early Second Coming, although he did not believe that all Christians would be alive. The dead had died in Christ, and the living have no advantage over them. Paul feared that, like those "who have no hope" (4:13), the Thessalonians would despair about deceased relatives and friends. He assures them the Lord will unite in himself all Christians, living and dead.

Having explained the situation of the dead, Paul turns to the living, using a vivid image: ". . . the Day of the Lord will come like a thief in the night" (5:2), and so the Thessalonians must continue to live in faith, hope, and love (5:8) and be ready for the Lord when he comes.

Paul closes with wishes that God will continue to bless the community. Although he says nothing about the community structures, he instructs the recipients of the letter to read it to all the brethren (5:27), suggesting that he sent the letter to the leaders of the community.

The Letter to the Galatians

I. Greeting (1:1-5)

II. Paul's Gospel (1:6-24)
- The only gospel (1:6-11)
- Divine basis of Paul's gospel (1:12-24)

III. Paul and other Christian leaders on Gentiles in the Church (2)
- Council of Jerusalem (2:1-10)
- Paul rebukes Peter (2:11-14)
- Justification of both Jews and Gentiles (2:15-21)

IV. Christianity and the Law (3:1–4:11)
- Galatians' experience of the Spirit (3:1-5)
- God's promise to Abraham (3:6-18)
- The Law and faith (3:19-29)
- Liberation in Christ (4:1-11)

V. Exhortation to Christian living (4:12–6:10)
- Friendship in the community (4:12-20)
- Allegory of Hagar and Sarah (4:21–5:1)
- Futility of circumcision (5:2-12)
- Love, flesh, and spirit (5:13-26)
- Mutual aid in the community (6:1-10)

VI. Conclusion—admonitions and blessings (6:11-18)

This letter was most likely written during what Luke portrays as Paul's third missionary journey, and from Ephesus. Scholars disagree as to who "the Galatians" were. Some think recipients of this letter lived in the southern part of the Roman province of Galatia, in cities such as Derbe and Lystra, which Luke says Paul evangelized. But Paul does not mention those cities, and "the Galatians" would most likely mean the descendants of Celtic tribesmen, called Gauls by the Greeks and Romans, who gave their name to the region. The identity of the recipients does not affect our understanding of the letter in any case. As for the date, it cannot be pinpointed and most scholars would settle for the mid- to late 50s.

This letter is both brief and important and should be read in its entirety; at the least please read chapters 1 to 4.

We discussed this letter earlier because of its value for charting the life of Paul, but he did not write it to be autobiographical. A crisis occasioned the letter. Paul had preached in Galatia, but unintentionally. He says that "it was because of a physical infirmity that I first announced the gospel to you" (4:13), and the Galatians accepted his preaching and converted to Christianity. But after Paul had left the community some other missionaries arrived, very conservative ones who told the Galatians that they must accept the requirements of the Jewish Law in order to be Christian. The Galatians accepted this "different gospel" (1:6). When word of this reached Paul, he reacted furiously. This angry letter has no thanksgiving, and Paul invokes his authority immediately. He calls the Galatians "fools" (3:1) and stoops to vulgarity in criticizing his opponents (5:12). The Gospel had been betrayed in Galatia!

Or had it?

Paul, of course, is Saint Paul, hero of early Christianity, the first great theologian, and patron saint of churches, cathedrals, schools, colleges, and even cities. Surely he must have been right and his opponents wrong. This is how later generations of Christians came to view the situation in Galatia, but it was hardly obvious then. We must consider three facts. First, we have only Paul's account of what happened, and so we cannot really know what his opponents thought. Second, these other missionaries were Christians, like Paul, and they were risking life and limb to promote the faith. They were hardly evil people. Third, we must recall that all the first Christians were Jews who had followed the Law. The specific issue was male circumcision, for Jews the sign of God's covenant with Abraham and thus with the Jewish people (Genesis 15), a sign carried by Jesus himself (Luke 2:21). The other missionaries were obviously Jewish Christians since Paul will refute them by citing his dealing with James of Jerusalem. Like all good Jews, they could not believe that a covenant made by God would ever become non-binding on his people, and so they thought that Gentiles converted to membership in God's people had to follow the Law.

Furthermore, although Paul takes these missionaries' work as a personal attack, there is no proof that they deliberately went to Galatia to counter his work. They may well have been passing through to someplace else, stopped in Galatia, became concerned about the Galatians' indifference to the Law, and so did something about it.

But their actions provoked Paul to write and explain his own views. He correctly recognizes that the central issue was not the Law, but authority. The Law carried the authority of the covenant with Abraham and of observance by the earliest disciples. What authority did Paul have? Paul strikes immediately, insisting that he is "an apostle—sent neither by human commission nor from human authorities, but through Jesus Christ and God the Father . . ." (1:1). He quickly repeats this. "For I did not receive it [his Gospel] from a human source, nor was I taught it, but I received it through a revelation of Jesus Christ" (1:12).

Paul took this revelation to heart and, as we have seen, he stood up to James and Peter and anyone else from Jerusalem who disagreed with him. He insisted that the Jerusalem disciples accept the truth of his Gospel, that is, the Gentile converts must only have faith and do not need to follow the requirements of the Law. Further, these leaders, these pillars of the church (2:9), ". . . saw that I had been entrusted with the gospel for the uncircumcised" (2:7).

After Paul has established the authority (God and Christ) for his Gospel and has demonstrated that the leaders of the Jewish Christians acknowledged both his Gospel and his apostolate, he next turns to the two central problems that dominate the letter. What exactly is his Gospel? How is it related to God's Law given to the Jews? The answers to these two questions are intertwined.

Paul states his view boldly and succinctly: ". . . a person is justified not by the works of the law but through faith in Jesus Christ" (2:16). Note the passive voice, "is justified." So who does the justifying? God. That is quite a statement to make. Can Paul support it? Yes, and in the Torah itself. "Abraham 'believed God, and it was reckoned to him as righteousness'" (3:6, here citing Gen 15:6).

Paul was not, of course, the only Christian who had read Genesis, but he was the one who read it this way, and no one knows why. Possibly the practical engendered the theoretical. The missionary saw that circumcision and other aspects of the Law deterred Gentile converts, and so the theologian was led to wonder about the necessity of the Law. Whatever the cause, Paul came to this important conclusion.

Ramifications quickly followed. People could obey the Law, which was written down and interpreted, but only God could engender both justification and faith. Both were freely given gifts of God, given with no intermediary, somewhat parallel to Paul's reception of Christ's revelation without the mediation of other apostles. This faith enabled the convert to see that God redeemed the world through Jesus Christ, not through the written Law or any other means.

But, one might ask, why not have faith and keep the Law as well? In Paul's interpretation no one can keep the entire Law, and thus everyone who lives under the Law eventually falls under its curse (3:10-14). But God gave the Law to God's people Israel. Could God give what was not sufficient? Paul believes that it was sufficient but only for a time (2:19-29). It guided the Jews along the paths of righteousness until the promised progeny of Abraham, that is, Christ, came.

Yet Abraham was both reckoned righteous by faith and made a covenant with God. Who then are his true descendants? To answer that question (4:21-31), Paul returns to Genesis, to the two women who bore sons to Abraham. The first was Hagar, a slave and mother of Ishmael, and the second was Sarah, his wife and mother of Isaac. Paul sees here an allegory, a narrative with a real historical meaning but also with a higher, spiritual meaning. The two women represented two covenants, Hagar the Jerusalem covenant which is enslaved to the Law, and Sarah "the Jerusalem above; she is free . . . while you, brothers and sisters, are children of the promise, like Isaac" (4:26, 28). Astonishing though it is to Jews and to many Jewish Christians, these Gentile Galatian Christians who do not keep the Law are the true children of Abraham. We can almost imagine the groans coming from the Jerusalem Christians at that, even if Paul does claim that they approved of what he taught (2:6).

But could not such a view lead to moral chaos? If people were not bound by the Law, couldn't they do anything they wanted since there was nothing to guide or restrain them? Not so, says Paul. Christian love will prevent believers from falling into self-indulgence, that is, lack of restraint. He then goes on with a rather impressive list of vices to which the self-indulgent would fall victim (5:19-21), making the reader wonder what was really going on in Galatia. He next pleads that his readers have understanding toward others and perseverance in keeping the faith.

He opens his farewell in a striking way. "See what large letters I make when I am writing in my own hand" (6:1). Most likely he wrote only that sentence and possibly what comes after, otherwise relying, as he usually did (Rom 16:22), on a secretary. He wants to emphasize that this sometimes harsh letter contains his own views and has not been modified or misunderstood by the secretary. He finishes up with a return to the argument about circumcision, which he compares to the crucifixion of Jesus, which in turn he compares to own sufferings for the Gospel (6:14-17).

Direct and forceful as this letter is, it did not settle the question of Christians and the Law. Paul would return to the theme again in 1 Corinthians and more so in Romans, but Galatians presents his earliest views on the topic. It also, as we have seen, provides some valuable biographical information.

A final observation. Modern Catholics and other Christians like to cite Galatians 3:28: "There is no longer Jew or Greek, there is no longer slave or free, there is no longer male and female; for all of you are one in Christ Jesus." Those are admirable sentiments, but they were ideals rather than realities: for example, Paul did not condemn slavery. Yet recognizing its historical climate does not prevent us from applying the ideals of this statement to our modern world.

The Letter to Philemon

    I. Greeting (1-3)

    II. Thanksgiving (4-6)

    III. Plea on behalf of Onesimus (7-22)

    IV. Farewell (23-25)

The shortest of Paul's letters and, to many Christians, his most disappointing, the Letter to Philemon deserves careful study.

Please read this letter in its entirety.

This letter was written about 56 from Ephesus, during the same prison stay (1, 9) in which Paul wrote the letter to the Philippians. This is a personal letter, although it begins with a greeting to the church that meets in the house of Philemon, Apphia, and Archippus. As we saw earlier, when Paul says "your house" he uses the Greek plural form of "your" and so includes Apphia, presumably Philemon's wife but definitely a woman.

Onesimus, Philemon's slave, has run away and come to Paul at Ephesus. There he converts to Christianity and becomes a genuine help and comfort to Paul, who would like Onesimus to stay with him. But the apostle follows Roman law. The slave belongs to Philemon, and so Paul writes to tell Philemon that he is sending Onesimus back to him, although he makes it clear that he would like the slave to stay. Paul cleverly says that if Onesimus owes Philemon anything, he (Paul) would pay back what is owed, even though Philemon owes Paul his very salvation (18-19)!

Modern Christians are naturally disappointed that Paul did not ask Philemon to free his slave. After all, how can a Christian own another human being? But, strange to say, Paul does not think of Onesimus as a slave, because his conversion has made him something more. Paul tells Philemon to consider Onesimus "no longer as a slave but as more than a slave, a beloved brother—especially to me but how much more to you, both in the flesh and in the Lord . . . . welcome him as you would welcome me" (16-18). This theological interpretation sees all humans as transformed in Christ so as to rise above human social distinctions.

But, critics say, isn't this just a rationalization to justify Paul's failing in this matter? There are two contexts to consider. The first is that, with the end of the age imminent, Paul and other Christians saw no need to change society. In fact, they feared that doing so would make Christianity look like a social revolution and impede the spread of the Gospel. The second context is that within the Roman empire slaves worked in many contexts, the lowest being those toiling in mines or on plantations or as rowers in galleys, the highest being those who managed affairs for their masters and who lived, materially, very well. Philemon knows who Onesimus is, proving that he was at least a household slave, and Paul may have thought that he was well-treated. Certainly Paul's request that Philemon welcome the slave as if he were Paul himself means that the apostle expected kind treatment of Onesimus. (And in fairness to Paul we must recall that large numbers of Christians, including American Catholics, laity and clergy, owned slaves into the nineteenth century. Its loathsome immorality, so obvious to us, was somehow not obvious to them.)

On the other hand, it is impossible not to note that Paul was a free man himself, and we only wonder how he would have viewed the question if he were a slave. But this should not keep us from seeing the central theological point of the letter, that faith in Christ transforms all human relationships.

One historical question stands out. Why did Onesimus go to Paul? Why not just keep on running? "It was a legally recognized practice for a slave who had incurred his or her master's wrath to flee to one of the master's trusted associates to plead for his intervention and assistance" (Bart D. Ehrman, *Historical Introduction*, 317). Making a pun on the name Onesimus, which means "useful" in Greek, Paul says (11), "Formerly he was useless to you, but now he is indeed useful both to you and to me," suggesting that Onesimus may have botched an important job and that is why he ran away. Knowing the respect his master had for Paul, Onesimus thought him an ideal person to ask for help.

The Letter to the Philippians

I. Greeting (1:1-2)

II. Paul's prayer for the community (1:3-11)

III. Paul's struggles for the gospel (1:12-30)

IV. Christological hymn (2:1-11)

V. Advice to the community (2:12-18)

VI. Timothy and Epaphroditus (2:19-29)

VII. Warnings and exhortations (3:1–4:1)

VIII. Personal acknowledgments of community members (4:2-20)

IX. Farewell (4:21-23)

Although not a particularly theological letter, Philippians shows Paul dealing with a community for which he had a deep and genuine affection. It also gives an idea of how modern scholarship has been able to expand our understanding of Scripture with both historical and literary analysis.

To understand the historical and literary issues involved with this letter, it helps to read it in its entirety.

Paul wrote this letter to a community he had founded in the Macedonian city of Philippi, an important commercial and military center. Paul encountered hostility there (1 Thess 2:2) but eventually triumphed. Luke (Acts 16) gives a vivid account of Paul's experiences there, including the conversion of the dye merchant Lydia, Paul's overnight imprisonment, and even an earthquake. Paul does not mention any of this. He does refer to his sufferings for the faith, and it seems odd that he does not refer to his imprisonment in Philippi, suffering the Philippians would have known about.

Whatever the case for Acts, here is Paul's situation at the time of this letter, around the year 57. Paul has been imprisoned (1:7, 13). The Philippians heard of this and sent Epaphroditus to him. But Epaphroditus became ill (2:19-30). The Philippians heard of that, too, and became worried, so Paul sent Epaphroditus and his own disciple Timothy to Philippi to assure the community that their ambassador and friend was well again.

Here is the historical problem: where was Paul in prison? Acts tells us that Paul was imprisoned in Caesarea in Palestine (23:33–26:32) before being sent to Rome for trial, and he was subject to house arrest in Rome (28:15-31), so presumably Paul wrote this letter from one of those two places. But he tells us that the Philippians learned of his imprisonment, sent Ephaphroditus to him, learned of his illness, communicated their concern about him to Paul, who in turn sent Epaphroditus and Timothy to Philippi—a total of five contacts between the apostle and the community. Caesarea lies almost 1000 miles from Philippi, Rome almost 900. Frequent communication at those distances is simply impossible, so scholars believe that Paul must have been imprisoned in some third place. Paul himself speaks of being imprisoned more than once (2 Cor 6:5; 11:23) in a letter he wrote *before* his imprisonment in Caesarea and Rome. Acts 19:23-41 tells of civic difficulties arising from Paul's stay in Ephesus, and most scholars believe Ephesus was the place of his imprisonment. It is 400 miles from Philippi, hardly a short journey in the first century but certainly a feasible and safe one, by land or sea. Furthermore, Paul tells us that Timothy was with him at Ephesus (1 Cor 4:17).

This is a good example of how scholars work. The Bible presents a problem, and some careful hypothesizing can provide an answer. Have scholars proved that Paul was in Ephesus? No, but they have demonstrated the difficulty of using either of the two known places of imprisonment. And if not Ephesus, then where?

Another example of scholarly probing involves Philippians 2:6-11. Scholars noticed that Paul's Greek suddenly becomes lyrical in these verses, and they concluded that Paul is here quoting an early Christian hymn, possibly one he wrote himself but far more likely one that predates him and that he knew would be familiar to the Philippians. This christological piece is the oldest surviving Christian hymn.

Another literary question surrounds Philippians: is it one letter or two or three? The letter survives only in its current form, and many scholars defend its unity. The problem lies in the first half of verse 3:1: "Finally, brothers, I wish you joy in the Lord," suggesting that Paul has begun the conclusion of the letter. But next comes a long paragraph on how to live a Christian life and to avoid the temptation to be circumcised (3:2), hardly a conclusion. In 4:1-20 Paul urges the end to a local dispute and gives thanks for a gift, items more fitting for a conclusion, followed (4:21-23) by a formal farewell. Many scholars believe that the third and fourth chapters come from another letter that an ancient editor of Paul attached to a letter that consisted of two chapters. Others suggest that chapter four is also part of this other letter, since it is not until then that we learn that Epaphroditus brought Paul a gift from the community, something we would have expected Paul to mention earlier in connection with Epaphroditus' illness. Finally, notice how naturally the letter ends after two chapters; if there were not two more chapters we would not suspect that the letter was incomplete.

There is an old joke in scholarship that you never want to solve a problem, because if you do, you can't write about it any more. That is not likely to happen here. Eminent scholars have lined up on both sides of the question. While I personally find the multiple letter hypothesis more convincing, this question may never be settled. So let us turn to the letter as it exists.

Paul opens on an apocalyptic note, urging his readers to keep the faith "[until] the day of Jesus Christ" (1:6). Part of this keeping the faith involves suffering; the Philippians "all . . . share in God's grace with me, both in my imprisonment and in the defense and confirmation of the gospel" (1:7). But this suffering can profit the church because "most of the brothers and sisters in the Lord [have] been made confident by my imprisonment" (1:14), that is, they have been inspired by Paul's sufferings and now evangelize with more fervor. All struggle involves suffering, but Paul will struggle alongside them (1:27-30).

Yet how can Christians struggle against outside pressure when they fight among themselves? Some people "proclaim Christ from envy and rivalry" (1:15). This rivalry has gotten so bad that two women, Evodia and Syntyche, who "have struggled beside me in the work of the gospel" (4:3), have become rivals. So acute a problem demands that Paul mention them by name and publicly ask someone named Syzygus to mediate. Additionally, an old problem has resurfaced: Christians from outside the community who insist the Philippians, converts from paganism, have to observe the Jewish Law. The furious Paul refers to them as "dogs" and "those who mutilate the flesh" (3:2). Lest his motives be questioned, the apostle assures his readers that no one could be more Jewish than he was. "Circumcised on the eighth day, a member of the people of Israel, of the tribe of Benjamin, a Hebrew born of Hebrews; as to the law, a Pharisee; . . . as to righteousness under the law, blameless" (3:5-6). *No one* can lecture him about what it means to be Jewish. But all Paul's previous efforts at keeping the Law pale in comparison to his acceptance of Jesus Christ. Finally, some who have rejected the Law have drawn the conclusion that there are no laws at all and simply do what gives them pleasure, and Paul asserts that "their god is the belly; and their glory is in their shame . . ." (3:19).

In the face of all this, how can the Philippians maintain communal unity? In humility, imitating the humility of Christ. Paul cites the christological hymn. It is a beautiful piece, and one often quoted liturgically.

> *. . . who, though he was in the form of God,*
> *did not regard equality with God*
> *as something to be exploited,*
> *but emptied himself,*
> *taking the form of a slave,*
> *being born in human likeness.*

But Christ's humility extended beyond just taking "the form of a slave."

> *. . . he humbled himself*
> *and became obedient to the point of death—*
> *even death on a cross.*

Acceptance of this humiliating and excruciatingly painful death caused God to raise him on high and elevate his name above all others. The phrase "equality with God" strikes us, but Paul here refers to Adam and Eve ("you will be like God"), contrasting their pride with Jesus' humility as well as reminding readers why Jesus had to die.

But can we really imitate Christ? Yes, says Paul, because he himself has suffered for others (2:17) as have Timothy (2:19-24) and the Philippians' own Epaphroditus. If they devote themselves not to self-aggrandizement but to service, so can his readers.

If the Philippians abandon factionalism for unity they will experience "the peace of God, which surpasses all understanding" (4:7).

Paul closes in a somewhat surprising manner. He thanks the community for a financial gift. But is this the same Paul who so consistently insists (cf. 1 Thess 1:9) that he took no personal gain from his work? What happened? Has he let his ethics slip? Actually, just the reverse. This is a community so close to him that he can safely accept a needed financial gift without anyone thinking that he has profited from it. The gift represents a remarkable testimony of mutual trust. As for its practical value, no doubt an occasional "donation" to prison authorities made it easier for Paul to receive visitors like Epaphroditus and to keep in contact with disciples like Timothy as well as to have the freedom to write to the Philippians.

Three final points about this letter. First, Paul greets church leaders in Philippi (1:1), including *epískopoi*, traditionally translated "bishops." But this word has specific connotations for modern Catholics, implying a more structured office than was possible in newly established communities. Furthermore, Paul uses different titles, like *proïstaménoi*, literally "those over you" in 1 Thess 5:12, and *kybernéseis*, "administrators" in 1 Cor 12:28. Therefore most modern Catholic editions of the Bible use the word "overseers" or "presiding disciples" to translate *epískopoi*. Second, Paul's description of himself as a Pharisee (3:5) is the *earliest known usage of that word*. And note that he uses the title proudly, a hint that the traditionally negative image of the Pharisees was not so widespread in earliest Christianity. Third, Paul's imprisonment marks the earliest known action of the Roman imperial officials against the Christian mission, the opening action of a centuries-long struggle.

Chapter Five

Paul's Longer Letters

The First Letter to the Corinthians

    I. Greeting and thanksgiving (1:1-9)

    II. Divisions with the community (1:10-17)

    III. Paul's response to the divisions (1:18–4:21)

    IV. Moral problems (5–6)

    V. Marriage, virginity, widowhood (7)

    VI. Food sacrificed to idols (8)

    VII. Paul as the model apostle (9)

    VIII. Warnings about arrogance and idolatry (10:1-22)

    IX. Paul a model to be imitated (10:23–11:1)

    X. Moral problems (11:2-34)
- Proper dress for women and men (11:2-17)
- Proper behavior at the Lord's Supper (11:18-22)
- Account of the institution of the Lord's Supper (11:23-34)

    XI. Spiritual gifts, especially speaking in tongues (12–14)

    XII. The resurrection of Christ and of believers (15)

    XIII. Conclusion (16)
- Collection for Jerusalem community (16:1-4)
- Paul's proposed itineraries (16:5-12)
- Exhortation, greetings, farewell, blessing (16:13-24)

For too long we have idealized the earliest Christian period, seeing it as a time of saints and martyrs, a heroic era never to be matched, but this attitude makes that era irrelevant to sinners like us. It is also all wrong, as Paul's First Letter to the Corinthians shows. In this remarkable letter we meet Christians—whom Paul calls "saints" (1:2)—who bicker, form cliques, engage in sexual immorality, get drunk, eat gluttonously, and drag others into court for petty reasons. If these were the saints, who were the sinners?!

First Corinthians gives us a picture of the life of an early Christian community, warts and all, and of an apostle who struggled with people he loved.

Since this is a long letter, please read chs. 1–7, 11–13, 15

Corinth was an important city in central Greece, the capital of the Roman province of Achaia. Paul had evangelized there for a year and a half, supporting himself as a tentmaker (Acts 18:1-11). Acts says little about Paul's stay, mentioning a few people he converted and his difficulties with the local Jews who brought him before the Roman proconsul Gallio, who dismissed the quarrel as a minor religious matter (Acts 18:12-17), probably in the year 52. After Paul left Corinth and was at Ephesus, probably around 54, he received word from "Chloe's people" (1 Cor 1:11) about trouble in Corinth and that prompted him to write to the community. The Greek phrase "those of Chloe" implies that these persons were slaves or employees of Chloe, who is otherwise unknown. She may have been a businesswoman (like Lydia of Acts 16:12-15) who lived in Ephesus and had interests in Corinth. Paul wrote a letter to the Corinthians, which he refers to at 5:9 but which has not survived (although see our discussion of 2 Corinthians). Some of the Corinthians wrote back to him (7:1) and had three members of the community (16:17) bring their letter to him. Paul wrote again, probably in the year 54, and this is the biblical 1 Corinthians.

Paul writes in his own name and that of Sosthenes, a synagogue official in Corinth (Acts 18:17) who had apparently become a Christian. But the letter is all Paul.

He greets the Corinthians as "saints," which often surprises Catholic readers for whom the term is restricted to those deceased Catholics canonized by the papacy after an elaborate investigative procedure. Yet Paul is using the term for people who are still alive. The Greek means "the holy ones" who have decided to follow Christ. Paul tells the Corinthians that he thanks God for them and that he worries that they will

not be ready to face "the day of our Lord Jesus Christ" (1:8), that is, the Second Coming, so he urges them to rely on God.

Then he gets down to business. How can the Corinthians have let themselves fall into factions, some claiming to "belong to Paul" or to Apollos, another missionary, or to Cephas (Peter), who had never even visited the community, and some, rather pretentiously, to Christ himself? Significantly, Paul does not side with the "Paul" faction but blasts the Corinthians for dividing the community, a division he finds rooted in their pride.

He points out that he preached only Christ crucified, that is, a Jesus who redeemed the world by dying the miserable death of a criminal. What a foolish idea by human standards, but this is how God works. And this is how God is now working through the Corinthians, "not many of [whom] are wise by human standards, not many . . . powerful, not many . . . of noble birth" (1:26). "For Jews demand signs and Greeks desire wisdom" (1:22), but the Christians live by different standards, standards set by God. The Corinthians' faith should "rest not on human wisdom but on the power of God" (2:5).

Paul seems to have wandered from the point, but he wants to establish that factionalism is a human response to problems: "as long as there is jealousy and quarreling among you, are you not of the flesh, and behaving according to human inclinations?" (3:3). As for that faction that claims to follow him, Paul declares: "I planted, Apollos watered, but God gave the growth" (3:6). The apostles to the Corinthians are one in insisting that the community be one. In fact, at the end of the letter Paul says that he urged Apollos to go to Corinth but he declined to go at this time, probably to avoid encouraging factionalism by his presence. Paul did, however, succeed in getting Timothy to go (4:17), although he had not yet arrived, and Paul would soon come himself (4:19).

Having settled the basic question of communal unity, Paul can turn to other problems, although he will insist upon the principle of community in dealing with some of them. He starts off with the case of a man who had married his deceased father's second wife (5:1-13), likely a younger woman about the man's age. This violated biblical principles (Lev 18:8; 20:11) as well as accepted moral standards, and Paul insists the community have nothing to do with the man, an early form of excommunication, although the man could repudiate what he had done and rejoin the community.

Paul next turns to Christians who have taken one another to court (6:1-11). He does not question their exercise of their legal rights, but he wants to know why Christians cannot settle things among themselves without involving the pagan-run law courts, an application of the principle of unity.

Paul returns to the matter of sexual immorality, a problem he may inadvertently have aggravated. He quotes a saying the Corinthians attribute to him: "All things are lawful for me" (6:12). Paul probably preached to the Corinthians that Gentile converts did not have to follow the Jewish Law, and he may have used a phrase similar to that, although with the understanding that true Christians would use their freedom for the good. Paul now finds that some Corinthians have concluded that they can do whatever they like. He gets to the point quickly: "Shun fornication!" (6:18).

Recall that the Corinthians had written to Paul, and now he answers their questions. Chapter 7 deals with marriage. Apparently some Corinthians had concluded that marriage was wrong, a giving in to the demands of the flesh or a worldly concern for producing heirs, and Paul concedes, "'It is well for a man not to touch a woman.' But because of cases of sexual immorality, each man should have his own wife and each woman her own husband" (7:1), hardly a ringing endorsement of matrimony. But Paul goes on to defend marriage and recommends that husband and wife treat one another equally, hardly a common view in that era. He speaks against divorce, which was often rather casually done in those days, and he believes that a Christian spouse could win over a pagan one to the faith and thus to sanctification. Yet he says that it is better not to be married (7:8, 38), and he goes on to give a rationale for the celibate life (7:32-35), although he gives it a practical rather than a theological rationale, that is, an unmarried man can more freely serve the Lord if he is free of the cares of marriage. He also believes that marriage often results from an inability to control sexual passions (7:9).

Some scholars believe that here Paul was practicing "eschatological ethics," that is, he was recommending forms of behavior that were appropriate for Christians living in anticipation of the imminent end of the age. Supporting this view is his recommendation that unmarried people should remain that way (7:8) and slaves should not try to change their lot: "even if you can gain your freedom, make use of your present condition now more than ever" (7:21). Simply put, ". . . let each of you lead the life that the Lord has assigned, to which God called you" (7:17) because "the present form of this world is passing away" (7:31). As usual, Paul has expressed his views strongly, but slaves could hardly have appreciated the recommendation to remain slaves, and married people would not have appreciated the parallel to slavery. Obviously the Church has not accepted Paul's views on either of these points.

From 8:1 to 11:1 Paul deals with a pressing issue for the Corinthians: what to do with food offered to idols? Hardly a relevant topic today, this does give some insight into the Corinthians' problems and also provides a good lesson of charity and unity. Pagan temples used to sell excess food offered to the gods at a discount. Many Christians, like Paul, thought that the pagan gods did not exist and food offered to them was just plain food. But others believed that food offered to the gods was tainted. Paul sees no harm in eating the food, but he does see harm in offending community members who think it tainted. He urges the Corinthians to exercise charity, to keep the community unified, by not eating food offered to idols if such an action would offend others.

This may give us a clue to the factionalism in the community. Paul says that "not many" (1:26) members were socially important or noble, but some clearly were. They may have been better educated and more sophisticated than the others and thus saw no harm in eating the food offered to idols. After all, the gods don't exist, so who cares? This scenario receives reinforcement from Paul's discussion of the liturgical meal. Some people arrived early (11:33) and started eating and drinking before everyone else arrived, with the result that some had gotten drunk (11:21) by the end of the meal. Very likely those who could afford to come early were the wealthy who did not have to wait until finishing work to attend. The factionalism may have had social and educational roots.

Unfortunately Paul does not deal with the other part of the question. The educated should try to avoid offending their less sophisticated brethren, but for how long should the entire community be forced to follow the views of the uneducated? Why not educate those who don't know? No easy answer exists to this question, and it plagues churches even today.

Paul's discussion of liturgical decorum includes a passage (11:2-16) about how women should dress, even to telling them to wear veils; he also tells men not to have long hair! He really does not have any good reason for these prohibitions, and so he justifies them by saying that all the other churches forbid them. Clearly these represent Paul's personal views, and they would not be considered normative today. Indeed, many scholars believe these are not Paul's views but were inserted by a later editor.

Yet inside this discussion of liturgical decorum is a historical gem, *the earliest description of the institution of the Eucharist.* Paul reports the tradition given to him, presumably by the Jerusalem church: ". . . the Lord Jesus on the night when he was betrayed took a loaf of bread, and when he had given thanks, he broke it and said, 'This is my body that is for you. Do this in remembrance of me.' In the same way he took the cup also, after supper, saying, 'This cup is the new covenant in my blood. Do this, as often as you drink it, in remembrance of me'" (11:23-25). Although most of us know the words of institution from the gospels, Paul wrote before any of the evangelists, recording here the traditional words of Jesus. The gospels do not have exactly the same wording (see, e.g., Mark 14:22-25), but the teaching is similar. By participating in the Eucharist we are partaking of the body and blood of Jesus.

Not surprisingly, these words have caused controversy over the centuries. Some (but not all) Protestant denominations do not accept what Catholics call the Real Presence, that is, the belief that the bread and wine actually constitute the body and blood of Christ. These denominations believe that they symbolize the body and blood, although, of course, the positions of these denominations are more nuanced than that. Ecumenical Catholics respect those views but still hold to the straightforward meaning of the words, that *is* means *is*, and so the bread and wine *are* the body and blood of Christ. (After the biblical period generations of theologians would create an extensive theology to go along with this belief, for example, the concept of transubstantiation.)

Further along (11:29) Paul emphasizes the importance to the community of "recognizing the body." He has a twofold purpose. People should recognize the body of Christ in the Eucharist, but they should also recognize that the church is the body of Christ, another way to emphasize the importance of unity. The Eucharist can be celebrated by a priest at a private Mass, and it can be given privately to people such as shut-ins and those hospitalized, but the Eucharist is the community meal of Catholics. That is why it occupies a central place in the liturgy.

In chapter 12 Paul turns to a controversial topic. The community is divided not only over the importance of human standards (influence, prominence) but also over purely spiritual gifts. Paul believed that the Holy Spirit manifested itself in the community in a variety of ways, quietly by entering people's souls at baptism and more vigorously by specific "gifts," the most controversial being *glōssolalia* or "speaking in tongues," by which someone would speak in a language (tongue) either unfamiliar or incomprehensible to the speaker, which we will consider in detail very soon. Paul recognizes that people will consider some gifts more important than others, thus making them a source of contention.

The apostle rightly insists that spiritual gifts take all forms, from the spectacular like working miracles (12:10) to the gift we all share, faith (12:9), but since all are from the Spirit, they are equally good. He compares the community to a human body, which functions well when all parts work well: "there are many members, yet one body" (12:20). More importantly, "you are the body of Christ and individually members of it" (12:27). Surprisingly, he then ranks some of the offices in the community, rather unhumbly putting apostles first. (Teachers come in third!)

But there is a spiritual gift that ranks above the rest: love. Chapter 13 contains some of Paul's most effective writing, a beautiful hymn to love that is widely used at weddings. The famous last line (v. 15), which extols love above faith and hope because of its permanence, has traditionally been understood as referring to the Beatific Vision: that is, when we are one with God we will need neither faith nor hope, but love will abide.

Now Paul returns to *glōssolalia*. In some communities this signified a gift of the Spirit, one that Paul himself possessed to a high degree (14:18). But he recognizes how divisive this gift can be. If someone is speaking in tongues and no one can understand or interpret what is being said, how can this gift build up the community? The person who speaks in tongues can claim it as a gift of the Spirit, but how can a gift of the Spirit be of no use to the community as a whole? "For you [the speaker] will be speaking into the air" (14:9). Better, then: ". . . since you are eager for spiritual gifts, strive to excel in them for building up the church" (14:12). That should have settled the matter, but Paul keeps on going, a witness to how important this phenomenon was at Corinth. Not only can *glōssolalia* divide the community, it can discourage converts. "If, therefore, the whole church comes together and all speak in tongues, and outsiders or unbelievers enter, will they not say that you are out of your mind?" (14:23), an experience occasionally had by modern believers who visit extreme charismatic communities.

Clearly on the defensive, Paul insists on the importance of regulating spiritual gifts, a difficult task in any era. He wisely makes the principle of unity the standard. He does not deny the validity of certain gifts, but he makes it clear that true gifts build up the community; they do not divide it. The apostle had to find a way to be both diplomatic and firm. This passage also provides a good example of how crucial problems for the earliest church may not affect us today, but we cannot ignore them if we wish to understand the NT.

But two questions remain. First, what exactly is *glōssolalia*? Frankly, no one really knows. We have only the descriptions here and in Acts

(2:1-4; 10:46; 19:6), but all these say is that people began to speak in languages they did not know and did not understand and in some cases were understood by no one. The communities considered these to be spiritual gifts, probably because of the enthusiasm of the speakers. Some modern charismatics have claimed to possess this gift. Second, how can one tell when some unusual phenomenon is a true gift of the Spirit and when it is just some psychological phenomenon or demonic possession? Paul never really explains, but later generations would develop the discipline of discernment of spirits.

An old problem reappears in chapter 15. As in Thessalonica, people in Corinth had died before the Second Coming and the survivors wondered about the resurrection of the dead, which some even doubted. Characteristically, Paul meets the challenge head on, first dealing with the fact of the resurrection (15:1-34) and then with the manner of the resurrection (15:35-58). Clearly, disbelief in the resurrection could divide the community, but Paul does not deal with that, focusing instead on the resurrection itself.

Paul reminds the Corinthians of how essential the resurrection is to their faith. His list of witnesses (15:5-8) not only demonstrates the fact of Christ's resurrection but also the centrality of this belief to the church right from the beginning. And the resurrection of Christ presages our own resurrection; one is unthinkable without the other: "If Christ has not been raised, your faith is futile" (15:17). Notice that he is not trying to prove scientifically that Christ rose from the dead; this is a matter of faith, an essential matter of faith, because without it we can have no faith. A modern, scientifically-oriented reader might want proof, but Paul is preaching faith, not science. For him, Christ's resurrection is as much a fact as daylight or darkness, but a fact that we reach only by faith, something to which he must recall the Corinthians.

But even people who believe in the resurrection have to wonder what it will be like, since dead bodies decompose. Furthermore, most Corinthians were Gentiles, and the great Greek philosopher Plato (ca. 429–347 B.C.E.) had considered the body to be the prison of the soul, which at death finally escaped from the prison. The bodily resurrection made little sense to educated Gentiles. No one can really explain the exact nature of the resurrection, but Paul, as a Jew, believed that the body, which God created and considered good, was necessary for full humanity, even in the risen state. It was not contradictory to him to envision a risen body, but it could not be like the body we all know. Making a comparison to seeds in the ground turning into plants, he contends,

"It is sown a physical body, it is raised a spiritual body" (15:44). Paul does not know what this spiritual body will be like, but he does know that we will continue to be whole persons in our eternal life with God. Whether or not this satisfied the worried Corinthians, it represents the first Christian attempt to understand the nature of the resurrection.

No doubt with some relief, Paul finishes what he has set out to do. He has emphasized the importance of unity over factionalism; he had answered some difficult questions; he has tried to be firm, fair, judicious, and understanding. This was probably his most difficult letter to write. Unfortunately, it had limited success, as 2 Corinthians demonstrates. But for now let us let Paul relax and say his goodbyes.

He finishes (ch. 16) by asking for contributions to a collection for the poor of the Jerusalem community. He then gives the Corinthians his travel plans, which include a visit to them as well as to the Macedonian churches. He commends Timothy to them, compliments some individual members of their community, and forwards greetings from the churches of Asia Minor. Possibly fearful that someone might claim that the many points made in the letter were not all his, he announces, "I, Paul, write this greeting with my own hand" (16:21). As with his letter to the Galatians, Paul has used a secretary, but he writes this verse himself. Appropriately, he closes with a blessing.

All Christians believe that God chose Paul to be an apostle and that the Spirit guided Paul in his work, but divine election and assistance in no way mitigated the burden the apostle had to carry. First Corinthians certainly proves that.

The Second Letter to the Corinthians

   I.   Greeting and thanksgiving (1:1-11)

   II.   Paul's relationship with the community (1:12–2:13)

   III.   Paul's understanding of ministry (2:14–5:15)

   IV.   Personal notes (5:16–7:4)

   V.   Paul and the Corinthians reunited (7:5-16)

   VI.   Collection for the Jerusalem community (8–9)

   VII.   Paul on the defense again (10:1–12:18)
   - Respond to accusations of weakness (10)
   - Paul preaches humbly and takes no fee (11:1-15)

- Paul recounts his labors for the Church (11:16-29)
- Paul boasts of his weakness (11:30–12:10)
- Paul labors selflessly for the Church (12:11-18)

VIII.   Paul's impending visit (12:19–13:10)

IX.   Farewell and blessing (13:11-13)

Second Corinthians remains a controversial letter, not because of what it says but because of its apparent lack of unity. In chapters 1 to 9 Paul speaks very warmly of his relations with the Corinthians, of their support for his apostolate and of his work for them. Then in chapter 10 he suddenly becomes harsh, striking out at people he derisively calls "super-apostles" and getting defensive about his work. Many scholars believe that this letter may in fact be two letters, and some think it may be even more. The apostle himself remarks on another, earlier letter he wrote to the Corinthians (1 Cor 5:9), and he also refers to a painful letter (2 Cor 2:4). Is it possible that one of these letters now makes up 2 Corinthians 10–13? Yet every ancient manuscript of 2 Corinthians contains all the chapters we have now, so there is no written evidence that this one letter was ever actually two.

This technical issue seems to have little place in an introductory text, but we wish to alert the reader that some problems in NT study involve very technical matters and not just those of interpretation. We also wish to alert those readers who may read the entire letter and wonder what happened at chapter 10.

Please read chapters 1:1–6:10, 10–13.

Paul wrote this letter after 1 Corinthians, probably around 55, and although few of the issues raised in that letter reappear here, Corinth still presented a problem for the apostle. Someone was rude to him on his most recent visit to the community, and community members had apparently disciplined the offender for doing so. Paul considers his punishment just, but wisely and charitably advises his readers to have mercy (2 Cor 2:5-11). Recall that in 1 Corinthians Paul worried about how factions split up the community; here he personally recommends reconciliation: no need for more division. Later in the letter he will lament how other apostles had tried to harm his reputation. But Paul puts the problems aside and writes (chs. 1–9) a thankful, affectionate, and eloquent letter to the Corinthians.

He writes in his own name and that of Timothy, his trusted associate. He deals with personal matters but places them against a larger background or uses them as examples of Christian living. He speaks of hardship (1:4) and suffering (1:5) but immediately cites the encouragement that God and Christ give to believers, and he knows the recipients of the letter share this: "Our hope for you is unshaken; for we know that as you share in our sufferings, so also you share in our consolation" (1:7).

Paul reviews some recent events, especially his failure to visit Corinth in spite of his promise to do so. But his plans are not made "according to ordinary human standards" (1:17), and for him "Yes" and "No" are not decisions that just he makes. To God he can only say "Yes," and human plans take a second place to God's will. Furthermore, Paul did not want to go to Corinth, since his visit would have been a painful one that he wished to spare the Corinthians, and he did not relish a confrontation with the man who had insulted him on a previous visit. Instead he wrote the painful letter to which we just referred.

But now things are different. Paul enjoys a good relationship with the community, which he expresses in a very imaginative way. He does not need letters from the Corinthians to attest to their strong relationship; on the contrary, "You yourselves are our letter, written on our hearts, to be known and read by all; and you show that you are a letter of Christ, prepared by us, written not with ink but with the Spirit of the living God" (3:2-3).

Yet in his very next paragraph Paul sounds a negative note, comparing how poorly the Jews understood God's teaching in comparison with the Christians; "a veil lies over their minds." This can upset ecumenical Catholics, but we must look at this historically. Paul's teaching disturbed many Jews, and conflict between them and Paul was inevitable. Paul and his Jewish opponents both wrote in a heated environment, and we must allow for that. Furthermore, ecumenism does not require that we ignore all differences. Catholicism and Judaism are two different religions, and we take different approaches to the Old Testament, just as Paul and the first-century Jews did. (The name alone shows the difference: the Hebrew Bible is not the Old Testament for Jews because there is no New Testament.) We must make sure that phrases like Paul's do not justify anti-Semitism, but we must also avoid trying to fit Paul into a modern church.

Paul initially brings up the Old Testament to show the Corinthians how their religion differs from Judaism, and he goes on to show how it differs from paganism as well. He laments all those who cannot see "the light of the gospel of the glory of Christ, who is the image of God" (4:4).

Paul could not visit Corinth because of the demands of his work, and now he recounts the difficulties and joys of the apostolate. He writes in general of some of the troubles he has encountered, but he always emphasizes the benefits of his work: "Though our outer nature is wasting away, our inner nature is being renewed day by day" (4:16). The apostolate offers its followers an eternal reward, but Paul does not engage in otherworldly polemics against life on earth. God made our human nature; it is good both here and in the hereafter. We cannot be guided solely by our bodies, but they are part of our human nature and are good, as long as we understand them rightly. Recall that in 1 Corinthians Paul expresses his faith in the resurrection of the body. Paul senses both the "now" and the "yet to come."

From 5:11 to 6:10 Paul shows the apostolate in action, but with a spiritual emphasis that he achieves literarily by using contrasts and paradoxes. In 5:14-15 he says, ". . . the love of Christ urges us on, because we are convinced that one has died for all; therefore all have died. And he died for all, so that those who live might live no longer for themselves, but for him who died and was raised for them." The contrast is between death and life, and the paradox is that the death of one leads to life for all. But notice that he says that the love of Christ "urges us on" (sometimes translated "compels"). How can love "urge" or "compel"? That implies power, but love does not use power. True, but the love of Christ is so great that it is irresistible, and so the paradox of an urgent or compelling love. Paul uses the same approach in 6:10, describing his fellow apostles and himself: "sorrowful, yet always rejoicing; as poor, yet making many rich; as having nothing, and yet possessing everything." Rarely does Paul display his eloquence so well.

Returning to the autobiographical mode, Paul recounts his journey to Macedonia, his meeting with his fellow apostle Titus, and his joy over his reconciliation with the Corinthians, specific examples of the general principles he had been discussing.

But then he turns to a surprising topic, a collection for the poor Christians in Jerusalem. He spends much space on this. Helping the poor was not a Christian idea; Jewish piety demanded aid for the poor. But why are Gentile Christians being asked to help the poor of Jerusalem? Surely Corinth had poor people?

Recall from the letter to the Galatians that several Jewish Christians, even Peter and James, had reservations about Paul's mission to the Gentiles, and they were not alone. Paul wants to show the Jewish Christians that the Gentiles are indeed their sisters and brothers; he may also want to emphasize to the Gentiles that they owe something to the courageous Christians who formed the first church at Jerusalem. The collection would bridge these potential gaps, and in a masterful way. Finally, we should not overlook a personal element. James and Peter were courageous men who risked their lives as much as Paul did (and who also died as martyrs), and Paul had challenged them. What better way for him to show the Jerusalem Christians that his mission to the Gentiles was not severing relations between Jewish and Gentile Christians?

Paul's exhortation to the Corinthians includes an immortal line, widely used by religious fundraisers: "God loves a cheerful giver!"(9:7).

A Second Letter?

The plea for the collection ends chapter 9, and in chapter 10 Paul takes a different tone. He is angry, and he does not hide it. He replies to accusations that he is weak, that he comes on formidably in his letters but is unimpressive in person (10:10), that he takes too much pride in his authority. He threatens the community: "We are ready to punish every disobedience" (10:6). He even resorts to sardonic self-justification: "We do not dare to classify or compare ourselves with some of those who commend themselves" (10:12). Clearly something has happened to infuriate him so, yet for the first nine chapters all seemed to be fine. What is going on?

Most scholars believe that chapters 10–13 come from another letter that was added on to chapters 1–9. These four chapters do not represent a complete letter since there is no salutation; chapters 1–9 also do not represent a whole letter since there is no conclusion.

A problem like this has inevitably generated innumerable scholarly theories, but two have won the most support. The first is that chapters 10–13 represent the painful letter Paul speaks of at 2:4. As 2:1-11 shows, Paul encountered distrust and even insult, and a harsh, angry letter like this would be a painful one both to write and receive. The second theory is that after Paul wrote chapters 1–9 and sent that letter to Corinth, a crisis arose that occasioned a second letter, much of which is preserved in chapters 10–13. The matter cannot be settled with finality, but most scholars believe that someone at Corinth who valued all of Paul's writings put the two together. There is no way to be sure.

This letter tells us a lot about Paul and Corinth. As in Galatia, other apostles arrived and impressed the Corinthians so much that Paul derisively calls them "super-apostles" (11:5). Oddly, he does not discuss their teaching, although when he defends himself by comparing himself to his critics, he writes, "Are they Hebrews? So am I. Are they Israelites? So am I. Are they descendants of Abraham? So am I" (11:21-22). Most likely some old opponents have returned, Jewish Christians who disagree with Paul's preaching. But whatever they preached, they infuriated Paul, who is driven to sing his own praises. He finds this distasteful, yet by so doing he gives us much autobiographical information, especially about the trials of the apostolate: "Five times I received from the Jews the forty lashes minus one. Three times I was beaten with rods. Once I received a stoning. Three times I was shipwrecked, for a night and a day I was adrift at sea . . . . And, besides other things, I am under daily pressure because of my anxiety for all the churches [he had founded]" (11:25-28). (Deuteronomy 25:3 specified thirty-nine lashes as a maximum punishment.)

Paul now turns from his physical sufferings to his spiritual experiences, once again reluctantly: "It is necessary to boast" (12:1). He says that he knows a man who fourteen years earlier had been caught up to the third heaven, that is, the highest heaven, and heard words that could not be spoken. He is speaking of himself, and of a deep spiritual experience that validates his apostleship. But such an experience could lead to spiritual pride, so Paul was given "a thorn . . . in the flesh, a messenger of Satan to torment me, to keep me from being too elated" (12:7). In spite of Paul's pleas to the Lord to remove this "thorn," Paul still suffers from it. Yet he accepts it because God's grace enables him to overcome any weakness.

Now Paul turns to the super-apostles, challenging their authenticity. "The signs of a true apostle [Paul] were performed among you [the Corinthians] . . . . How have you been worse off than the other churches . . . ?" (12:12-13). Paul concludes his letter by asking the Corinthians to put aside all divisions, and he promises that he will pray for them. He acknowledges that he may disappoint them when he comes for his third visit, but "we rejoice when we are weak and you are strong" (13:9).

Did Paul's letter(s) succeed? Did his visit succeed? We do not know. Paul does not write again to Corinth, and no other early Christian source tells us. Given Paul's remarkable personality and indomitable faith, he probably did succeed.

A footnote to the Corinthian correspondence: the oldest datable Christian work outside the New Testament is the First Letter of Clement to the Corinthians, dated about 95 and attributed to Clement of Rome, traditionally the third pope after the apostle Peter. The letter takes a fraternal tone as it advises the Corinthians to stop breaking up into factions, in this case younger presbyters overthrowing the authority of older ones. We do not know if the letter succeeded in its purpose, but it does show us that forty years after Paul's letters the Corinthian Christians were still divided into factions. Some things never change.

The Letter to the Romans

I. Greeting and thanksgiving (1:1-15)

II. Divine wrath and judgment (1:16–3:20)
- Gentiles dominated by sin (1:16-32)
- Judgment under the Law (2)
- Objections to common understanding of the Law (3:1-8)
- Both Jews and Gentiles under judgment (3:9-20)

III. Justification for all (3:21–4:25)
- Justification apart from the Law and works (3:21-31)
- Abraham justified by faith (4:1-12)
- Our inheritance in Abraham (4:13-25)

IV. Christ and Adam (5)
- Believers saved through Christ (5:1-11)
- Sin and death from the first Adam (5:12-14)
- Grace and life through Christ the new Adam (5:15-21)

V. Grace, sin, and the Law (6–7)
- If sin brings grace, should we sin more? Absolutely not (6:1–7:6)
- Does the Law bring sin? Absolutely not (7:7-25)

VI. Law and love (8)

VII. Jews in the divine plan (9–11)
- Israel specially privileged by God (9:1-5)
- Children of the promise are Israel's true descendants (9:6-29)
- Righteousness based on faith (9:30–10:21)
- Remnant of the Jews follows the gospel (11:1-10)
- Salvation offered to the Gentiles (11:11-24)
- God stays with the Jews and offers them mercy (11:25-36)

VIII.   Daily life in the community (12–15)
- Service in many forms (12:1-8)
- Love and forgiveness (12:9-21)
- Obedience and respect for legitimate rulers (13:1-7)
- Love all to fulfill the Law (13:8-10)
- Always remember that the End is near (13:11-14)
- Considerate treatment of those weak in faith (14:1–15:6)
- Christ's message for all people (15:7-13)

IX.   Paul's friends and co-workers in the Roman community (16:1-20)

X.   Farewell and doxology (16:21-27)

The letter to the Romans is Paul's longest, latest, and most theological work. It is also unusual in being a letter to a community the apostle had neither founded nor visited. Clearly Paul wonders how the Roman Christians will receive his letter; in the last chapter (16) he lists no fewer than twenty-eight people (twenty-seven by name) in the community whom he knows, trying to make himself look less like a stranger.

Please read chapters 1–7, 13, 15–16.

Why did Paul write to this community? Because he expected to visit it on a projected missionary journey to Spain (15:24). Although the Roman writer Clement, about the year 95, said that Paul went to the farthest end of the West (presumably Spain), modern scholars do not believe that Paul got there. When he did get to Rome he arrived in chains and never left the city, being executed either as a result of losing his legal appeal or in Nero's persecution (see the life of Paul in Chapter Three). As for the when and where, most scholars date the letter around 58 and believe that Paul wrote it from Corinth.

As we also saw in Chapter Three, the emperor Claudius had expelled some Jews from Rome in 49, but Nero had readmitted them in 54. The Roman community apparently had a large number of converted Jews (7:1), and much of this letter deals with the Law, the relationship of the new faith to the old one, and Jewish-Gentile relations. For us this makes much of what Paul says historical in nature and not so relevant to the twenty-first century, but there are some perennial concerns raised in the letter, and Jewish-Christian relations still make demands upon us. Yet Paul also places the Romans among the Gentiles (1:13), suggesting that most believers there were Gentile.

Paul opens the letter by affirming his call directly by Christ to be an apostle and then gives a lengthy thanksgiving for the Romans' faith. He wants to make a good impression on the Romans, and gives a brief encapsulation of his Gospel, his "good news" (1:3-7) of which he is not ashamed. The word gospel now means a written document, but Paul's Gospel means the basic message he preached, what he considered the most salient points. He preaches Christ crucified and risen. Since he learned the faith in and around Jerusalem, his Gospel may reflect a Jewish-Christian understanding of the Christian message and may well have been familiar in Rome.

In this letter he does not speak of a problem to be solved, a typical feature of his letters to churches he founded, but he has no hesitation about imparting his views to his readers. He announces his central theme immediately: justification through faith (1:17).

Paul warns the Gentiles against divine retribution for their sins and makes an unusual argument: that the Gentiles had to know of God's existence because it can be "understood and seen by the things [God] has made" (1:20), known today as the argument from design. Why would Paul use a philosophical argument here? Probably to make it clear that paganism has no value because it denies the true God, and so God spurns those who refuse to know him. They then turn to immorality and injustice. Clearly Gentile Christians should rejoice in their conversion.

But surely the Jews are better off, since they got the Law from the one true God? No, says Paul, they too face divine retribution because the Law has no value for them if they do not live up to its precepts. "Circumcision indeed is of value if you obey the law; but if you break the law, your circumcision has become uncircumcision" (2:25). "Rather, a person is a Jew who is one inwardly" (2:29). This is rather standard moral teaching, but it gives Paul a segue into his real topic, faith and the Law.

"But now, apart from law, the righteousness of God has been disclosed, and is attested by the law and the prophets, the righteousness of God through faith in Jesus Christ for all who believe" (3:21-22). The Jews cannot be justified merely by observing the Law; more is required, and God alone can give it. But is this just Paul's understanding of the question? Does it have a biblical foundation? It certainly does, Paul replies: the figure of Abraham, father of the Jewish people.

Chapters four and five constitute the doctrinal heart of this letter. "For if Abraham was justified by works he has something to boast about, but not before God. For what does the scripture say? 'Abraham believed God, and it was reckoned to him as righteousness'" (4:2-3; quoting Gen 15:6). Male circumcision represents the sign of the covenant between God and God's people. But God promised this righteousness to Abraham *before* he was circumcised, and "he received the sign of circumcision as a seal of the righteousness that he had by faith while he was still uncircumcised" (4:11). Indeed, the Law becomes a burden to those without faith since it is impossible not to violate the Law: "for the Law brings wrath; but where there is no law, neither is there violation" (4:15). The uncircumcised Abraham is the ancestor of the Gentiles as well as of the Jews, and his salvation and theirs depends not on the Law but on faith—in the case of the Romans, faith in Jesus Christ. Abraham's faith in God models the Romans' faith in Christ.

But how does God's righteousness work in the contemporary (that is, Paul's) era? Through Jesus Christ. "But God proves his love for us in that while we still were sinners Christ died for us." (*Note the parallel to Abraham's having been saved while still uncircumcised.*) "Much more surely, then, now that we have been justified by his blood, will we be saved through him from the wrath of God" (5:8-9).

Since Paul spoke of Abraham sinning without the Law to violate, he now turns to the source of sin, Adam. "Therefore, just as sin came into the world through one man, and death came through sin, and so death spread to all because all have sinned—sin was indeed in the world before the law, ... Adam . . . is a type of the one who was to come. . . . For if the many died through the one man's trespass, much more surely have the grace of God and the free gift in the grace of the one man, Jesus Christ, abounded for the many" (5:12-14). Paul just says that God reckoned Abraham as righteous, but here he makes it clear that we are reckoned righteous before God by the work of Jesus, the Second Adam, and the one who makes up for the harm done in the Garden of Eden. And Jesus did not do this once and for all; he continues to work on our behalf: "where sin increased, grace abounded all the more, so that, just as sin exercised dominion in death, so grace might also exercise dominion through justification leading to eternal life through Jesus Christ our Lord" (5:20-21).

This is an important concept but not an easy one. Paul does not wish us to think that if God reckons us as righteous we are free to sin as we will and pay no consequences; he also does not want us to think that the Law, given by God, has no more value, so he turns now to some practical spiritual problems.

If grace comes to us because of sin, "should we continue in sin in order that grace may abound? By no means! . . . Do you not know that all of us who have been baptized into Christ Jesus were baptized into his death? . . . The death he died, he died to sin, once for all; but the life he lives, he lives to God. So you also must consider yourselves dead to sin and alive to God in Christ Jesus" (6:1-2, 10-11). Being justified, we are not free to sin but dead to the very idea of sinning. We should lead lives that reflect this new state. We were slaves to sin and now we are free of it, and we should be careful not to return to that state. "For the wages of sin is death, but the free gift of God is eternal life in Christ Jesus our Lord" (6:23).

Since faith and not the Law saves us, we are free from the Law. In a surprisingly personal passage Paul the Pharisee explains what the Law did to him. Knowing the Law proved spiritually dangerous to him: ". . . if it had not been for the law, I would not have known sin. I would not have known what it is to covet if the law had not said, 'You shall not covet.' . . . The very commandment that promised life proved to be death to me. For sin, seizing an opportunity in the commandment, deceived me . . ." (7:7, 10-11). The great apostle tells of his struggle with sin: "I do not do the good I want, but the evil I do not want is what I do" (7:19). But he finds hope: "Wretched man that I am! Who will rescue me from this body of death? Thanks be to God through Jesus Christ our Lord!" (7:25).

Paul stays with his spiritual topic, and chapter eight includes some of his most impressive statements about the spiritual life. "Those who live according to the flesh set their minds on the things of the flesh, but those who live according to the Spirit set their minds on the things of the Spirit" (8:5). "[It] is that very Spirit bearing witness with our spirit that we are children of God, and if children, then heirs, heirs of God and joint heirs with Christ—if, in fact, we suffer with him so that we may also be glorified with him" (8:17). "If God is for us, who is against us?" (8:31). "For I am convinced that neither death, nor life, nor angels, nor rulers, nor things present, nor things to come, nor powers, nor height, nor depth, nor anything else in all creation, will be able to separate us from the love of God in Christ Jesus our Lord" (8:39). Freedom, uprightness, the Spirit—these do not just free us from sin but transform us into a new life, one difficult for us to understand and simply inaccessible to those who deny God or who live only under the Law.

But Paul cannot get away from the Law, and so he turns to it again. He deals with a sizeable problem: if Christ fulfills the plan that God started working centuries ago via the people Israel, then why have the Jews rejected Christ? Aware that this rejection could lead to anti-Semitism, Paul insists he would do anything to help his people (9:3).

One explanation is that God failed to keep the promises to Israel, but Paul rejects this soundly by arguing that "not all Israelites truly belong to Israel, and not all of Abraham's children . . . are his true descendants [because] it is not the children of the flesh who are the children of God" (9:6-8). We (Christians) are that people "whom [God] called, not from the Jews only but also from the Gentiles" (9:24). Paul then gives a list of OT passages showing that God knew Israel would forsake his message and the message would go to the Gentiles.

How does Paul think the Jews went astray? By trying to please God with works and not in faith. They failed to see that God, not works, makes people holy. In fact, "Christ is the end of the law so that there may be righteousness for everyone who believes" (10:4). (Paul here uses a double meaning of "end": the finishing of something, but also its perfection, the fulfillment of its purpose.) But surely the Jews can be forgiven for not recognizing this new message? Paul argues that they did hear the message and did understand it (10:18-19), but he cites OT examples of the people's refusing to understand. This means that they have no excuse for not accepting the message. He knows this is harsh, and he emphasizes his oneness with the Jews: "I myself am an Israelite, a descendant of Abraham, a member of the tribe of Benjamin" (11:1). He points out that God never abandoned God's people, and even when the people drifted away, God always preserved a sacred remnant through which to effect salvation. "So too at the present time there is a remnant, chosen by grace" (11:5). For Paul the Jews remain God's chosen people, and he believes that as the Jews see the Gentiles reaping the fruits of their acceptance of Christ, the Jews will eventually turn to Christ as well. In a sense this is deserved because the Jews are like the branches of a plant—some branches withered and were replaced by new ones grafted on (the Gentiles), but some branches remained strong, and God has the power to graft the withered ones back onto the plant.

Paul's reasoning can be difficult, and he knows that he has hardly deciphered God's will, so he ends this section with one of his most famous sayings about God: "How unsearchable are his judgments and how inscrutable his ways!" (11:33).

Now Paul turns from doctrinal issues to ones relating to daily Christian life. Paul's experience in Corinth weighs heavily upon him because he emphasizes unity and respect for diversity. "For as in one body we have many members, and not all the members have the same function, so we, who are many, are one body in Christ, and individually we are members one of another" (12:4-5). "Live in harmony with one another; do not be haughty, but associate with the lowly" (12:16). "Why do you pass judgment on your brother or sister [that is, another Christian]? Or you, why do you despise your brother or sister?" (14:10) "Each of us must please our neighbor for the good purpose of building up the neighbor" (15:2). But does this concern result solely from the factionalism at Corinth, or did Paul know or think that the Roman community also suffered from factionalism? There is no way to answer that question.

Some other familiar issues appear: gifts and food. We all have different gifts, and we must use them in grace. The apostle lists prophecy, practical service, teaching, and encouraging others (12:6-8). As for food, "I know and am persuaded in the Lord Jesus that nothing is unclean in itself; but it is unclean for anyone who thinks it unclean" (14:14). Yet "it is good not to eat meat or drink wine or do anything that makes your brother or sister stumble" (14:21), the view he endorsed in 1 Corinthians. Although we can see that unity must come first, we must wonder why Paul again sides with the ignorant on this issue. If he really believes that no food is unclean, why not teach the ignorant that it is not, instead of making everyone else change their diets to accommodate them?

Paul is writing to the church in the imperial capital, and he must address the question not so much of church and state but of how the Christian should view governmental authorities. The reigning emperor was Nero, who would later persecute the Christians in 64, but at this point he had not harmed them. Paul urges his readers to "be subject to the governing authorities; for there is no authority except from God, and those authorities that exist have been instituted by God. Therefore whoever resists an authority resists what God has appointed, and those who resist will incur judgment" (13:1-2). Paul worries that the Christian movement, essentially spiritual, could be misunderstood as a social or political one, so he leans too far in the other direction. To say that "those authorities that exist have been instituted by God" validates any ruler, and clearly Paul would not have said that after Nero had persecuted the Christians. Even worse, a line like that could be applied to the worst governments in existence today, causing Raymond Brown to write: ". . . it is unwarranted to absolutize the Pauline instruction as if his were the NT view applicable to governing authorities of all times" (*Introduction to the New Testament*, 572). Modern Catholics should recall how often clergy and laity have stood up to repressive regimes in many parts of the world. Catholics like Thomas More and Maximilian Kolb gave their lives in opposing tyrannical rulers. But we can understand Paul's concern, even if we cannot accept his views totally.

Most of us know the famous line, "Give to Caesar the things that are Caesar's" (Mark 12:17), and apparently Paul encountered a similar question about whether it was lawful to pay taxes. "For the same reason you also pay taxes, for the authorities are God's servants, busy with this very thing" (13:6). Since this is the only particular issue Paul mentions concerning obedience to authorities, we must assume it was a problem at Rome.

But that last line leads us to another question: why did Paul presume to give the Romans lectures about Christian life? There was a flourishing community there, and obviously the local leaders could urge the people to Christian living without Paul's help. Did Paul write at the request of the Roman leaders, lending his authority as apostle of the Gentiles (11:13) to their teaching? Possibly, but there is no reason to think that, especially since Paul rarely takes a commanding tone in this letter. Most likely Paul's experience in Corinth led him to believe the problems there might replicate themselves elsewhere.

Paul finishes his letter by describing his ministry, including this important saying: "I make it my ambition to proclaim the good news, not where Christ has already been named, so that I do not build on someone else's foundation" (15:20). Paul acknowledges that there are other fine missionaries and that one or more of them had evangelized in Rome, but he does not mention anyone by name.

He then gives the Romans his travel plans. He hopes to stop in the city on his way to Spain (15:24), an intriguing reference. Clearly Christianity has taken hold in the imperial capital, but why does Paul plan to go so far west? Is there no more evangelizing to do in Italy? And why does Paul plan to bypass the Roman province of Gaul (modern France) to get to Spain: are missionaries already in Gaul? And does he have the language skills to evangelize in Spain? Yet he mentions this goal a second time (15:29), so he clearly intends to go there, although modern scholars do not think he did.

Before he can go to Spain he must take funds for the Jerusalem church that he has collected among his churches. Why mention the collection to the Romans, whom he has not asked for funds? Maybe he hopes for Roman good will in dealing with other churches, probably even Jerusalem itself since he expresses the hope "that I may be rescued from the unbelievers in Judea, and that my ministry to Jerusalem may be acceptable to the saints" (15:31), that is, he fears that the Jerusalem church leaders will not even accept his gift—a reference to some unknown hostility between them and him?

The last chapter of Romans presents a problem for scholars. It is undoubtedly authentically Pauline, and all but one ancient manuscript of the letter includes it, but some scholars doubt if it was originally part of the letter. Why? Scholars question how Paul could possibly have known twenty-eight people in a community he had never visited. But against that interpretation is the ending of chapter 15, "The God of peace be with all of you. Amen." That is not how Paul ends his letters, whereas the farewell wishes of chapter 16 fit Paul's style much better. And as for the twenty-eight people, there is no reason why he could not have known them. Paul's letters and the Acts of the Apostles show Christian missionaries on the move—from Jerusalem to Antioch and on to Cyprus, Asia Minor, Greece, Alexandria, and Rome. Paul thinks it no impossible task to go to Spain, and we know that he is not the only one who travels: Barnabas, Silas, Mark, Timothy, and Titus are the ones Paul mentions, and Acts speaks of others, such as Lydia. Priscilla and Aquila went from Rome to Corinth, and now they are back at Rome (16:3). Can anyone say with finality that no others from Rome joined them on the trip to Corinth where they could have met Paul and later returned to Rome? Most scholars believe that chapter 16 is an integral part of the letter and Paul has included it because he wants to convince the Romans that he is well known among community members.

A list of names sounds dull, but we can learn a lot from it. The first person Paul mentions is a woman, "our sister Phoebe," who is a deacon. He also mentions a woman named Junia, who is an apostle (16:7). As Raymond Brown points out, "This verse is a problem chiefly for those who, *contrary to the NT evidence,* confine apostolate to the Twelve" (*Introduction to the New Testament,* 574). Paul cites several other women who are co-workers of his, such as Prisca, Tryphaena, Julia, and the unnamed sister of Nereus, proof that women had a significant role to play in the earliest communities.

Paul names many men, including "my kinsman Herodion" (16:10), but he does not specify the relationship. Most of the names are Greek, implying a community of mostly immigrants from the eastern Mediterranean, although there are several Latin names such as Rufus and Julia.

He makes one last reference to the need for unity, and then we find a surprising statement: "I, Tertius, the writer of this letter, greet you in the Lord" (16:22), proving that Paul dictated this letter as he did some others. The end of the letter is a doxology, a liturgical prayer of praise to God, possibly one in use at Rome.

Appendix: Peter in Rome

Catholics cannot help but notice that Paul does not include Peter among the Christians at Rome whom he greets. Why not? There are several possibilities, including one unworthy of Paul, that is, that he was still angry at Peter (Galatians 2) and declined to mention him. Even if this were the case, he could hardly have ignored the leader of the Twelve in a communal letter. Possibly Paul did not know that Peter was there, which would be very unusual, given the prominence of these two men. The most likely possibility is that Peter had not yet arrived in Rome.

Many traditions grew up around the New Testament figures, and while there is nothing wrong with that, we must distinguish the traditions from what Scripture itself says. A medieval Roman tradition says that Peter served as bishop of Rome for twenty-five years. Since Nero's persecution occurred in 64, that would put Peter in Rome by the year 39, a very early date. This tradition became so well known that traditions grew up around it, such as the notion that no pope would ever reign longer than Peter, a notion seemingly validated by eighteen centuries of papal history until Pius IX (1846–1878) finally broke the barrier.

But traditions do not always preserve history, and Paul probably did not mention Peter because he had not arrived in Rome by 58. Paul tells us that Peter was definitely in Antioch and that he had an apostolate to the circumcised (Gal 2:7-8), which implies that Peter did missionary work among Jewish Christians in the Diaspora. Paul further says that there was a party in Corinth claiming allegiance to Peter (1 Cor 1:12), and although he does not say that Peter himself had ever been in Corinth, this reference suggests some activity by Peter in the Corinth area. These sparse references show that Peter worked as a missionary in the eastern Mediterranean for a while before going to Rome.

But how can Peter then be the founder of the Roman church? The Catholic Church has never understood the term "founder" in a purely chronological sense, that is, that Peter was the very first Christian to set foot in Rome. Rather, "founder" means that when Peter went to Rome— and Catholic, Protestant, and Orthodox scholars accept that he did—he, as leader of the Twelve, became the most prestigious member of the

Roman community, uniting the community and serving as its first *epís-kopos*, giving it form and focus, and thus founding it. In fact, some scholars believe that Peter was an *epískopos* and more, that is, that his stature prevented him from having to get involved in the day-to-day operation of the local church; rather, he was appealed to primarily on important matters. This is a conjecture, but a logical one. We should see Peter exercising overall authority, providing the community with a living link to Jesus, and recounting many personal recollections of the Lord, his words, and his deeds. Despite many ancient and medieval legends as well as famous novels, such as *Quo Vadis?* by the Polish novelist Henryk Sienkiewicz (1846–1916), we really know little about Peter in Rome. But we do not doubt that he was there and served as head of the community.

Chapter Six

Introduction to the Gospels

Biographies of Jesus?

The gospels are the most important books in the New Testament. Believers know much of their contents, but the gospels still present many problems, mostly because of misunderstandings. Before the modern era Christians considered the gospels to be "lives of Christ," and many still think that. Actually the gospels are theological accounts of Jesus' public career, and not biographies in the modern sense of the term. When we get to the individual gospels later in the book we will examine these points in detail, but for now let me demonstrate why the gospels cannot be considered biographies of Jesus.

The most obvious point about these "lives" is that, except for an account of the twelve-year-old Jesus in the Temple (Luke 2:41-50), they tell us nothing about Jesus between his birth and his public career, and only two of them, Matthew and Luke, mention his birth. One might respond that this period of Jesus' life was not important. That may be, but the point is that a true biography would not start when the subject was an adult but would instead cover the person's entire life.

Furthermore, the gospels never tell us what Jesus looked like. Thanks to movies we all know that he was tall and handsome and strong with a mass of flowing hair, *et cetera et cetera et cetera,* but actually we do not know what he looked like. Jewish men of his era wore beards, so he would have done so. As a carpenter in an age with no power tools, he would have been physically strong. The gospels show him constantly outside and walking long distances, so he was in good health, but that is really about it. Was he short, medium height, or tall? We simply do not know; we are not going to know; and we should agree with the gospel writers that this does not really matter to believers (no matter how much it matters to movie directors).

But even if we focus just on Jesus' public career, there are still problems with the gospels as "lives." Modern biographers writing about the same figure may disagree on how to interpret the person's life and career, but they at least agree on the facts. Yet the gospels often do not. For example, all four gospels record how Jesus drove the money changers from the Temple, but Matthew, Mark, and Luke place this event *at the end of Jesus' public career* (Matt 21:12-13; Mark 11:15-19; Luke 19:45-48), while John places it *at the beginning of his public career* (John 2:13-17). It is not important for now which episode is correct; rather, the point is that either one or three of the gospels got the fact wrong.

Matthew, Mark, and Luke all tell the story of Jesus' calming the storm (Matt 8:23-27; Mark 4:35-41; Luke 8:22-25). Matthew and Luke also contain Jesus' words about the nature of discipleship ("Foxes have holes, and birds of the air have nests . . ."). In Matthew's Gospel (8:18-22) Jesus utters these words *before* he calms the storm, while in Luke's Gospel (9:57-60) he utters them not just *after* the calming of the storm but *after he does several others things as well,* such as the cure of the Gerasene demoniac and the woman with the hemorrhage (8:40-56). It is likely that one of the gospels has the correct chronology, but they obviously *both* cannot, so one of the gospels is wrong on the chronology. Examples like these could be multiplied, and they prove that the gospels cannot be considered modern biographies.

Does this mean that we do not have reliable information about Jesus? Not at all. It does mean that we have to be realistic about the gospels by understanding what they are and how they came to be.

The evangelists composed their gospels after the career of Paul. They wrote about a Jesus who is alive, out of their belief in the Risen Christ. This belief impacted their works. For starters, the gospels, like all NT books, *were written by believers for believers,* and they include material that can only be discerned by faith and not by history. In his opening verse Mark says that Jesus Christ is the Son of God. No historian could prove that. One could prove historically that Jesus existed, but that he is the Christ, the Messiah, and the Son of God is a matter of faith. All four evangelists profess their belief in Christ and try to explain for their readers who he was, who he is, what he has done for us, and how God works through him. Biographical details have much importance, but they are not the ultimate goal of the gospel accounts. Raymond Brown summed up the situation well: "The notion that Christian faith should depend upon reconstructions of the historical Jesus is a dangerous misunderstanding" (*Introduction to the New Testament,* 106).

It is also important to recognize how the gospels came into being. Jesus himself did not write anything, and his words were passed along orally for decades before being written down by his followers. The same applies to accounts of his deeds. This is not unusual for the ancient world and especially not for religions. The first "lives" of the Buddha appeared five hundred years after his death, while the first accounts of Mohammed's life date to two centuries after the prophet's death. Almost inevitably some event would slip loose from a larger chronological framework, and words could become detached from their setting. One of Jesus' best known sayings is, "it is better to give than to receive." Teachers use this for a trick question when they ask students, "In what gospel does this appear?" It does not appear in any of the gospels, but rather in the Acts of the Apostles (20:35), where Paul simply quotes it without a context, so we have no idea where or when Jesus said it. In his first letter to the Thessalonians Paul cites another saying of Jesus out of context (1 Thess 4:15). When we realize that sayings and deeds were often preached and repeated without chronological and physical contexts it is easy to see how their sequence could become unsettled.

Before we get to an outline of Jesus' life, let me refer back to the first chapter where we saw that a lot of factors (liturgical readings, media) impact our understanding of the NT. The same is true here. A lot of erroneous information has circulated for a long time, and scholars often find themselves playing the role of bad guys who have to disillusion people. That is not a role anyone likes, but the real problem is the misinformation, not the people who have to correct it.

Oral transmission partly explains something else that bothers many people: that Jesus' words don't match in all the gospels. For example, there are two versions of the Lord's Prayer, Matthew 6:9-13 and Luke 11:2-4 (Matthew has the familiar "Our Father"). Doesn't that mean that we have lost Jesus' authentic teaching? No, and on two counts. First, the most important words of Jesus (for example, "This is my body") would have been carefully preserved by his disciples. Second, we don't have the "authentic" words of Jesus anyway. Jesus traveled about Galilee, preaching to the people, and he did so in their own language, Aramaic, a Semitic dialect widely used in the Near East. Although the occasional Aramaic word survives, the gospels preserve the words of Jesus *in Greek,* that is, the "authentic" words of Jesus survive in a translation.

And most Catholics read the Bible translated into their own language. So when we read that Jesus said something like "Give to Caesar the things that belong to Caesar," we are actually reading an English translation of a Greek translation of Semitic words preserved by oral tradition.

This upsets very conservative Christians, but it is not a problem for Catholics. Recalling that Jesus never wrote anything himself, we realize that *we have always been dependent on his disciples and the earliest community, that is, the church, to preserve his words and accounts of his deeds.* The modern historical mind might prefer the original Aramaic words, but no amount of wishful thinking will bring them back. Even if we did have sayings of Jesus in Aramaic, we would still get them *through the community that preserved them,* that is, we would still be dependent on the church to recount Jesus' words. Our trust—our faith—rests on the church, and we modern Catholics share the faith of the first Christians. Let me also note that many other important documents from the ancient world survive in translation. The preservation of Jesus' words in Greek is simply not a big problem.

What about his life? Here again misinformation abounds. So many people think that Jesus was born at midnight as the era passed from b.c.e. to c.e., that he began his public career at age thirty in the year 30 c.e., and that, after a three-year public ministry, he died at age thirty-three in the year 33. A nice little account, but, unfortunately, completely unhistorical.

Only Matthew and Luke have accounts of Jesus' nativity, and *neither gives the year of his birth,* but the gospels do give a clue. Matthew (2:1) and Luke (1:3) tell us that he was born during the reign of Herod, and Matthew suggests that the birth occurred shortly before Herod's death (2:19). So when did Herod reign? From 37 to 4 b.c.e. (or, as others would say, b.c. = before Christ. Scholars now use b.c.e. = Before the Common Era, and c.e. = of the Common Era, out of respect for people of other religions who do not date everything in terms of Jesus). Yet this means Christ was born *before* Christ. How can this be? The answer lies in the sixth century when a monk at Rome, Dionysius Exiguus, prepared a new calendar centered around the birth of Christ. This calendar is now universally used, even by non-Western nations. Later generations of scholars realized that Dionysius had simply made a mistake in judging the death of Herod and thus the date of Christ's birth, which has now been correctly recalculated. That is how Christ came to be born no later than 4 b.c.e. Since Matthew tells us that Herod asked the Magi exactly when the star appeared (2:7) and later put to death all boys in Bethlehem up to the age of two (2:16), Jesus could have been born as much as two years before Herod's death, as early as 6 B.C.E.

As for Jesus' being thirty when he started his public ministry, that derives from an imprecise reading of Luke 3:23 which says that Jesus was *about thirty* years old at the time he began his ministry. "About thirty" could mean 28 or 29 or 31 or 32 as well as 30. Luke did not know exactly how old Jesus was, so he gave the approximate date. No other gospel mentions Jesus' age, not even approximately.

The three-year public ministry derives from John's Gospel, which mentions three Passovers (2:13; 6:4; 11:55), and since Passover occurs only once a year, this means a three-year ministry. But Matthew, Mark, and Luke mention only one Passover during the public ministry, which suggests a ministry of only one year. For reasons we will discuss later, scholars generally believe that these three gospels give a more historical view of Jesus' career than John does, and most scholars think Jesus' public ministry lasted one year or maybe two, given the time he would have needed to travel so much on foot.

So if we cannot be sure that he was exactly thirty when he began his ministry and scholars question a three-year ministry, when did Jesus die? We know that his public career occurred during the governorship of Pontius Pilate, that is, from 26 to 36, so it occurred sometime during that period. But from non-biblical sources we know that Pilate owed his appointment to a confidante of the emperor Tiberius, a man named Sejanus, who fell from power in 31. Very likely Pilate moved carefully after the fall of his patron, and his execution of a man he believed to be innocent was motivated by his fear of looking too lenient. John 19:12 reports that the mob shouted to Pilate, "If you release this man (Jesus), you are no friend of the emperor." If this theory is correct and Jesus' execution did occur after the fall of Sejanus in 31, then the traditional date of 33 is most likely correct. No scholar dates the crucifixion later than 33.

So, if the gospels are not modern biographies, what can we say about Jesus' life? There are many points about which the gospels agree and which we can consider biographical:

- Jesus' parents were named Mary (Miriam) and Joseph.
- Joseph was a carpenter.
- Jesus followed his father's trade, normal for a boy of that era.
- He was born in Bethlehem in Judea during the reign of Herod.
- He grew up in Nazareth in Galilee.

- The public ministry of John the Baptist preceded his.
- His ministry was spent almost completely in Galilee.
- He was a popular preacher and miracle worker.
- He had disciples of both sexes who followed him.
- He chose twelve male disciples for special roles.
- He had conflicts with the Pharisees.
- He was careful not to let people believe he had political goals and always stressed that his ministry was religious.
- He traveled constantly with his disciples, even into non-Jewish territories.
- After a ministry in Galilee he went to Jerusalem, where some of the local authorities banded together against him.
- His enemies engineered his condemnation by the Roman governor, Pontius Pilate.
- He was crucified.
- He rose from the dead.

As for the many individual elements, such as his telling the parable of the Good Samaritan or debating with the Pharisees about picking grain on the Sabbath, there is simply no way to place them exactly in his ministry. We may safely assume that his preaching became more complex as he moved more and more among the people and that he probably preached differently in Jerusalem than in small towns like Capernaum or Nazareth, but we cannot say that he told a specific parable on a specific date or between two specific events.

Let us consider one other issue, not about Jesus, but about his family. All four gospels (Matt 12:46; Mark 3:31; Luke 8:19; John 2:12) speak of Jesus' "brothers," and they used the standard Greek word *adelphós* for a full-blood brother, that is, someone who had the same parents as Jesus. This seemingly contradicts Catholic teaching that his mother Mary was perpetually a virgin, but Catholic scholars have pointed out that *adelphós* is a translation of an Aramaic word that can mean male relatives other than a full-blood brother. Thus the doctrine of Mary's perpetual virginity does not contradict the gospels.

(There is an interesting sidelight to this. Catholics are not the only Christians who accept Mary's perpetual virginity. In the second century some Christians in Syria who believed in her perpetual virginity tried to explain Jesus' brothers by claiming that his father Joseph had been previously married and had sons by a then-deceased first wife. Although no one takes this seriously today, many medieval and Renaissance artists did, which is why so many paintings of the Nativity show Joseph as much older than Mary, even having gray or white hair.)

Understanding the Gospels

Even when we know the gospels may not be biographies, they still present problems, again because of misunderstanding. The gospels of Matthew and John give us particularly valuable testimony because two of the twelve apostles wrote them, right? Unfortunately, no. We will discuss each gospel separately, but it is best to clarify this misimpression here.

Unlike Paul, the evangelists did not put their names on their work. In the second century Christians named the evangelists. That does not necessarily mean that the names are wrong, but the names do not derive from the gospels themselves.

"Matthew" cannot have been written by one of the Twelve because, as we shall see, Matthew copies material from Mark. To ask the obvious question, why would an eyewitness to Jesus' life copy material from someone who was not there? There is also the problem of Matthew's Greek. Clearly the evangelist was a native Greek speaker, not a Galilean who learned Greek as a second language.

As for John, the Gospel of John never mentions an apostle named John, speaking only of "the Beloved Disciple," whom second-century Christians identified as John. And if the Beloved Disciple were John, he still could not have written the gospel since the gospel itself says that *it derives from the testimony of the Beloved Disciple* who apparently had already died (21:23). As with Matthew, John's Greek is a problem since this "Galilean fisherman" wrote very sophisticated Greek. We simply do not have eyewitness accounts from any of the Twelve, but we will follow standard practice and use the traditional names.

Since we do not have eyewitness accounts, we can see again the importance of oral tradition and of the church as the preserver of that tradition. Mention of the church brings up another important point: the evangelists wrote for particular communities, and the gospels often tell us about those communities. Every author writes for an audience, as I am doing now, and naturally enough she/he arranges the material for that audience. For the evangelists this means that they often portrayed Jesus in a way that met the needs of their audiences, and thus we get four portrayals of Jesus.

This also shocks conservative Christians, but it shouldn't. All of us are different people to different people. I am my wife's husband, my children's father, my brothers' brother, my students' teacher, and so on.

My students do not see me as my family members do, and the reverse is equally true. Thus it is no surprise that the evangelists understood Jesus in varying ways. Although we will see this in more detail further along in the book, let me note that Matthew puts much stress on Jesus as the one who fulfilled the prophecies of the OT because the evangelist wrote partly for converted Jews for whom this carried much weight. Luke, on the other hand, emphasizes the good non-Jew in both the gospel and Acts (for example, the Good Samaritan), because he wrote for converted Gentiles. Clearly Jesus can be both the fulfillment of the Israelite prophecies and the redeemer of all nations and still be one and the same person. So it is only natural that evangelists writing for diverse communities will stress different aspects of who Jesus is.

The evangelists also wrote differently. Mark writes at a breathtaking pace, with events piled one on top of the other, and he often uses the word "immediately" to move the text along. Matthew frequently presents Jesus as the rabbinic teacher who likes to make formal pronouncements; this evangelist often adds to passages where Mark provides just the facts. Luke prefers a refined style, and in his gospel everyone from illiterate beggars to Roman governors speaks the same high-quality Greek. John uses many symbols to get his message across. The evangelists did not just report the basics; they were conscious literary artists who cultivated particular styles.

Earlier on I suggested that the best way to understand the gospels is to read them in their entirety at least once. Another good way is to examine particular passages side by side—which we will do from time to time in this book—because then these literary traits become obvious.

One final point: Like many teachers in Catholic institutions, I have occasionally been asked by people, "Should you really let the students know how complicated the gospels are? Won't it harm their faith?" The people asking that question mean well, but the answer can never be "Yes," and for four reasons:

First, faith and learning do not contradict each other. Many simple, even illiterate people became saints, but so did great scholars like Augustine of Hippo and Thomas Aquinas. Illiteracy or ignorance never made anyone a saint nor has learning ever detracted from sanctity. People's lives, not their educations, make them saints.

Second, if learning is not important, why does the church have elementary schools, high schools, colleges, and universities? Why not just keep people theologically illiterate?

Third, if people read the Scriptures, as the church urges them to do, they will eventually notice that the Lord's Prayer in Luke differs from the familiar "Our Father," and they will certainly wonder why. So even if someone wanted to keep people ignorant, it just would not work.

Fourth, and most importantly, teachers have a moral obligation to give their students at all levels and ages the most accurate information they have. To tell people that the gospels are straightforward biographies is to tell an untruth, even if it is done to "protect their faith." Ignorance is no friend of faith—never was, never will be.

So let's now look at the Gospel of Mark.

Chapter Seven

The Gospel According to Mark

I. John the Baptist (1:1-13)

II. Galilean Ministry (1:14–6:6)
   - Calling disciples and first miracles (1:14-45)
   - First conflicts with Jewish authorities (2:1–3:6)
   - True followers and true kindred (3:7-35)
   - Parables (4:1-34)
   - Healing miracles (4:35–5:43)
   - Rejection at Nazareth (6:1-6)

III. Journey to Jerusalem (6:7–10:52)
   - Mission of the Twelve and death of the Baptist (6:7-29)
   - Miracles of healing and feeding (6:30-56)
   - Teaching about the Law (7:1-23)
   - Miracles of healing and feeding (7:24–8:26)
   - Disciples' confession of faith and prediction of Passion (8:27–9:1)
   - Transfiguration and Elijah (9:2-13)
   - Healings, teachings, and predictions of Passion (9:14–10:52)

IV. Jesus in Jerusalem (11–13)
   - Triumphal entry and cleansing of Temple (11:1-19)
   - Teaching in Temple and conflicts with Jewish authorities (11:20–12:44)
   - Apocalyptic discourse (13)

V. The Passion and Death of Jesus (14–15)
   - Last Supper and Gethsemane (14:1-52)
   - Trials before Sanhedrin and Pilate (14:53–15:5)
   - Crucifixion and Death (15:6-47)

VI. Resurrection (16)

It is important to read at least one gospel in its entirety. Since Mark is the shortest gospel, this is a good one to read.

Mark is both the earliest gospel and the shortest. Scholars date it around the year 70. Although it often has a rather brusque style, it shows considerable theological acumen. Clearly Mark wrote after the career of Paul, when christology was becoming a theological discipline, indicating a date no earlier than the 60s. Scholars set it no later than 70 because the Markan Jesus predicts the destruction of Jerusalem by the Romans, which occurred in that year, but Mark's description does not correspond exactly to the actual destruction. On the other hand, in the gospels of Matthew and Luke the prediction matches the reality more closely, suggesting that the event had already occurred and that the two evangelists put in some realistic details. This in turn means that Mark wrote before the destruction, so he wrote no later than the year 70. Clearly this does not provide exact dates, but scholars can only work with available evidence.

Where did Mark write? The gospel mentions no place of writing. Internal evidence suggests a Gentile locale. For example, Mark has to explain Jewish customs to his readers (7:3-4) and translates Aramaic words for them (3:17; 7:34), which suggests that they were not Jewish converts, yet he uses Jewish words like "rabbi" and "Satan," so his readers knew something about Judaism. Mark uses several Latin loanwords (5:19; 6:37; 14:5), which suggests a location where Latin was spoken along with Greek. That could mean any place where a Roman garrison was stationed, but many scholars think the locale was Rome itself because we know from Paul that the community there had a Jewish base. Yet no scholar can prove an exact location.

Can we say anything about the author? Several scriptural passages speak of a John Mark or Mark; in the Acts of the Apostles he is a fellow-missionary of Paul and Barnabas; in the First Letter of Peter he is with Peter (5:13), while 2 Timothy makes him an associate of Paul (4:11), as he is briefly in Acts. It is not implausible that this Mark wrote the gospel, but there is no proof for it, and most Catholic scholars conclude that an identification cannot be made. Nor is that important. Mark found a place in the NT because the church believed the book to be inspired, not because of a tradition that Mark of the NT wrote it.

How do we know that Mark is the earliest gospel? Because Matthew and Luke knew his gospel, which can be proved by setting Mark side by side with Luke and Matthew and noting how the other two gospels change his text. Mark 4:35-41 tells how Jesus calmed a storm at sea. This account says that "other boats were with him" (v. 36) but never says what happens to the other boats. The Matthean (8:23-27) and Lukan (8:22-25) versions omit the other boats. What is more logical, that Mark added a confusing and unexplained detail or that Matthew and Luke eliminated it? In addition, Mark has a confusing passage (v. 39): "*They woke him up* and said to him, 'Teacher, do you not care that we are perishing?' *He woke up* and rebuked the wind, and said to the sea, 'Peace! Be still!'" In Matthew's and Luke's gospels Jesus wakes up only once!

When the Pharisees challenge Jesus as his disciples pick grain on the Sabbath (2:23-28), Jesus defends them by citing the example of David's doing something similar when Abiathar was high priest (v. 26). But the high priest in David's day was Ahimelech (1 Sam 21:1-7), which means Jesus made a mistake. In the Matthean (12:1-8) and Lukan (6:1-5) accounts there is no mention of Abiathar. Is it more likely that Matthew and Luke corrected a mistake or that Mark added it? Accounts such as these, which could be multiplied, demonstrate that Matthew and Luke wrote after Mark.

(Some readers may be disturbed that Mark shows Jesus making a mistake. The letter to the Hebrews (4:15) spells it out clearly: Jesus is as completely human as we are, "yet without sin." A fully human Jesus could make a mistake in citing the Scriptures; there is nothing sinful about a slip of the memory. If there were, we would all be hopeless sinners. Mark does not demean Jesus when he shows him as human in this regard.)

But is it not possible that since his gospel is the shortest, Mark came after Matthew and Luke and abbreviated some of their material? Not really, because there are passages where Mark's account is longer than that of the other two, such as the Parable of the Sower (Mark 4:13-20; Matt 13:18-23; Luke 8:11-15) and the Gerasene demoniac (Mark 5:1-20; Matt 8:28-34; Luke 8:26-39), so clearly he did not abbreviate material from the other two.

Finally, if the other two came before Mark he made some startling omissions, most obviously the infancy narratives (Matthew 1–2, Luke 1–2). Why would he ever have omitted material like that? Or the Good Samaritan or the Prodigal Son?

The cumulative evidence becomes overwhelming. We can understand why Matthew and Luke might change or add to Mark's text, but we just cannot explain why Mark would change or subtract from their texts. Catholic and Protestant scholars overwhelmingly agree that Mark's is the earliest gospel.

Why did Mark write a gospel? He does not tell us, and scholars have suggested a variety of reasons, including the deaths of the first generation that knew Jesus. The evangelist may also have wanted to record the oral traditions he knew, lest they be lost or altered. Most likely he wanted to give a solid organization and structure to his community's understanding of Jesus. Whatever the reason, the written gospel proved popular since several other early Christian writers imitated him.

When we looked at Paul's letters we followed the text, explaining it along the way. We cannot do that with the gospels because of their length. This shortest gospel is thirty-six percent longer than the longest letter (Romans); any two gospels are longer than all of Paul's letters combined. Instead, we shall highlight the main themes of the gospel and see how these appear in the text.

Mark begins his gospel by saying that it is the good news of Jesus Christ, that is, Jesus is the *christos*, "the Anointed One," "the Messiah." But Jesus cannot be understood by the traditional meaning of "Messiah," one who will come in clouds and power to liberate the Jews from Roman domination. This Messiah has a different calling, one that few people will understand, not even those closest to him. Mark uses a literary device known as the "omniscient reader," which means that the reader knows things that the characters in the story do not. He tells us in 1:1 that Jesus is the Messiah, but the "characters" in this tale have trouble grasping that. Throughout this gospel Jesus will try to bring them to the true understanding of who he is. Mark implies that Jesus' disciples should have been able to grasp who he was. The social reforming preacher, John the Baptizer, proclaims his coming (1:7-8), and God the Father acknowledges Jesus to be his Son (1:11). The forces of evil, symbolized by Satan, try to tempt him away from his calling (1:12-13), but to no avail.

Before his public career Jesus goes on a retreat in the desert. He then sets about fulfilling his calling. He proclaims that the reign of God is close at hand (1:15), and he recruits disciples who can assist and then carry on his work when he is gone. Mark's omniscient readers knew that his disciples had continued his work.

Jesus claims authority from God, and the people recognize this. When he speaks in a synagogue, "they were astounded at his teaching, for he taught them as one having authority, and not as the scribes" (1:22). Others recognize his authority. At the synagogue in Capernaum he cures a man possessed by an evil spirit. This spirit defies him: "I know who you

Synagogue at Capernaum

are, the Holy One of God" (1:24). But Jesus tells the spirit to be silent and to come out of the man, which it does. Mark shows Jesus having power over supernatural beings and simultaneously being charitable to the poor man who was possessed. His reputation begins to spread.

Jesus demonstrates his power over natural forces as well, curing the illness of Simon Peter's mother-in-law at the house of Peter and Andrew. "That evening, at sundown [that is, after the Sabbath] they brought to him all who were sick or possessed with demons. And the whole city was gathered around the door. And he cured many who were sick with various diseases, and cast out many demons; and he would not permit the demons to speak, because they knew him" (1:32-34). After leaving the house "he went throughout Galilee, proclaiming the message in their synagogues and casting out demons" (1:39). A particular cure was that of a man with a skin disease; Jesus tells him, "See that you say nothing to anyone; but go, show yourself to the priest" (1:40). The man ignored the injunction to be silent about the cure, and so "people came to him from every quarter" (1:45).

And thus we come to the end of Chapter One!

This introduces us to several things about Mark's Gospel. First, he writes at an absolutely breakneck pace, often focusing on deeds without many words. For example, his account of Jesus' temptation by Satan does not include the mini-debate familiar from Matthew and Luke. Mark portrays Jesus as relentlessly active, driven by a sense that time is short and he has much to do. Things inevitably slow down after this remarkable opening chapter, but Mark will still move his narrative along.

Second, we see the importance the evangelist puts upon Jesus' authority. He differs from everyone else. He is unique. The world has never seen his like and never will again. Human history has changed because of him, although few knew it at the time.

Third, one reason few people knew him was that Jesus kept cautioning those he healed as well as the evil spirits to tell no one about the work he did. On the surface this makes little sense. How can he cure someone in a synagogue or when the whole town is present and expect word of that not to get around? The answer is that this is a Markan literary device. Jesus does not wish people to consider him the Messiah because their understanding would be incorrect. He is a different kind of Messiah, and he needs time to bring people to knowledge of that. This was a difficult task. The demons, by contrast, do not need to be brought to that knowledge; they already know who Jesus is. Although Jesus wishes people to recognize his true identity, he will not accept recognition from evil sources. Maybe he cannot stop people from spreading knowledge of him, but he can and does stop the demons.

In the next and subsequent chapters Jesus continues to do what he did in the first one, curing people who then acknowledge, "We have never seen anything like this!" (2:12), and the crowds following him constantly grow. But a new element appears. Among the many who do not understand him are the religious authorities who fear his growing influence with the people. They go after him on a major point: how to keep the Sabbath. They criticize his disciples for picking grain on the Sabbath. Jesus gives a brief defense of his disciples, but the real point of the story is his assertion, "The sabbath was made for humankind, and not humankind for the sabbath; so the Son of Man is lord even of the sabbath" (2:27-28). Significantly, he does not justify this but proclaims it. He has authority, and he exercises it.

Some readers may have noticed that in his exchange with the Pharisees over the Sabbath, Jesus referred to himself as the "Son of Man." This title will appear several more times in this gospel. What does it mean?

Bart Ehrman points out that modern believers often think that "Son of Man" means a human and "Son of God" a divine being, "but this is just the opposite of what the terms meant for many first-century Jews . . ." (*Historical Introduction*, 70). All humans were sons and daughters of God, although Mark understands Jesus as God's son in a unique way. "Son of man" could also be a description of a human, but for ancient Jews it referred to a mysterious, apocalyptic figure in the second-century B.C.E. book of Daniel, in which the visionary prophet, famous for his experiences in the lions' den, says, "I saw one like a Son of Man coming with the clouds of heaven. . . . To him was given dominion and glory and kingship, that all peoples, nations, and languages should serve him. His dominion is an everlasting dominion . . ." (Dan 7:13-14). Since we have only oral tradition to take us back to Jesus, Catholic scholars cannot be sure whether he used the term of himself—certainly there is no reason why he could not have done so—but we can see why Mark uses this designation: Jesus receives heavenly acknowledgment. By the time Mark wrote, Christianity had spread to many people besides the Jews, and the title had faded. Significantly, Paul never used it, but he did use "Son of God" (2 Cor 1:19; Gal 2:20).

Keeping this theme, Mark tells how Jesus cures on the Sabbath, but only after he challenges the Pharisees by asking them, "Is it lawful to do good or to do harm on the sabbath, to save life or to kill?" (3:4) They simmer silently and then leave to plot against him, even joining forces with supporters of the Roman puppet king Herod Antipas, a man for whom the Pharisees had no regard—proof of their anger and fear.

Since the reader knows how this will end, Mark introduces (3:16-19) the Twelve, Jesus' special disciples (Mark never uses the phrase "twelve apostles"). Eleven familiar names are there, but Mark mentions Thaddeus third from last, as does Matthew (10:3); Luke omits Thaddeus but puts in Jude (6:16); John's Gospel does not include a list of the Twelve. Later generations sometimes called this disciple Jude Thaddeus, a clumsy attempt to reconcile the lists, but Raymond Brown observes: "(by the time Mark wrote) recollection of the minor members was uncertain" (*Introduction to the New Testament,* 130). But most importantly Jesus now has a core group upon whom he will depend and whom he can entrust with the true meaning of his calling.

He will need them, because the misunderstanding has even reached his family. "When his family heard of it [the sensation Jesus was creating], they went out to restrain him, for people were saying, 'He has gone out of his mind'" (3:21), an accusation that could mean he was possessed by a demon, and one the scribes will soon make against him. Needless to say, this shocking verse is rarely if ever read liturgically, but Mark means what he says: literally no one understood who Jesus truly was. Some verses later, in a different scene, his mother and his brothers come to see him, which leads Jesus to redefine the notion of family. "Whoever does the will of God is my brother and sister and mother" (3:35). This passage disturbs some Catholics, who see it as a rejection of the Blessed Mother, but Jesus does not reject physical relationships; rather, he expands the notion of family. This verse also has in mind a problem Paul had to deal with—insisting that the true descendants of Abraham are not physical descendants—so Mark is here addressing a contemporary problem. Note that while humans can be understood as Jesus' mother or siblings, only one person can be understood as his Father.

After these events Mark adds a new element. Jesus now speaks in parables, starting with the famous one of the sower (4:1-9). But he includes a troubling verse in which Jesus tells the Twelve, "To you has been given the secret of the kingdom of God, but for those outside everything comes in parables; in order that 'they may indeed look but not perceive . . .'" (4:11, quoting Isa 6:9). Matthew (13:13) and Luke (8:10) mitigate the bluntness of this, and they are right to do so. Mark is probably looking backward at the disbelief of the earliest hearers of Jesus' words, because in 4:33 he says, "With many such parables he spoke the word to them, as they were able to hear it."

Jesus preaches in parables whose basic point is that he has come to change the world, and "Let anyone with ears to hear listen!" (4:23). The miracles continue, demonstrating Jesus' power over nature (the storm at sea) and over the supernatural (curing the Gerasene demoniac). In 5:21-43, the cure of Jairus' daughter, Jesus demonstrates his power over death, foreshadowing his resurrection. This also illustrates the point we made in Chapter One: Jesus performs miracles only after people (in this case Jairus and his wife) have faith. In the middle of this story Jesus cures a woman suffering from hemorrhagia, that is, persistent bleeding. This illustrates a technique used often in Mark's Gospel, the insertion of one story between two halves of another.

The stories of Jesus' cures also serve to introduce us to Jesus' idea of community. We have already seen how he extended the notion of family to all believers. He did the same for community. The strict Jews who produced the Dead Sea Scrolls "excluded or dismissed to the periphery by the purity standards of the Quman community . . . the deaf, the blind, the lame, those with a bloody flux, and those in occupations that compromised their ethnic loyalty and their ritual purity . . ." (Howard Clark Kee, *Cambridge Companion*, 459). *These are precisely the people Jesus welcomes.* Indeed, the community can help those on the outside to be accepted. When four friends lower a paralytic through the roof of a house so that Jesus can cure him, Mark tells us, "When Jesus saw *their* faith" (2:5), he cured the paralytic. For Mark, not only is Jesus different from anyone the world has ever seen, so is the community that he establishes, a community for whom Mark was writing his gospel.

But not all communities will receive him. When he returns to Nazareth his neighbors say, "Is not this the carpenter, the son of Mary and brother of James and Joses and Judas and Simon, and are not his sisters here with us?" (6:3). This skepticism and rejection lead to one of Jesus' most famous sayings, "Prophets are not without honor, except in their hometown, and among their own kin, and in their own house" (6:4). We also get an insight into Mark's understanding of miracles: "And he could do no deed of power there . . . . he was amazed at their unbelief" (6:5-6). Jesus had the power to work miracles, but miracles require faith—otherwise people think of them as magic tricks—and the Nazarenes lack faith.

In chapters 6 to 8 opposition to Jesus begins to mount. To foreshadow the impending danger, Mark tells his readers what happened to John the Baptizer. Jesus defies the Pharisees on several issues, including ritually clean food (shades of Paul), and he moves from legal righteousness to personal righteousness: "It is what comes out of a person that defiles." Mark points out that Jesus made all foods clean (7:19-20). He refuses to give the Pharisees a sign from heaven that they demand. The lesson is obvious—no signs without faith. He even links them with their old enemies, the supporters of Herod Antipas who has executed John the Baptizer. Jesus makes no compromises when asserting his authority.

He also continues to perform miracles, demonstrating his power over illnesses and even the forces of nature when he walks on water (6:45-52), which includes at 6:50 his use of the phrase *I am*, the same phrase YHWH used from the burning bush to identify himself to Moses (Exod 3:14). Obviously people use the phrase all the time, but here Jesus uses it to let us know who he is. Mark does not claim divinity for Christ, but this verse has serious overtones. This man does not just *do* more than ordinary people, he *is* more than ordinary people. This doctrine will be developed in John's Gospel.

Of the miracles, two stand out. The only one of Jesus' miracles that appears in all four gospels is that of the loaves and fishes (Mark 6:30-44; Matt 14:13-21; Luke 9:10-17; John 6:1-15). It provides a good model for understanding a text in its original Jewish context and then in a Christian one. As Daniel Harrington, s.j., points out, "The miraculous feeding points back to God's feeding of his people in the wilderness and to Elisha's feeding of 100 men . . . . It points forward to the idea of life in God's kingdom at which the Messiah will preside . . . . Mark and his readers saw this incident as an anticipation of the Last Supper and the messianic banquet, both of which were celebrated in the community's eucharists" (*NJBC*, 610). Since Mark wrote for Christians, he echoes the Last Supper: "he looked up to heaven, and blessed and broke the bread" (6:41). At the end of the meal the disciples collect twelve baskets of fragments (6:43).

Mark and only Mark repeats the story (8:1-10), but the second time the people number 4,000 instead of 5,000. Scholars consider these two accounts to be of the same event but with an important difference. This time seven baskets of bread remain (8:8). When Jesus warns his disciples against the yeast of the Pharisees (8:14-21), he points out that first there were twelve baskets and then seven, and he challenges them, "Do you not yet understand?" (8:21) Apparently the twelve meant the people of Israel (who came first), while seven meant the Gentiles, symbolized by seven, the complete number in the ancient world.

The second miracle is the strangest one in all the gospels, but only if taken literally. Jesus cures a blind man (8:22-26), but in two stages. Jesus lays his hands on him and the blind man can see partially; Jesus tries again and the man can see completely. On the surface level this makes no sense. Jesus has already driven out devils, cured sick people, even raised Jairus' daughter from the dead. Why couldn't he do this right the first time? The answer is that the story must be taken symbolically. The blind man symbolizes those, including the disciples, who have heard Jesus' message and who do not understand it fully at first but gradually come to realize who Jesus is.

Having established the point, Jesus "asked his disciples, 'Who do people say that I am?'" When they say John the Baptist or Elijah, he insists, "But who do you say that I am?" On behalf of the group, Peter says, "You are the Messiah" (8:29). Jesus then forbids them to say anything about that.

There are several points to note. First, the word "disciples" includes more than just the Twelve; Jesus had many disciples, some of whom would have been women. Second, Peter emerges as the group leader for the first time. Third, the disciples recognize Jesus as the Messiah, something the reader has known since the opening verse of the gospel.

But we quickly learn that their understanding has a long way to go. "Then he began to teach them that the Son of Man must undergo great suffering, and be rejected . . . and be killed, and after three days rise again. He said all this quite openly" (8:31-32). The disciples do not want to hear this, and when Peter rebukes Jesus for it, Jesus calls him Satan: "For you are setting your mind not on divine things but on human things" (8:33). In fairness to Peter we must recall that the Jews expected the Messiah to come in glory, not to suffer and die; furthermore, the disciples cared for Jesus and naturally did not want him to suffer. But Jesus will have none of that. This is his calling and he cannot turn from it. He now tells the disciples what kind of Messiah he must be, and, to their distress, what kind of disciples they must be: "If any want to become my followers, let them deny themselves and take up their cross and follow me. For those who want to save their life will lose it" (8:34-35). These words targeted not just Jesus' own disciples but also Mark's readers. Being a Christian makes demands on people, and they must realize it.

Yet a suffering Messiah is no less a Messiah, and Jesus' three closest disciples have a mystical experience of Jesus transfigured (9:1-8); in attendance upon him are Moses and Elijah, symbols of Law and Prophecy, and the voice of God affirms Jesus, just as at his baptism by John.

Jesus has not misunderstood his calling. The divine plan, evident in the OT, will be fulfilled by a suffering Messiah.

Jesus continues his mission, curing an epileptic boy possessed by a demon. Jesus drives out the demon but does not impose silence upon it, since he has already acknowledged to his disciples that he is the Messiah. He knows how difficult this is for them to comprehend, so he gives a second prediction of the Passion (9:30-32), "but they did not understand." Mark shows their lack of understanding by telling how the Twelve argued over who would be the greatest in the kingdom; they still think that greatness rather than suffering will be their lot (9:33-37).

The Pharisees continue to harass Jesus, trying to get him to violate the Law on the question of divorce, but Jesus again outwits them. He also demonstrates the new standard, insisting that marriage is inviolable, thus providing a NT basis for the church's opposition to divorce: "Therefore what God has joined together, let no one separate" (10:9). Having told his disciples about this new standard, he now has to tell a rich man that to be saved he must also suffer, in this case giving up his wealth, which the man cannot do. He follows the Law faithfully, but he cannot take the next step. Jesus uses this incident to remind his disciples that the old order is passing; he makes new and different demands upon people with the result that "Many who are first will be last, and the last will be first" (10:31).

This notion of suffering now leads Jesus to the third prediction of the Passion, but Mark again insists that the disciples just do not understand. James and John, the sons of Zebedee, want to know where they will sit when Jesus reigns in glory. But he ominously replies, "You do not know what you are asking" (10:38), and then makes it clear to all the disciples that the goal is not glory but service: ". . . whoever wishes to be first among you must be slave of all" (10:44). The modern mind cannot understand how this repelled free people—to think that they must be like slaves, literally chattel in the eyes of society, property to be disposed of at the owner's whim. Who would seriously want to follow that call? But Jesus gives them no choice. As Mark has been saying throughout the gospel, there has never been anyone like this before. No one, then or now, particularly liked those demands—after all, better glory than slavery—but Jesus not only insisted on sacrifice from his disciples, he himself made the ultimate sacrifice.

The Passion

Mark has set the stage for the ultimate drama. Jesus now turns his face toward Jerusalem and his destiny. He leaves behind the small towns of Galilee and enters the world of the Temple, the aristocratic high priests, and the Roman governor. No doubt the Temple clergy have already heard of this country preacher and wonder-worker, and what they heard has not been good. Jesus' arrival in Jerusalem does not reassure them.

On what we now observe as Palm Sunday, Jesus enters Jerusalem on a colt to cheers of "Hosanna" from the crowd, who throw down their cloaks and put leafy branches on the road. The misunderstanding continues as the crowd cries out, "Blessed is the coming kingdom of our ancestor, David" (11:9), but the reader knows that David's kingdom, a powerful political state, is the furthest thing from Jesus' mind.

Fearful of the crowd's reaction, the Temple priests stand by as Jesus drives the money changers—legitimate businessmen—from the Temple, since he wants no commercial transactions there. Significantly, he quotes Isaiah 56:7, "My house shall be called a house of prayer *for all the nations*," hardly the sentiment of the priests, whom Jesus has just compared to a barren fig tree. Clearly Jerusalem did not intimidate Jesus; clearly he would preach his message as he always had; clearly the authorities would try to stop him. The Pharisees disappear from the picture; they are mentioned only once more (12:13) when the Temple priests send them to ask Jesus about tribute money. The Temple priests and their scribes will now challenge this unexpected and unwelcome Messiah.

Initially they take the Pharisees' approach, challenging Jesus' authority (11:27-33) or trying to trap him on points of the Law (12:13-17), only to find that this country preacher can handle himself quite well. Now the Sadducees make their appearance, challenging Jesus on the resurrection (12:18-27). He does not win them over, but he does give them a strong answer, explaining that in heaven "they neither marry nor are given in marriage, but are like angels in heaven" (12:25). One scribe who hears all this honestly acknowledges that Jesus has answered well. Seeking genuinely to learn, he asks him, "Which commandment is the first of all?" Jesus responds with the now familiar words, "'You shall love the Lord your God with all your heart, and with all your soul, and with all your mind, and with all your strength.' The second is this, 'You shall love your neighbor as yourself.' There is no other commandment greater than these" (12:30-31). Although these are now considered the archetypal Christian commandments, Jesus is, as always, a good Jew, quoting from Deuteronomy 6:4-5 and Leviticus 19:18. The scribe recognizes this and compliments him, acknowledging "'this is much more important than all whole burnt offerings and sacrifices.' When Jesus saw that he answered wisely, he said to him, 'You are not far from the kingdom of God'" (12:33-34). Mark well establishes that, different as Jesus' ministry might be from what the crowds and his disciples expected, he does not renounce the religion of his parents. God worked through God's people Israel and now works through God's Son; there is continuity here, even if it is not easily apparent.

The struggle continues, leading Jesus to warn his disciples against the Temple scribes and, by way of contrast, to praise a poor widow, a lowly person by human standards, who understands the true meaning of Judaism and gives money that she needs in order to help others. Jesus calls her gift "all she had to live on" (12:44), a parallel to the sacrifice he would make, giving all that he had.

Chapter thirteen contains Jesus' eschatological discourse in which he tells Peter, James, and John about the end of the age. In general one should not interpret apocalyptic literature literally, as we shall see in detail when we get to the book of Revelation. Apocalyptic statements include visions and claim fulfillment of prophecies, and there is no justification for trying to map out the future by analyzing any of this as history. Jesus clearly had foreboding about the eventual fate of the Temple, about the fates of his disciples, and about the fate of his movement. All these appear in this chapter, starting with the blunt assertion that when the Temple has been torn down, not a single stone will remain standing (13:2).

Jesus initially speaks very generally about wars and rumors of wars, about nations battling nations, material found in Jewish apocalyptic literature, and he warns about false teachers and prophets, an experience Mark's community may have had (13:5-8). But then Jesus turns to the suffering his disciples will experience, including being hauled before numerous government bodies and enduring beatings, but, continuing a theme found earlier in the gospel, Jesus insists that such suffering is needed for the Gospel to reach all nations. While the disciples should see themselves as heroically standing up to persecutors, they must realize that standing up for Jesus will divide families in almost unspeakable ways. "Brother will betray brother to death, and a father his child" (13:12). And as for any thought of earthly reward: "you will be hated by all because of my name" (13:13). But the Holy Spirit will inspire them and "the one who endures to the end will be saved" (13:13).

He next turns to the destruction of Jerusalem. He paints a frightful picture. Recognizing that a time of trial might produce religious leaders who try to explain it, he warns of "false messiahs and false prophets" (13:22).

When all these terrible things have been accomplished, "they will see 'the Son of Man coming in clouds' with great power and glory. Then he will send out the angels, and gather his elect from the four winds, from the ends of the earth to the ends of heaven" (13:26-27). The glory denied the earthly, suffering Jesus will be accorded to the heavenly Jesus; the suffering of his disciples will be rewarded in this new age.

But when will this happen? Jesus can only warn his disciples, "Beware, keep alert; for you do not know when the time will come" (13:33). It could come during this generation, but "about that day or hour no one knows, neither the angels in heaven, nor the Son, but only the Father" (13:32). This last saying has caused problems: why would the Son not know? Because Mark speaks here of the human Jesus.

Yet the Son of Man coming in glory lies in an unspecified future. The present reality for Jesus is the Passion.

The accounts of the Passion and resurrection make up the most important parts of the gospel. As we saw earlier, each gospel writer will take a unique approach to Jesus' ministry. But when we read Mark's Passion narrative we still wonder why he does not mention Jesus promising paradise to the "good thief" or why Jesus does not ask the Beloved Disciple to take his mother Mary into his home. In fact, only Luke tells of the "good thief," while only John tells of Mary and the Beloved Disciple. If Mark knew of these accounts, he had a good reason for not including them, and we can only understand Mark if we focus on what he wrote.

We Catholics should also be aware that over the centuries many pious people have added to the Passion narratives, and we can easily think that these additions are actually in the Scriptures. This in turn can lead us to misunderstand the Scriptures. The most obvious example is the devotion called the Stations of Cross, which dates as early as the fourth century. It includes accounts of Jesus falling and of meeting his mother while carrying the cross, neither of which is in the gospels, and it also includes the fourteenth-century story of Saint Veronica. Let me be clear. I am not criticizing the stations, which I consider to be a very effective Passiontide devotion I practice myself, but rather I am saying that we must read the gospels for what they say and not for how later generations magnified them.

Into this same category must fall the celebrated Shroud of Turin, which many Catholics and other Christians believe to be the shroud that covered Jesus' body (Mark 15:46). In fact, the church has never officially proclaimed this famous cloth to be authentic or inauthentic, mostly because it is impossible for now to determine conclusively that this is the shroud of Jesus himself and not that of some other first-century Jew whom the Romans executed in the same way they executed the Lord. Like all believers, I would be thrilled if scholars could someday prove conclusively that the Shroud is authentic, because it would be wonderful to see the face of Jesus, but until that authenticity has been proven conclusively and authoritatively accepted by the church we cannot factor the Shroud into any discussion of the Passion narrative.

The Passion narrative in Mark's Gospel puts much emphasis on Jesus' having to face his trial alone, deserted by his disciples. The chief priests, scribes, and elders have decided to do away with the troublemaker; the Pharisees have left the scene and play no role in Jesus' death. Yet before that happens Mark recounts how a woman anointed Jesus' head with ointment while he was at the home of Simon the leper. This is a good touch. Just as the upholders of the Law plot to kill him, Jesus associates with a leper and an unknown woman, bluntly violating ritual purity but demonstrating again that the Son of Man transcends the Law. But the evangelist quickly returns to his narrative as Judas, one of the Twelve, decides to betray Jesus for money (14:10-11).

A quick note on Judas: everyone *knows* that Judas always had an interest in money because he took care of the group's funds. Actually not. That detail appears in John 13:29, that is, in a not-yet-written gospel, so Mark's readers would not have known that. The evangelist mentions Judas in 3:19 as one of the Twelve and the one who would betray Jesus, but he gives no reason for the betrayal. Scholars have speculated endlessly on this, accusing Judas of base reasons (the money) or even of almost good reasons, for example, that he believed that Jesus had the power to drive out the Romans and that betraying him into the hands of his enemies would force his hand and he would unleash his power. The fact is that we simply do not know what motivated Judas. Mark says it is the money, and it is best to accept that. The chief priests accept Judas' offer (14:11).

Jesus has the Passover Supper with the Twelve, during which he forecasts Judas' treachery (14:18-21), thus indicating that the betrayal must happen and is part of God's plan, because he makes no attempt to escape.

Verses 14:22-25 often surprise Catholics, whose liturgy centers around the Eucharist and who practice eucharistic adoration. Mark describes the institution of the Eucharist in the briefest terms. Matthew also has a brief account, Luke a somewhat longer one, while John does not even include it in his account of the Passion, although Luke and John also refer to it elsewhere. On the other hand, we have seen that Paul makes the Eucharist central to Christian worship (1 Cor 11:23-25). We must recall that the evangelists focused on the historical Jesus, about to face his greatest trial, while Paul dealt with problems at liturgies and wished to emphasize what really counted at the services. We experience the Eucharist liturgically, and it brings us into one-to-one contact with the Body of Christ. However briefly, Mark does make that clear, and he does so in such matter-of-fact language that it is difficult to see how some Christians cannot believe that the Body of Christ is indeed really present in the Eucharist.

Judas has left to betray Jesus, but Peter assures Jesus of his fidelity, only to be reproached by the prediction of a threefold denial by the time the cock crows twice (14:30). But Mark does not single out Peter, reporting that "they all said the same" (14:31).

Jesus' isolation quickly begins. Only three disciples accompany him to Gethsemane, and they fall asleep there. Jesus is alone with his Father, and Mark tells us he "began to be distressed and agitated" (14:33). Anyone who doubts the humanity of Jesus should read these verses. This is not a supernatural being for whom death holds no terror; for good reason Jesus prays "that, if it were possible, the hour might pass from him" (14:35). But that cannot be so, and Jesus accepts the final stage in his mission—no more predictions, the Passion has now come upon him.

Judas leads a body of armed men to the garden and betrays Jesus with a kiss. "But one of those who stood near drew his sword and struck the slave of the high priest, cutting off his ear" (14:47). Peter was the one who did it, right? No, not here. That reference also appears in the not-yet-written Gospel of John (18:10). Mark does not even say it was one of the Twelve, but rather "one of those who stood near," suggesting confusion or even chaos. This provides a good reminder to us not to conflate the accounts from all four gospels, no matter how natural that seems. Each gospel must be understood on its own. If Mark wanted to say Peter, he would have; clearly he did not, and we must try to understand what he intended.

Now completely alone, Jesus quietly accepts arrest. Next follows one of the most confusing passages in the NT. Mark 14:51-52 speaks of a young man wearing only a linen cloth who follows the fleeing disciples, losing the cloth along the way and thus fleeing naked. For generations people thought this might be Mark himself, but Raymond Brown offered an insightful symbolic interpretation: "Those who have left everything to follow him have now left everything just to get away from him" (*Introduction to the New Testament*, 146).

Events move quickly. First brought to the high priests, Jesus is soon transferred to the Jerusalem council, the Sanhedrin, for an immediate trial. So hastily has this fraudulent assembly been called that the "false witnesses" do not even agree with one another; "their testimony did not agree." (14:56-59). The high priest decides to settle matters by asking Jesus if he is the Messiah, to which Jesus replies, "I am," recalling the self-identification of Yhwh to Moses, used once at the walking on water (6:50) and now again, but once again not an outright claim of divinity. The high priest rather dramatically tears his robe and declares Jesus guilty of blasphemy, and the assembly agrees. By the way, many people think the Sanhedrin could not pass a death sentence. It could for matters of blasphemy, but the high priests and his associates do not want to shoulder the blame for executing a man popular with the people. They cleverly bring him to Pontius Pilate.

Simultaneously a smaller drama is being acted out in the courtyard. While Jesus affirms to the Sanhedrin who he is, Peter denies he is a disciple of Jesus—an effective Markan contrast.

Mark shows how differently from the priests Pilate treats Jesus, getting immediately to the central question for Rome: "Are you the king of the Jews?"—that is, do you represent a political threat? Jesus neither denies nor accepts the title; he remains silent. Pilate knows the priests accuse him from envy, but the Roman must work daily with the priests and has no interest in taking a risk for this prisoner. He resorts to a clever ploy, asking the crowd to choose between Jesus and Barabbas, a rebel and thus someone appealing to the crowd. Incited by the priests, the crowd demands Barabbas and insists that Pilate crucify Jesus. The governor willingly "gives in."

After an abusive scourging Jesus must carry the cross bar (not, as is often shown in paintings, the entire cross) up the hill to Golgotha, helped only by a complete stranger, Simon of Cyrene, whose sons Alexander and Rufus were known to Mark's community (15:21), a surprising personal touch from Mark.

Mark offers a stark crucifixion scene—no family members, no disciples, no good thief, just endless abuse from strangers and from Jesus' enemies (15:29). In an apocalyptic sign, darkness covers the land at the sixth hour (noon) and lasts for three hours, when Jesus utters his only words from the cross, "My God, my God, why have you forsaken me?" (15:34), emphasizing his human feeling of desolation. Then, uttering a loud cry, he dies. Simultaneously the veil of the Temple sanctuary is inexplicably ripped in two, paralleling the high priest's ripping his clothing at Jesus' supposed blasphemy and thus indicating the end of the old dispensation by removing its sense of mystery and holiness. Significantly, a Gentile, a Roman officer, recognizes who Jesus is: "Truly, this man was God's Son" (15:39), symbolizing the faith's going from Jews to Gentiles.

Some women disciples, including Mary Magdalene, here mentioned for the first time and with no negative reference, watch from afar while a hitherto secret disciple, a prominent Jew named Joseph of Arimathea, arranges for Jesus' burial in a newly hewn tomb. He does this partly because the Sabbath is the next day (15:42), and as a pious Jew he knew the body must be buried before the sacred day. Joseph also wishes to do Jesus honor by preventing his body from being dumped in the common grave for criminals. Mark finishes his Passion narrative by noting that Mary Magdalene and another woman "saw where the body was laid" (15:47).

The Resurrection

Of all the Markan passages, none disappoints us more than the resurrection.

But before getting to that, let us note two elements common to all the gospel narratives. First, there is no account of the resurrection itself, but rather of the empty tomb, although all the gospels use other ways to establish that Jesus did indeed rise from the dead. Second, all four accounts list women as the primary witnesses at the tomb, one of many elements to which modern scholars point when demonstrating that the role of women in the earliest church was greater than often thought.

On Sunday morning three women go to the tomb; Mark identifies them as Mary Magdalene, Mary the mother of James, and Salome. They wish to anoint the body but wonder how to roll back the huge stone over the tomb entrance. They find the stone rolled back, suggesting a more-than-human intervention, and then they encounter a young man who tells them that Jesus has risen and will go to Galilee where he can be seen. The women are commissioned to tell the disciples and Peter, whose being singled out for mention indicates his denial of Jesus has been for-given—and again showing him as the group's leader. The young man should probably be understood as an angel; Jesus' presence in Galilee fulfills a prediction he made in Mark 14:28: ". . . after I am raised up, I will go before you to Galilee." In spite of this commission the frightened women run away and say nothing to anyone because of their fear, which means that the evangelist never tells us how the Twelve came to know about the resurrection. Mark's Gospel comes to an abrupt end at 16:8.

What a disappointing ending! Many scholars have attempted to ex-plain this away, saying that Mark assumed that people knew of other accounts and so he did not have to put them in (yet why leave them out?), but Raymond Brown, the authority on the Passion, commends Mark: "Mark's theology is consistent: Even a proclamation of the resur-rection does not produce faith without the hearer's personal encounter with suffering and carrying the cross" (*Introduction to the New Testa-ment*, 148). Mark, living decades after Jesus' death when the church was growing, knew that the disciples did indeed get the message about the empty tomb; he just chose not to include it here in order to make a theological point.

But modern believers are not the first to be disappointed. Your Bible probably has verses 16:9-20 under a heading like "an alternative end-ing" or "the longer ending." The editors of *The Jerusalem Bible* sum this ending up well: ". . . comparison with other gospels made the first Christian generation feel that this ending [at 16:8] was incomplete and also stylistically somewhat harsh. This led them to *add* the 'longer' end-ing" (p. 100). A quick perusal of this ending will demonstrate how it borrows from Luke (the ascension) and Matthew (preach to the whole world). It also includes the strange reference to believers being able to handle snakes and be unharmed (16:18), which has led some fringe congregations to practice snake handling! Even the most experimental Catholic liturgy has never included that.

This is not a gospel that believers like very much. It seems too bare, with no Infancy Narrative, no Lord's Prayer, no wedding at Cana, and no post-resurrection apparitions. Catholics particularly notice that Jesus' mother Mary is mentioned by name just once (6:3), and then only to identify Jesus. She makes only one actual appearance in the gospel (3:31-35), where she is not with Jesus but rather part of a crowd outside the house where he is. Other members of the crowd say to him, "Your mother and your brothers and sisters are outside, asking for you" (v. 32).

He does not go out to her but stays in the house and uses the occasion to downplay physical relationships, a much more restricted treatment of Mary than Catholics would expect.

But we must let Mark be Mark, and that is what he wrote. The ancient Christians concluded that this gospel provided an important witness to Jesus and so included it in the NT. We must take seriously Mark's presentation of a Jesus who is difficult to understand under any circumstances and impossible to understand without faith. This is a Jesus who faced his mission courageously but ultimately alone. Possibly the evangelist wrote for a community that had suffered persecution (Rome under Nero?), and he felt a need to highlight the potential suffering that Jesus' followers would have to endure.

We should also recall that this gospel contains most of the basics: the mission of John the Baptizer; Jesus' call of his disciples, the special role of the Twelve and the leadership role of Peter; Jesus' teaching, parables, and miracles; his suffering and death, and his resurrection. The gospel also includes references to the Father and the Spirit; it tells of the institution of the Eucharist; it provides guidelines for a number of community issues such as church and state (12:13-17) and wealth (10:13-16); it shows the mystery of the kingdom of God; and, most prominently, it proves beyond doubt the need for faith: Jesus had a difficult calling but never lost faith in his Father. We certainly do not have to face a calling like his, but being a believer in the modern world can often be challenging, and we must never lose faith in Jesus.

Chapter Eight

The Q Document

Throughout this book I have tried to avoid complicated scholarly approaches to the New Testament, but, on the other hand, what modern Catholics know about the NT derives from the work of scholars, and nowhere is this more evident than in the *Q* Document hypothesis.

As we noted before, Matthew and Luke both wrote their gospels after Mark and relied heavily on him. This reliance on Mark and consequent similarity of the three gospels led scholars to refer to the group of three as the Synoptic Gospels; that is, they can be "seen together," the literal meaning of the word "synoptic." This in turn generated the "Synoptic Problem" of how exactly these gospels are related. The basic answer is that Matthew and Luke relied on Mark but also, since Matthew's and Luke's gospels are longer than Mark's, they must have used other sources. Scholars can see how Matthew and Luke used Mark, and we will observe some of this when we look at those gospels. Scholars then had to explain the non-Markan sources for Matthew and Luke.

Two of those sources scholars label simply *M* and *L* to designate sources unique to those evangelists. For example, only Matthew (18:23-35) has the parable of the unmerciful servant and only Luke has the parable of the rich fool (12:13-21). No surprise here. The two evangelists were individuals and members of independent communities, and some accounts of Jesus' words and deeds would have differed because the earliest missionaries would have focused on the basic message (Passion, resurrection) and then would have included "optional material," that is, they would have recounted some narratives in one community and others in a different one. Let me note that this *M-L* theory is hardly foolproof because Matthew and Luke may both have known about the same parable but only one decided to use it, and so we think it was known only to that writer. But generally scholars believe that they had access to different traditions.

Yet that leaves another problem. What about those passages common to Matthew and Luke that do not appear in Mark, passages such as the parable of the lost sheep (Matt 18:10-14; Luke 15:3-7) and the lament over Jerusalem (Matt 23:37-39; Luke 13:34-35)? Scholars concluded that *the two evangelists drew from a common third source,* which they labeled Q, because a German scholar first discovered this and the German word for "source" is *Quelle.* As scholars went through these common passages they noticed three things: (1) often Matthew and Luke agree verbally, which suggests that Q was written in Greek, the same language as the gospels, and thus most likely composed outside Palestine; (2) most of the Q passages are sayings, leading some scholars to label it a Sayings Source, although there are narrative portions; (3) most of those sayings are eschatological in nature, that is, dealing with the end of the age and urging Jesus' followers to lead good lives since they could not know when the end would come. Significantly, Q includes no account of the nativity, Passion, or resurrection.

The Q hypothesis provides a good example of careful scholarship at work. Some critics point out that this document does not survive anywhere except in the minds of scholars, but such facile criticism simply overlooks the problem of common material between Matthew and Luke without Mark as a source. Few modern Catholic scholars doubt the existence of Q. The questions revolve around the date, authorship, locale, and widespread use of this source.

Since, as we shall see, scholars date Matthew and Luke to the 80s, Q must have been compiled before then. But there is more evidence to help us with the dating: the Gospel of Mark. About the year 70 Mark basically took what had been oral traditions and created a written, narrative framework, with much emphasis on the Passion and resurrection, also emphasized by Paul. Mark's approach appealed to people, since three other Christians followed his lead and also wrote gospels. To be sure, oral tradition continued into the second century, but clearly Mark represented the future. How then, scholars ask, would someone writing *after* Mark put together a document with little narrative framework and no account of the Passion or resurrection? This makes little sense, and so scholars believe that Q was compiled before Mark, possibly in the 50s and definitely no later than the 60s. As for the identity of the compilers and the location of the writing, no one can say, other than that the person (or persons) was a native Greek-speaker or group who probably lived outside Palestine.

Exactly how the evangelists used Q is impossible to determine. For example, suppose Matthew took a passage from Q and Luke did not. We would think the passage to be from Matthew's particular source rather than from Q. The Gospel of Mark has many eschatological passages, as does Q. Suppose Mark took a passage from Q and Matthew and Luke did likewise. We would think that the two later evangelists got the material from Mark rather than from Q. Given the prominence Paul gives to the crucifixion and resurrection of Jesus in the 50s, it is difficult to believe that any first-century Christian compiled a written source about Jesus with no mention of those. Did Mark take over the Passion narrative of Q?

Scholars do not ignore these problems, but they remain convinced that Matthew and Luke did indeed have access to a source other than Mark, a source consisting largely of eschatological sayings of Jesus.

Readers who wish to know more about Q can consult a biblical dictionary or encyclopedia. In his *Introduction to the New Testament*, Raymond Brown lists all the Q passages on pp. 118–19.

Chapter Nine

The Gospel According to Matthew

I. Genealogy and Infancy Narrative (1–2)

II. John the Baptist, baptism, temptation (3:1–4:11)

III. Galilean ministry (4:12–13:58)
- Call of disciples (4:12-25)
- Sermon on the Mount (5–7)
- Miracle cycle (8–9)
- Sending of disciples; missionary discourse (10:1–11:1)

IV. Rejection (11:2–13:58)
- Opposition from Jewish groups (11:2–12:50)
- Parables (13:1-52)
- Rejection at Nazareth (13:53-58)

V. Jesus travels to Jerusalem (14:1–21:11)
- Death of John the Baptist (14:1-12)
- Miracles of feeding and healing (14:13–16:12)
- Disciples, especially Peter, confess Jesus as Son of God (16:13-20)
- Predictions of Passion, Transfiguration, healing miracles (16:21–20:34)
- Triumphal entry (21:1-11)

VI. Jesus in Jerusalem (21:12–25:46)
- Cleansing the Temple (21:12-17)
- Messianic parable and teaching (21:18–22:45)
- Denunciation of the Jewish leaders and lament for Jerusalem (23)
- Apocalyptic predictions (24–25)

VII. The Passion and Death of Jesus (26–27)
- The Plot (26:1-16)
- The Last Supper (26:17-35)
- Gethsemane (26:36-56)
- Trials before the high priest and Pilate (26:57–27:23)
- Crucifixion and Death (27:24-66)

VIII. Resurrection and Post-Resurrection Appearances (28)

With Matthew's Gospel we enter familiar territory. For one thing, it is much longer than Mark, a full sixty percent longer. It has a nativity narrative, and we recognize the Sermon on the Mount with the Lord's Prayer and the eight beatitudes. But we must recall that these do not make Matthew "more" of a gospel than poor, old, brief, blunt Mark. This gospel has a different orientation, yet it depends heavily on Mark, using eighty percent of what is found in that gospel.

Please read chapters 1–12 and 24–28.

As with Mark, this gospel has no name attached to it, nor does it supply a date or place of writing. By the early second century Christian writers claimed the author was Matthew, one of the Twelve and identified in only this gospel as a tax collector (9:9). That sounds like a reliable identification, but these early sources also say that Matthew wrote his gospel in Hebrew (that is, Aramaic). Yet the surviving gospel is written in Greek, and its fluency as well as the plays on words in Greek indicate that this is no translation. Furthermore, as noted earlier, if Matthew was one of the Twelve and thus an eyewitness to Jesus' public career, why did he copy so much from Mark, who did not know the earthly Jesus? Catholic scholars believe that Matthew wrote sometime in the 80s of the first century, a date partially derived from his use of Mark, dated about 70. The rationale is that Matthew would not go out of his way to correct Mark if that gospel were not gaining in popularity, a process that would have taken some time. The place of writing? Probably Antioch or some place near Judea since, as we shall see, Matthew has concerns about what is happening there, although his community had a large Gentile element.

Let me just add here that I have given enough religious education presentations to know that learning that none of the Twelve wrote a gospel can upset people who were taught that they did. This results largely from an old educational approach that did not emphasize reading the Scriptures. One of the manifold consequences of Vatican Council II (1962–1965) was to increase emphasis on Scripture, and this goal has taken a while to achieve. But no modern Catholic exegete teaches that Matthew the tax collector wrote this gospel.

Scholars have searched this gospel for clues about Matthew's community, and many have emerged. Readers of the gospel note quickly how often Matthew quotes the OT, repeatedly emphasizing how aspects of Jesus' life fulfilled the prophecies of Isaiah especially, but also other OT writings as well. Matthew also compares Jesus to Moses and repeatedly emphasizes that Jesus was a pious Jew who reverenced the Law, as we shall soon see.

Clearly many of Matthew's readers took the OT and the Law very seriously, and we can easily determine who they were: converted Jews. Yet not all of Matthew's readers were Jewish. His community also contained many Gentiles—and we cannot speculate on the percentages of either—and so we will see in his gospel examples of how Jews misunderstood or even threatened Jesus while Gentiles (the Magi, the Romans under the cross) recognized who he was. Matthew's Gospel, and only his, closes with the famous exhortation by the risen Christ that the disciples evangelize all nations.

Most scholars believe that Matthew was Jewish, and we can sympathize with his plight—loyal to his people but frustrated and occasionally angry that they did not recognize Jesus; defending the Law while insisting Jesus superseded it; welcoming the Gentiles yet still hoping his people would convert. These tensions appear often in his gospel. And the tensions were not just theoretical. Only Matthew recounts how the Jerusalem leadership bribed the guards at Jesus' tomb to say that the disciples stole his body. "So they (the guards) took the money and did as they were directed. And this story is still told among the Jews *to this day*" (28:15). Clearly friction existed between Matthew's community and the local Jewish one.

Something else also becomes evident. Matthew writes for a settled community; significantly, he is the only gospel writer to use the word "church" (16:18; 18:17), a word well known from its use in all of Paul's seven epistles. Matthew agrees with Mark in believing in a Second Coming, but he wants to let Christians know how to lead their everyday lives. Thus he writes much about ethics and discipleship. Naturally he sets his examples in Jesus' time, but when Jesus warns about Jewish spiritual hypocrisy we must remember that the evangelist expected Christians to apply those words to themselves.

Much of what Matthew has comes from Mark, and we will not go over those passages very heavily. Instead we will concentrate on non-Markan material, although we will also look from time to time to see how Matthew has reworked the Markan material.

A final point before we get into the gospel: how can someone rewrite Scripture? Two answers. First, the OT offers several examples of rewriting previous works, the most important being the anonymous "Chronicler," about 400 B.C.E., who rewrote the earlier books of 1–2 Samuel and 1–2 Kings in 1–2 Chronicles. Second, Mark was not yet Scripture. As mentioned earlier, it was not until the first third of the second century that most Christians began to refer to specifically Christian books as Scripture. Only in the second century, when the four gospels gained apostolic stature, did their texts become inviolable.

Matthew 1–2 contains an infancy narrative, and it offers a good opportunity to show how modern views can impact how we view Scripture. Matthew recounts the first Christmas, right? No way. Matthew and Luke tell about the nativity, but Christmas is the feast in honor of the nativity and was not celebrated until the third century. So if Matthew did not write for a nonexistent feast, then why did he add an account of Jesus' birth to Mark's story of Jesus' public career? Probably because of Mark 1:9-11, the baptism of Jesus by John, when God the Father recognizes his Son. The passage lies open to misunderstanding: was Jesus not God's Son until baptism? Was there a causal relationship—that is, did the baptism somehow make Jesus God's Son? Matthew and Luke wished to make it very clear that Jesus was God's Son from his conception. Relying on some common traditions (virginal conception, birth in Bethlehem, childhood in Nazareth), they created what we now call the Infancy Narratives.

When we start Matthew's account, instead of finding an infancy narrative we find a genealogy. Why? First, ancient peoples took these very seriously and expected to know a great man's ancestry. The First Book of Chronicles begins with nine full chapters of "so-and-so begot so-and-so," a flawless cure for insomnia. Second, the genealogy includes Abraham, Isaac, Jacob, Jesse, David, and Solomon, so Matthew has placed Jesus squarely within Israel's history. Third, Matthew includes five women—an unusual touch—four of whom played major roles in Israel's history but were on the fringe, such as the Gentile Ruth. The fifth woman is Mary. Recall that Jewish stories about the theft of Jesus' body circulated in Matthew's day (28:15); possibly he had to counter questions about Mary's virtue, which he did by showing misunderstood women in Israel's history.

The nativity narrative introduces many themes important for the rest of the gospel. Events surrounding Jesus' birth fulfill no fewer than five OT prophecies. The Magi from the East introduce Gentiles into the story, Gentiles who followed a star and believed in Jesus while Herod and "all Jerusalem" disbelieved and even sought Jesus' death. Matthew returns to these themes in his Passion narrative. Only he mentions Pilate's wife (27:19) and the earthquake (27:51), paralleling the believing Gentiles and the natural phenomenon present at Jesus' birth. The evangelist also parallels the childhood of Moses, when an evil ruler killed all the young boys in the region but the bearer of the promise escaped (Exodus 1–2); Moses will later leave Egypt, the country to which the Holy Family fled. Note this verbal parallel: God tells Moses to return to Egypt because "all those who were seeking your life are dead" (Exod 4:19); the angel tells Joseph to leave Egypt and return to Israel because "those who were seeking the child's life are dead" (2:20).

We should also note that five dreams occur in this narrative (1:20; 2:12; 2:13; 2:19; 2:22), and every dream is a message from God. Today we understand dreams psychologically or as the consequence of too heavy a meal, but in the ancient world God routinely spoke to people through dreams. Jacob dreamed of a ladder to heaven (Gen 28:12), an angel spoke to the patriarch Joseph in a dream (Gen 31:11), and God appeared to Solomon in a dream (1 Kings 3:5). In the gospel Joseph, bearing the same name as the Hebrew patriarch, also receives and understands dreams. Matthew's readers would easily have grasped the sacred significance of a dream.

Of course, we cannot ever read this without thinking of Christmas, but it is clear what Matthew had in mind.

An ecumenical point: Matthew 1:25 says of Joseph that he "had no marital relations with her [Mary] until she had borne a son . . . ." This simply means that Jesus was not born as a result of marital intercourse; it does not imply that they had relations afterward. This passage also does not speak of Mary's perpetual virginity. That belief appeared for the first time in Christian Syria in the second century, was eventually adopted by the larger church and developed into Catholic doctrine. Protestants who accept only what the Scripture says explicitly do not accept the doctrine of Mary's perpetual virginity. As ecumenical Christians, we must just agree to disagree.

Proof that the infancy narrative provides a preface to the gospel appears immediately in chapter 3. Jesus is already an adult; Matthew shows absolutely no interest in his life between his birth and public career. At this point Matthew starts to follow Mark's narrative, but with his own emphases. He demonstrates that John is a forerunner of Jesus, something that John himself acknowledges (3:11). Thus there is no way that John's baptism caused God to acknowledge Jesus as his Son. Mark says that John preached "a baptism of repentance for the forgiveness of sins" (1:4), but Matthew drops the reference to sins, which he did not want anyone to attribute incorrectly to Jesus. John himself cannot understand why Jesus is there (3:14); when Jesus emerges from the water, the voice of God speaks not to Jesus but to everyone there, "This is my Son," rather than "You are my Son" as in Mark. John also presages Jesus' mission in another way by his excoriation of the Pharisees who appeal to their Abrahamic ancestry, which John considers a dodge by that "brood of vipers" (3:7-10). And—almost inevitably in Matthew—John's mission fulfills a prophecy (3:3).

The preparation for the public career continues in chapter four, where Matthew considerably expands Mark's bare account of the temptation. Matthew includes dialogue that shows Jesus outwitting Satan in a rather engaging way, a contest of scriptural quotations that shows the reader that this carpenter knew his Bible. Jesus then goes to Galilee, fulfilling a prophecy, and while there he calls his first close disciples, four fishermen. Note that the offer to become fishers of people is made to both Peter and Andrew. Matthew makes much of Peter's special calling, as we shall see, but not in this verse. Having this basic group, Jesus now goes public, "proclaiming the good news of the kingdom and curing every disease and every sickness among the people" (4:23), so that large crowds follow him. This large following sets up Matthew's masterpiece, the Sermon on the Mount, which occupies all of chapters 5 through 7.

But before we get to the content of the Sermon, let us consider how this shows that the gospel writers often did creative theology rather than passing along information. Most likely Matthew created the Sermon on the Mount in order to parallel Jesus with Moses; that is, just as Moses received the Old Law on Mount Sinai, so Jesus provides us with the New Law on a mount. But how can scholars make such an assertion?

Earlier in the book I mentioned that a good way to understand the gospels is to look at parallel passages. Matthew 5–7 parallels many passages in Luke, but note these examples (Matthew's all being from the Sermon on the Mount):

Sermon on the Mount

- Matthew 5:3-12 parallels Luke 6:17-23, but Luke sets these verses on a plain.
- Matthew 7:7-11 parallels Luke 11:9-13, which is set "in a certain place."
- Matthew 6:24 parallels Luke 16:13; Matthew 7:13-14 parallels Luke 13:23-24, which, when put together with the previous verses, means that passages in Matthew 5–7 parallel passages in Luke 6, 11, 13, and 16.

The problem scholars focus on is this: Is it more likely that Matthew took verses attributed to Jesus in a number of settings in *Q* and put them into one long sermon, or that Luke took one long sermon and broke it up into different pieces? The first makes far more sense, especially since *Q* was largely a sayings source with little indication of long, sermonic material. Furthermore, Matthew's desire to parallel Jesus to Moses is a better explanation of why he would collect this material than Luke's desire to break it up for no apparent reason. Since Matthew actually records five sermons by Jesus (5:1–7:29; 10:35–11:1; 13:1-52; 18:1-35; 24:1–25:46), some scholars believe he may be paralleling the Torah, the five books traditionally written by Moses. And when we get to Luke in the next chapter we will see that the corresponding passages in his gospel represent a more primitive tradition than those in Matthew. (These parallel sayings in different locations put yet another nail in the coffin of the gospels as modern biographies.)

Having established that, let us turn to the Sermon. Matthew starts with an ethical masterpiece, the Eight Beatitudes (5:1-10). They carry obvious and perennial spiritual relevance that needs no comment, but we can see how they fit into a settled community. Someone who is poor in spirit could still be financially wealthy; someone who hungers and thirsts for righteousness could always have a full stomach. Matthew still includes those who face direct suffering: "Blessed are those who are persecuted for righteousness' sake, for theirs is the kingdom of heaven" (5:10), but he clearly has in mind those who will prove their Christianity by their daily lives rather than by martyrdom, that is, people like us. Thus Matthew praises those who mourn, who show mercy, who make peace, and who have pure hearts. He offers a code of behavior for the ordinary believer.

He next turns to his Jewish-Christian readers for whom the Law still had relevance. Jesus the Jew states unequivocally that he has not come to destroy the Law, but to fulfill it (5:17). No true Christian can disparage the Law, which came from God to the Jewish people. But there is the Law, and there is its interpretation. Jesus makes it clear that a higher standard now applies; "unless your righteousness exceeds that of the scribes and Pharisees, you will never enter the kingdom of heaven" (5:20). He then gives a list of new standards—again, the ethical preacher—and among other things he recommends reconciliation rather than vengeance, humility instead of show.

But ethics without prayer has no value, and so Jesus teaches his disciples how to pray, a prayer we all know and one that, like the beatitudes, needs no comment from me. But in terms of Matthew's intention, we can see that this prayer fits our daily lives—"Give us this day our daily bread," an invocation for God's constant assistance, and "Forgive us our trespasses as we forgive those who trespass against us" [or: "forgive us our debts, as we also have forgiven our debtors"], recalling the beatitude that praises the merciful as well as the one that praises peacemakers because forgiveness fosters reconciliation. It is not, however, all peace and light; after the prayer Jesus warns that those who do not forgive others will find that God does not forgive them (6:15).

The Sermon continues with practical advice as Jesus explains what we must do to get along with others, such as fasting without show, placing spiritual treasures ahead of monetary ones. But do these things really do any good? Yes, Jesus asserts, but only if we have faith in God. In a famous simile, Jesus points to the lilies of the field, which, through God's grace, are more gloriously arrayed than Solomon, the Israelite king famed for his wealth (6:28-29). Returning to the practical advice, Jesus observes, "So do not worry about tomorrow . . . . Today's trouble is enough for today" (6:34).

The sayings on effective Christian living continue: "Do not judge, so that you may not be judged" (7:1); "Do not give what is holy to dogs" (7:6); and the immortal Golden Rule, "In everything do to others as you would have them do to you" (7:12). The Sermon finishes appropriately with advice on true discipleship, comparing the true disciple to the one who builds a house on a rock: rains, floods, and gales can do such a house no harm. Since every Catholic knows that later in this gospel Jesus will compare the disciple Peter to a rock we can see that Matthew here uses foreshadowing.

The great Sermon has now ended, and Matthew says, with some understatement, "the crowds were astounded at his teaching" (7:28).

Matthew now turns to Jesus' action in the community with a succession of ten miracles, some from Mark, others from *Q*, and these reflect some Matthean themes. The cure of the centurion's servant clearly reflects the movement of Christianity to the Gentiles as Jesus remarks, "in no one in Israel have I found such faith" (8:10). But, more subtly, Matthew invokes the theme of mercy. "Servant" in that era meant a slave, a piece of property to be used and discarded, yet this Roman officer cares even about a slave.

We can also see that in the account of the storm at sea (8:23-27) Matthew has dropped Mark's confusing reference to the other boats and focuses on the miracle, which, although from Mark, fits Matthew's Mosaic imagery because Moses too had power over the sea.

Jesus calls Matthew, the tax collector, which leads into an account of the Pharisees' criticism that Jesus ate with "tax collectors and sinners" (9:10). Matthew continues Mark's theme of Jesus' working with social and religious outcasts, and Jesus makes it unambiguous: "I have come to call not the righteous but sinners" (9:13), a great comfort to all of us.

Matthew closed the Sermon on the Mount with the need for faith and trust in God, and he returns to that theme with two miracles. Jesus cures the woman with the hemorrhage, saying to her, "Your faith has made you well" (9:22). He tells two blind men, to whom he gives sight, "According to your faith let it be done to you" (9:29). As we noted in the Introduction, despite the widespread belief that Jesus did miracles to give people faith, the gospels relate just the reverse. First the people believe, then Jesus performs the miracle.

In chapter ten Matthew moves from the general to the specific in the second great discourse, the Mission Sermon (10:1-42). Jesus summons the Twelve and instructs them on their particular calling, which differs from the calling of the ordinary believer. Appropriately, he starts with a list of the Twelve, and, like Mark, he lists Peter first and Judas last. First the disciples must go to the Jews, and God will support their work by enabling them to do miracles. They must trust God and not worry about material belongings, depending rather on hospitality, "for laborers deserve their food" (10:10). Inevitably the disciples will meet rejection, but surely they can handle that? Actually, Jesus goes on, they will face far more than rejection. They will endure outright persecution, being hauled into courts, scourged, driven from town to town, and "hated by all because of my name" (10:22). They hope to bring reconciliation, but instead, "Brother will betray brother to death, and a father his child, and children will rise against their parents and have them put to death" (10:21). (At the trial of Saint Perpetua in North Africa *ca.* 200, the Roman magistrate criticized Christianity for the way it divided families; Perpetua was a Christian and her father a pagan.)

But these trials cannot dissuade the disciples. "Do not fear those who kill the body but cannot kill the soul" (10:28). They must accept that Jesus' message is not one many people want to hear; Jesus compares it to a sword (10:34). Keeping up that imagery, Matthew quotes him, "Those who find their life will lose it, and those who lose their life for my sake will find it" (10:39). We can only wonder how the disciples reacted on hearing what lay in store for them. By the time Matthew wrote in the 80s things had settled down, and there is no recorded persecution at that time. But the possibility was always there, and Matthew wants his readers to know that, however much he is showing them how to live daily Christians lives, unexpected and frightening demands may be made upon them. If we think that this was so only in the ancient world, we should remember someone like Thomas More, wealthy, powerful, and a friend of the king, who had to give up all for his faith. And think of those Christians in occupied Europe in World War II who hid Jews from the Gestapo, often for years, risking and even losing their lives—how could they, as young believers, ever have envisioned the demands their faith would make on them?

Matthew returns to his narrative as Jesus meets disciples of John the Baptizer, who want to know who he is. Jesus tells them, and after they return to John, Jesus praises John but makes it clear that a new order beyond that envisioned by John is coming into being (11:11). Following Mark and *Q*, Matthew next recounts a variety of events, from denunciations to healings, although he gives the stories his own emphasis. In the account of picking grain on the Sabbath he follows Mark but quietly drops the reference to Abiathar the high priest; for Matthew, Jesus does not mistakenly cite Scripture. The evangelist also adds an additional example from the OT portraying Jesus taking the Scripture seriously in his debates with the Pharisees (12:5). Having challenged the Pharisees in one way about the Sabbath, Jesus next performs a miracle on the Sabbath, enraging the Pharisees (12:9-14). And as the Jewish leadership turns from Jesus, Matthew turns to the prophet Isaiah (12:15-21 [Isa 42:1-14]), who said that God's chosen one "will proclaim justice to the Gentiles. . . . And in his name the Gentiles will hope."

The Pharisees return, accusing Jesus of being in league with the devil, but Jesus asserts his power over the forces of evil. His enemies ask for proof, but he refuses to give them a sign, reminding us that he used his power when people had faith—hardly the attitude of those accusing him of being in league with Satan. Appalled by the self-righteousness of these Pharisees, Jesus then tells a number of parables that portray the kingdom of God as something small that will grow (the mustard seed, the leaven), but many people, such as his enemies, will not recognize it (the treasure hidden in the field). Then Matthew tells the reader of the death of John (14:1-12), contrasting the one who proclaimed who Jesus was with those who refuse to recognize him. And only Matthew portrays Jesus' purely human reaction to John's death: "Now when Jesus heard this, he withdrew . . . to a deserted place by himself" (14:13).

But the crowds seek him out; unlike the Pharisees, they believe, at least for now. Jesus feeds them with the loaves and fishes (14:13-21). Then he sends his disciples out in a boat, and he appears to them, walking on water (14:22-33). Matthew thus shows Jesus using his power, first to help people and then to overcome the forces of nature. With a strong display of faith, Peter asks Jesus if he can walk with him. Jesus agrees, and Peter walks to him, only to lose his faith at the end and start to sink. Jesus rescues him. Matthew here alerts us that Peter is more than just an ordinary member of the Twelve; his faith is greater. Yet even his faith fails, but Jesus does not fail him. The evangelist's Jewish-Christian readers would recognize an OT theme—no matter what the people of Israel do, God never deserts them. The disciples now recognize Jesus as the Son of God (14:33).

After a series of signs and wonders as well as more opposition from the Pharisees, Matthew gets to a crucial passage for Catholics. Jesus asks the disciples who they think he is. "Simon Peter answered, 'You are the Messiah, the Son of the living God.' And Jesus answered him, 'Blessed are you, Simon son of Jonah! For flesh and blood has not revealed this to you, but my Father in heaven. And I tell you, you are Peter, and on this rock (*pétra* in Greek) I will build my church, and the gates of Hades will not prevail against it'" (16:16-18). This is the basic scriptural text on which the pope's role in the church depends. Anyone who has been to Saint Peter's basilica in Rome has seen the Latin version of these words engraved in large gold letters at the interior base of the dome.

This is the major statement, but hardly the only one that singles out Peter's leadership. Matthew makes several references to Peter's significance, as we have seen, but so does Mark when the young man at the empty tomb of Jesus tells the women to report this to "his disciples and Peter" (16:7), separating Peter from the group. Luke gives Peter some prominence in his gospel, but far more in his Acts of the Apostles. For example, Peter receives a vision from Jesus telling him not to require Gentiles to follow Jewish dietary laws, a major breakthrough in the infant church's self-understanding as a commuity for all (Acts 10:9-16, 34-35). No modern scholar questions Peter's significance in the NT.

But that raises an important question. Why then do Protestant and Orthodox Christians not accept the papacy? Some conservative Protestants argue that the NT never says that Peter went to Rome, nor does it say he was its bishop. As we shall see, 1 Peter hints that he did go to Rome, and many ancient, non-biblical Christian sources cite his presence in the Eternal City. As for the title of bishop, we have already seen that the word *epískopos,* translated even by Catholics as "overseer" or "president," did not initially have the same meaning it later came to have, so this is an anachronistic squabble over terminology. For mainline Protestants and for the Orthodox, the problem is succession. Even if Peter had this authority, the NT does not say it passed on to his successors in Rome. Certainly it does not do so literally, but we must recall that Matthew wrote two decades after Peter had died in Nero's persecution. As we have said several times before, the evangelists wrote about past events for current (that is, first-century) audiences. Why then would Matthew and other NT writers give such prominence to the Petrine charism if it had no meaning after Peter's death?

The first pope to cite this Matthean passage as a basis for instructing the entire church was Stephen I (254–257), presumably after some development of this doctrine in Roman circles. Greek bishops rejected this then and have done so for eighteen more centuries; the Protestants joined them in the sixteenth century. This is yet one more point on which modern ecumenical Christians must agree to disagree, at least for the present. Maybe some future developments will unite us on this point.

But the commissioning of Peter did not make him into the perfect disciple. Having established a role of leadership for his disciples, Jesus now tells them how he must suffer. Peter cannot accept this and tells Jesus, "This [suffering] must never happen to you," thus earning the stinging rebuke, "Get behind me, Satan!" (16:23). This suffering will happen to Jesus, and when it does Peter will deny even knowing him. Matthew offers an important foreshadowing as well as a reminder that the church must always rely on frail, sinful people because those are the only people there are.

Logically enough, Matthew now recounts the conditions for discipleship, which we have seen before in Mark: the disciples too must take up the cross. But as a sign for what awaits them, Jesus is transfigured before Peter, James, and John, and Matthew adds a detail to Mark's account, telling us that Jesus' face shone like the sun (17:2). Why? Because in Exodus 34:30, when Moses came down from Mount Sinai, "the skin of his face shone because he had been talking with God."

Yet the glory of the transfiguration cannot hide the coming fate of God's Son. Jesus gives a second prediction of the Passion (17:22-23), and we again see the disciples misunderstanding it, wondering instead about their status in the kingdom of heaven. After telling them they should be as innocent as children, Jesus warns them about temptations in general and not just about dreams of greatness. As so often, Matthew gives a historical account but includes a lesson for his readers. He concludes his account of Jesus in Galilee with more community lessons, these on reconciliation.

With chapter 19 a new phase of Jesus' ministry opens: ". . . he left Galilee and went to the region of Judea beyond the Jordan." He now begins his fateful and fatal journey to Jerusalem. We know what will happen to him, yet we cannot wish that he had turned back. He told his disciples that he must redeem the world through their suffering. This is his calling, which, for our sakes, he cannot deny.

But the events of the Passion do not occur immediately. Matthew first records a full seven chapters of Jesus' teaching on a variety of issues. Most deal with practical issues or with opposition to Jesus; several come from Mark. We cannot analyze all of them, but we will look at some in detail.

As in Mark, Matthew repeats Jesus' teaching about divorce, once again emphasizing a more rigorous standard than the Pharisees allowed, but now he also adds a recommendation for continence "for the sake of the kingdom of heaven" (19:12). This theme continues in his encounter with the rich young man, as Jesus warns about riches and praises renunciation. Also as in Mark, Jesus here praises the simplicity of children, although Matthew drops Mark's reference to the disciples' trying to keep the children away from Jesus and his consequent indignation at them. Matthew wants to strengthen the image of the disciples because they would have to build the church (19:3-15; Mark 10:13-16).

Matthew continues with his theme of new values replacing old ones. He alone tells the parable of the laborers in the vineyard, a parable that often upsets believers because it seems unfair to pay people the same amount when they did different work. But its meaning is quite different. First, on a basic level it means that those who came late to God's revelation, the Gentiles, are on the same level as the Jews who received it centuries before. Second, God's standards are not those of humans.

God can forgive and welcome into the fold even those who come late, such as people who do not turn to God until well along in their lives. Matthew here shows God as a parent, not a judge. Third, Jesus overturns values again: "So the last will be first, and the first will be last" (20:16). That does not mean that those who have lived good lives since childhood will be behind those who repent on their deathbeds; recall that Matthew has spent much of the gospel providing a guide to Christian living. Rather it means that we cannot understand Jesus or his message if we use only human standards.

Overturning values continues with the third prediction of the Passion, followed by the now familiar clueless reaction of the disciples who want to sit on Jesus' right and left hand in the kingdom. Jesus responds by pointing out that "the Son of Man came not to be served but to serve" (20:28), an important adage for the disciples and the leaders of Matthew's community. We also see Matthew again improving the disciples' image in a small way. In Mark (10:35) the sons of Zebedee (John and James) made the request from Jesus; Matthew says that their mother did it (20:20).

It is the verse-by-verse comparison with Mark that enables scholars to see Matthew's goals in his gospel as well as demonstrating that he depended on Mark and not vice-versa. If Matthew wrote first and said the mother initiated the request, why would Mark make the disciples look bad by changing it to the sons?

The Messiah has now reached Jerusalem, and Matthew tells the story of Palm Sunday, following Mark but adding the fulfillment of a prophecy. He also changes Mark's chronology when Jesus cleanses the Temple on the day he arrives and not the next day (Mark 11:12). His actions in the Temple have challenged and offended the Temple priests, and their response is not long in coming. Indeed, from here until the Passion Jesus will be responding to challenges from religious authorities and giving parables about those who refuse to accede to the demands of this new revelation. Since Matthew records Jesus saying some very strong things about the Jewish leaders, we should note that these do not justify any kind of anti-Semitism. Jesus remained a good Jew until his death. He does not criticize Judaism, but rather those who have not lived up to its standards, who have abused it for their own purposes, and whose clinging to power prevents them from recognizing God's work in Jesus.

When he is in the Temple "the chief priests and the elders of the people" get to the basics, questioning Jesus' authority. But this small-town preacher outwits them by asking them what they think of John the Baptizer. They refuse to answer, so he does likewise. Remaining in the Temple, Jesus gives two brief parables, one praising "tax collectors and prostitutes" (21:32) who had the honesty to recognize John while the priests denied him, and then another one about wicked tenants who abuse their master and kill his son. "The chief priests and the Pharisees . . . realized that he was speaking about them" (21:45), but they could do nothing because the people thought Jesus was a prophet—something unique to Matthew.

Old opponents reappear. The Jerusalem Pharisees try to trip Jesus up on a question about taxes, but his answer, "Give therefore to the emperor the things that are the emperor's" (22:21), again demonstrates that divine and human values cannot be put on the same level. Acknowledging defeat, the Pharisees "were amazed; and they left him and went away" (22:22). Next come the Sadducees to trip him up with a question about the resurrection of the dead, in which they did not believe, and once again Jesus shows that God's standards differ from human ones. To the disappointment of the Sadducees, "when the crowd heard it, they were astounded at his teaching" (22:33).

Getting their second wind, the Pharisees return and insist he tell them what is the greatest commandment. Ever the good Jew, Jesus replies (as in Mark) by quoting Deuteronomy 6:5, "You shall love the Lord your God with all your heart, and with all your soul," adding "and with all your mind," but also going on to a second commandment, "You shall love your neighbor as yourself" (22:39)—not a minor commandment to the Pharisees who thought the Gentiles were inferior to them and that their own people did not match their holiness. Not giving up, the Pharisees try again, asking if the Messiah (the Christ) is David's son, which Matthew asserts in his genealogy (ch. 1). But again the standards differ. The true Messiah is more than David's son, something the Pharisees could not recognize.

This marks Jesus' last discussion with his opponents; "nor from that day did anyone dare to ask him any more questions" (22:46). Now they would exchange questions for plots, debates for violence. The Passion draws near, and Jesus knows it.

Jesus continues to speak to his disciples and to the people, but his tone has changed. Realizing he has little time left, he now denounces those who would lead the people astray and tries to prepare his disciples, who must continue his work after his death, for what is now upon them. These passages (chs. 24–25) do not make pleasant reading, but the evangelist has no choice. He has shown his Jewish converts that the leaders of the people denied this man sent from God. In true OT fashion, which Matthew's Jewish readers would recognize, God will wreak vengeance on the evildoers.

Six times Jesus calls the Pharisees "hypocrites" (23:13, 15, 23, 25, 27, 29) in a blistering attack that includes five indictments; he also denounces them as "blind guides" (23:16) and—a famous reference—"white-washed tombs" (23:27). Until the twentieth century the English word "pharisaic" meant hypocritical, mostly from this passage, which is only partly reproduced in Luke 20. Matthew no doubt reflects the historical reality, but he also attacks any kind of religious hypocrisy, including that in his own community.

Matthew's last discourse, on the Last Judgment, derives mostly from Mark and has a strong apocalyptic coloring, although there is a small original touch. To Mark 13:18, "Pray that it may not be in winter," Matthew adds for his Jewish converts, "or on a sabbath" (24:20). And whereas Mark ends with Jesus' discourse, Matthew includes the parables of the conscientious steward (24:45-51), the ten wedding attendants (25:1-13), and the ten talents (25:14-30), all of which deal with the need to be prepared, symbolizing the Last Judgment, "for you know neither the day nor the hour" (25:13).

Matthew alone provides a vivid account of the Last Judgment, filled with horrific imagery yet also including some Matthean touches. "Then the king will say to those at his right hand, 'Come, you that are blessed by my Father, inherit the kingdom prepared for you . . . for I was hungry and you gave me food, I was thirsty and you gave me something to drink, I was a stranger and you welcomed me.'" When the righteous ask when they did such things, the King replies, "as you did it to one of the least of these who are members of my family, you did it to me" (25:34-40). We gain salvation not by punctilious observance of religious minutiae but by how we deal with others, and here the others are the poor and the lowly, hungry, thirsty, and homeless. Contrarily, hell is reserved for those who did not care for others. Even in this apocalyptic discourse we can see Matthew showing his community how to act in Christ's name.

Jesus' public ministry has now ended, and his Passion begins.

The Passion

Matthew's Passion Narrative resembles much of the rest of the gospel, that is, he follows Mark but adds material on discipleship and for his Jewish readers. This appears immediately when he adds the detail, unique to his Passion account, that the high priest who led the plot against Jesus was Caiaphas (26:3), possibly known to his Jewish readers or a historical detail he thought would interest them. The plotters succeed when Judas agrees to betray Jesus for thirty pieces of silver (26:15), another detail unique to Matthew and alluding to Exodus 21:32 where that amount covers the indemnity for a slave who has been gored by an ox. The amount also appears in Zechariah 11:12 as a shameful amount the people offer to the good shepherd, the Messiah. Jesus will likewise be treated shamefully. Pushing the notion of the disloyal disciple a bit further, Matthew says that the conspirators paid Judas, whereas Mark says they promised to pay him (14:10).

The Last Supper also follows Mark, except for one element. When Jesus announces that one of the Twelve will betray him, "Judas, who betrayed him, said, 'Surely not I, Rabbi?' He replied, 'You have said so'" (26:25). Jesus does not say this privately to Judas, so wouldn't his words have been heard by the other disciples? This verse is not so much historical as an effective literary device, a face-to-face encounter of the betrayer and betrayed.

With the Last Supper, Matthew corrects Mark in a minor way. Instead of the Markan "Take; this is my body" (14:22), Matthew has "Take, *eat* . . ." (26:26). He does the same thing with Jesus' forecast of Peter's denials. In Mark, Jesus says the cock will crow twice (14:30), which raises the obvious question: when Peter heard the cock crow the first time, didn't that jar him into realizing what he was doing? Matthew mentions only one crowing of the cock (26:34), again clarifying Mark's prose.

The theme of discipleship returns in the account of the arrest. In Mark, Jesus says nothing to Judas, but in Matthew he says to him, "Friend, do what you are here to do" (26:50). Since Matthew has already told us that Jesus knew why Judas was there, the title "friend" shows that Jesus, even at this moment, will not condemn Judas. The evangelist also adds a rather debatable compliment to the disciples. As we saw, Mark does not specify who cut off the ear of the high priest's servant, but Matthew says that "one of those with Jesus" (26:51) did it, that is, one disciple made an attempt to save him. But this goes against all that Jesus stands for, and Matthew records an immortal ethical saying of the great teacher: "All who take the sword will perish by the sword" (26:52).

The arrest leads to two trials, one Jewish, one Roman. The conspirators ask if Jesus is the Messiah, and he acknowledges it; following

Mark, Matthew shows Peter simultaneously denying who Jesus is. The Jewish leaders decide to put him to death, but they seek the approval of the Roman governor Pontius Pilate. Another dramatic moment is coming, but first Matthew inserts a sad passage, unique to his gospel: the suicide of Judas (27:3-8). Peter denied Jesus but would eventually be reconciled to the Risen Christ. Judas, by contrast, despairs. Discipleship depends on faith, which Judas no longer has. Peter weeps but hopes; Judas cannot believe that he can be forgiven. He has become the total opposite of what a disciple should be.

Two points about Judas' suicide. First, while no other gospel mentions it, Luke says in Acts that Judas' stomach burst open "and all his bowels gushed out" (1:18). This was not suicide, but still a sudden death. There is no way to tell which account is historically accurate, although Matthew's seems more realistic. Second, some previous generations of Catholics linked the suicide with the passages in Mark (14:21) and Matthew (26:24) where Jesus says, "It would have been better for that one not to have been born," and they concluded this meant that Judas went to hell. It surely is a startling passage, but the church has never taught that any specific person has gone to hell.

The Roman trial includes three specifically Matthean elements, one of which is very famous. The first deals with Barabbas. Mark identifies him as one "who had committed murder during the insurrection" (15:7), a charge echoed by Luke (23:19), but Matthew says simply that he was "a notorious prisoner" (27:16). Why would he omit so dramatic a charge as "revolutionary"? Because he wants to establish that the crowd that called for Jesus' death preferred an evil man to a good one, but if Barabbas were a revolutionary, the crowd's choice would be more understandable. Furthermore, although his Jewish Christian readers would favor Christ, they too would not think so badly of a revolutionary against Rome. Thus Matthew settles for the amorphous designation of "notorious prisoner."

The second Matthean element we have seen already. Only he mentions Pilate's wife. She parallels the Magi by being a good pagan who recognizes who Jesus is while the Jewish leaders (Herod and his court then, the chief priests now) plot his death.

The third element is a disturbing one with a dreadful history. "[Pilate] took some water and washed his hands before the crowd, saying, 'I am innocent of this man's blood; see to it yourselves.' Then the people as a whole answered, 'His blood be on us and on our children!'" (27:24-25). This passage has been viciously used to promote anti-Semitism for two millennia. Not only, so the "reasoning" went, did God condemn the Jews, but they condemned themselves as well. Except for some fringe groups, no one takes that seriously today, but what does the passage mean?

The notion of perpetual guilt has no application here. In the Book of Exodus, God warns the people, "I the LORD your God am a jealous God, punishing children for the iniquity of parents, to the third and the fourth generation of those who reject me, but showing steadfast love to the thousandth generation of those who love me and keep my commandments" (20:5-6). In an era when knowing one's ancestors was important (recall that Matthew starts with a genealogy), the notion of children suffering for the sins of their parents was not unknown. But notice that God's wrath expires at most in the fourth generation, while God's love continues to the thousandth generation. *If* Matthew intended this as a curse—and that is far from certain—it would not have applied to all the generations of Jews and not even to all the descendants of those in the crowd. This passage can in no way justify anti-Semitism.

Yet the passage does deal harshly with the Jews. Modern Catholic exegetes, realizing that Matthew wrote after the Jewish War of 66–70, contend that he and many other Christians believed that the defeat of the Jews resulted from their demanding Jesus' death. While modern Catholics cannot agree with this ancient view, we can understand that the evangelist did not write of an endless vengeance against the Jews. Furthermore, this passage ends with Pilate delivering Jesus over to be crucified, so Matthew does not exonerate the Romans and blame only the Jews. And, of course, the central theological point of the Passion in all four gospels is that Jesus died for the sins of all humans, so all of us contributed to the need for his redemptive death.

Matthew differs little from Mark in his account of the road to Golgotha and on the crucifixion itself, but he does add details after the death of Jesus. He mentions an earthquake, recalling the natural phenomenon (the star) at Jesus' birth. Four decades ago, in the original *Jerome Biblical Commentary,* John McKenzie, s.j., spoke of "legendary features" in this account (p. 112), and it is obvious in Matthew's surprisingly clumsy handling of verses 52-53. He says that at Jesus' death the tombs of holy people of the past were open and "many bodies of the saints . . . were raised," but then goes on to say that they appeared to people only after the resurrection, which presents the odd picture of the resurrected dead sitting in their tombs from Friday afternoon until Sunday morning. McKenzie is correct; this should be understood as a literary device. The deceased "holy men . . . recognize [Jesus], but

Israel of the flesh does not" (p. 112). Like Mark, Matthew finishes off this passage with the pagan Gentile Roman centurion recognizing that "Truly this man was God's Son" (27:54).

Matthew continues to follow Mark, disagreeing with him on the identity of one of the women who watched where Jesus was buried. We also see a note to his Jewish readers. Mark notes that "when evening had come . . . it was the day of Preparation" (15:42), but Matthew does not mention the exact day since his readers would know that. He does, however, add an important passage, a result of his community's struggle with the local Jewish community (27:62-66). He tells how the Jewish leaders feared the disciples would steal Jesus' body and then claim that he rose from the dead, so they convinced Pilate to put a guard on the tomb. This sets up 28:11-20 when, after Jesus has actually risen from the dead, the leaders bribe the guard to say that the disciples stole his body—the upholders of righteousness have hypocritically descended to lying and bribery. Importantly, "this story is still told among the Jews to this day," showing that Matthew is worried not about a historical event so much as its relevance to Jewish-Christian relations in his day.

Like Mark, he does not describe the resurrection, but only the empty tomb. Mark says three women went to the tomb (16:1), while Matthew says two (28:1), suggesting that the tradition had already become uncertain by the time he wrote. Mark's lapidary account displeases Matthew, who recounts a glorious one: "And suddenly there was a great earthquake; for an angel of the Lord, descending from heaven, came and rolled back the stone [that closed the tomb] and sat on it. His appearance was like lightning, and his clothing white as snow. For fear of him the guards shook and became like dead men" (28:2-4). Mark's implied angel has now become one, but instead of being there when the women arrive, he is announced by an earthquake as he descends from heaven. The angel rolls back the stone, which presumably means that Jesus then rose, but Matthew makes no mention of that, which is a bit confusing literarily, though the basic intent is clear. This passage also shows the danger of relying on non-biblical works to understand the Bible. How many paintings have you seen of Jesus' rising from the dead as the guards fall over backward in awe and terror? But that is not what the gospel says. Fear of the angel is what causes the guard to tremble and become like dead men. There is *never* a substitute for reading the Scriptures.

Not surprisingly, Matthew rejects Mark's abrupt ending with frightened women ignoring the command to tell the disciples Jesus is risen, especially since, decades earlier, Paul had spoken about not only his experience of the risen Christ but that of hundreds of other people (1 Cor 15:5-8). Clearly the disciples knew of the resurrection.

Matthew tells of Jesus' final words to his disciples, what scholars call the Great Commission (28:16-20), suitably set on a mountain, maintaining the Mosaic imagery and recalling the Sermon on the Mount. Yet even at this supreme moment the humanity of the disciples seeps through because "when they saw him, they worshiped him; but some doubted" (28:17). Benedict Viviano, o.p., calls this mingling of faith and doubt "a common psychological experience which gives hope to moderns" (*NJBC*, 674). Jesus tells the disciples, "Go therefore and make disciples of all nations, baptizing them in the name of the Father and of the Son and of the Holy Spirit." "All nations" means that the message goes to everyone, not just the Jews, but the term also includes the Jews. Like Paul, Matthew recognizes that the faith cannot be limited to one people, but this people is still God's chosen people and cannot be left out. We also see here one of the rare Trinitarian passages in the gospels and possibly a formulation later than Jesus' day. And, ending on an appropriately Jewish Christian note, Jesus assures the disciples, "Remember, I am with you always," just as the God of Israel was always there for his people—an excellent ending combining, as Matthew so often does, the old and the new in God's providential dealing with his people. And it recalls more than the beginning of Israel. It recalls Jesus' own human beginnings, his birth reminiscent of Isaiah 7:14: "'They shall name him Emmanuel,' which means, 'God is with us'" (Matt 1:23).

This gospel quickly became popular with the early Christians. To be sure, much of that popularity derived from the belief that the author belonged to the Twelve and provided an eyewitness account. But even beyond that, Matthew tells us so much more about Jesus than Mark did, and he wrote the only words in the NT that every Christian knows by heart, the Lord's Prayer. He presented the Christian message in a form that all Christians could access. He did not deny that Christians might have to die for their faith—Nero's persecution had occurred barely two decades before he wrote—but he also realized that most Christians would live and die in peace, and so he created a gospel filled with ethical maxims that guided Christians in daily life. Catholics especially note Matthew's emphasis on the role of Peter as well as his being the only evangelist to attribute the word "church" to Jesus.

He also recognized that Jesus' work had been continued by his disciples, and so he emphasized discipleship. Occasionally he did it clumsily, as when he "corrects" Mark to make the disciples look less unreliable, but overall he gets the message across: discipleship is an honored but difficult calling. Disciples do God's work, but that does not save them from fallibility: confusion (what thrones do we get in heaven?), lack of faith (the doubt at the Great Commission), and even denial of Jesus. But the only people in the church are the sinners, and God relies on them, just as God relied upon the Chosen People who often deserted him for foreign gods. As Jesus often says in this gospel, God works through the most unlikely people.

Chapter Ten

The Gospel According to Luke

I. Prologue and Infancy Narrative (1–2)

II. John the Baptist; temptation of Jesus (3:1–4:13)

III. Galilean ministry (4:14–9:50)
- Ministry in Nazareth and Capernaum, call of disciples (4:14–6:11)
- Discourses and miracles (6:12–9:50)

IV. Jesus' journey to Jerusalem (9:51–19:27)
- Discourses and parables (9:51–12:3)
- Signs and warnings about the End (12:4–13:35)
- Miracles and more parables (14:1–19:27)

V. Jesus in Jerusalem (19:28–21:38)
- Triumphal entry and cleansing of temple (19:28–48)
- Conflicts; warnings about destruction of Jerusalem (20–21)

VI. Passion and Death (22–23)
- Last Supper (22:1-46)
- Gethsemane (21:47-71)
- Trials (23:1-25)
- Crucifixion and Death (23:26-56)

VII. Resurrection (24)

Please read chapters 1–2, 10–19, 22–24.

This is the gospel most people like best because of its presentation of Jesus. Luke shows Jesus forgiving people, extending his message to everyone, and praying at times of great crisis. The other gospels do

136

likewise, but not as much and not so obviously. Furthermore, Luke had real literary ability. He offers the best organized of the Synoptic Gospels, no small feat since he had to work with two existing sources, Mark and Q. Luke also knows how to tell a story. His three best-known parables, the Prodigal Son, the Good Samaritan, and the Pharisee and the Tax Collector, are the ones that come most easily to mind. While we can never know how they sounded in Jesus' native Aramaic, in Luke's Greek they are masterpieces. So who was Luke, when did he write, and where?

As you have probably already guessed, who knows? As usual, the gospel itself carries no name. In the second century Christian scholars identified the author with a man named Luke who is mentioned in several letters (Philemon 24; Col 4:14; 2 Tim 4:11). Colossians mentions that he was a physician, which led earlier generations of Christians to look for medical terminology in the gospel, but nothing other than well-known words appear, the way many modern people with no formal psychological training use words like "complex." The Luke of the letters may be the author, but this cannot be proven and, as with Mark and Matthew, it does not matter. What matters is that the church accepted this gospel as inspired. As with the other two evangelists, we will use the traditional name.

Can we say anything definite about this evangelist? Yes, and it is very important. He wrote a second book, the Acts of the Apostles, as a continuation of his gospel, and he did not do so in a haphazard way. When he wrote the gospel he had Acts in mind, and some of his concerns in the gospel foreshadow Acts. For example, Luke knows how the disciples struggled to establish the church against fearsome obstacles, and so he treats the disciples less harshly in his gospel than Mark did in his. Of course the disciples let Jesus down at crucial moments, and Luke records some of these, but he also treats the disciples' failings with understanding and mercy.

Luke also knew the Roman world well (something more evident in Acts than in the gospel), which suggests he was a Gentile; his knowledge of Palestinian geography and Jewish Law is less certain—more indication of his Gentile origins—although he may have been a Gentile considering a conversion to Judaism.

As for the place of writing, several possibilities exist. Antioch seems likely, but most scholars would place Matthew there. It is unlikely that two gospels would emerge from the same milieu and virtually impossible that the two evangelists would be unfamiliar with each other's work, which is clearly the case, as we shall see. Some ancient sources say Luke lived in Greece, a plausible location. The date is also uncertain, but definitely after Mark, and Acts presumes that local churches have become well organized. Most scholars opt for a date in the 80s.

As we shall see in Acts, Luke admired Paul's universalism very much, and he adopted the apostle's view of the church: it is open to everyone. But whereas Paul worried about making Gentiles at ease with Christianity, Luke's universalism extends far beyond the ethnic and geographical. It is also social. This new faith appealed to people of all socioeconomic classes, although Luke focuses much on the poor. Equally important, Luke focuses on another marginalized group: women. In this gospel and in Acts women appear frequently, and they often have important roles to play. This applies most to Jesus' mother Mary. Most of what Catholics know about her (the annunciation, the visitation, the Magnificat, the nativity, the presentation in the Temple, the lost Jesus in the Temple) comes from the first two chapters of this gospel. Luke also shows women initiating merciful acts by Jesus, who, in contrast to Mark's Gospel, rarely appears stern or harsh. Luke does include some fearsome parables, such as the rich man who goes to hell, and he also records Jesus' sermon about the Last Judgment, but his emphasis falls on mercy, forgiveness, and reconciliation.

We will consider Luke in two ways, as we did with Matthew. We will see how he has reworked the Markan material, although he uses less of it than Matthew, and we will see what unique, independent traditions he recorded.

Luke opens with a dedication to someone named Theophilus. That may be a proper name, but since it means "one who loves God" in Greek, it may be an honorary title. Luke addresses him as "your excellency," showing that Theophilus was an aristocrat and probably Luke's patron, the person who paid for the publishing of the book, a common practice in an era when authors could rarely live off their writings. Luke assures his patron that he consulted reliable sources (1:2) and then collected the material he gathered in orderly fashion; that is, he did not write down all that he knew, but tried to make sense of it for Theophilus and his other readers. This also alerts us that Luke is not writing a modern biography but rather presenting his understanding of Jesus, his christology, in an effective and convincing way.

Now the evangelist turns to the annunciation (1:5-25), but not of Jesus; rather, he starts with John the Baptizer. Like Matthew, Luke included an infancy narrative to show that Jesus had always been recognized as God's Son and not first at his baptism. But Luke also carries John's story back to his infancy. The story is well known and easily read, but it can best be understood in comparison with the annunciation of the birth of Jesus. The pattern of the two is identical: the angel Gabriel appears, the recipient of the apparition is startled, Gabriel says not to fear, announces the birth of a boy against severe obstacles (Elizabeth's age, Mary's virginity), gives the boy's name, a prediction of his greatness, and a sign that all this is true (Zachary's dumbness, Elizabeth's pregnancy). But clearly Jesus emerges as the greater. First, while Elizabeth is old, several OT women of great age had children (Sarah the most famous), so she fits a pattern, whereas a virginal conception appears nowhere in the OT; this is the greater event. Second, the predictions show that John will do great things; "He will turn many of the people of Israel to the Lord their God" (1:16). But Jesus "will be called the Son of the Most High . . . . He will reign over the house of Jacob forever" (1:32-33). Third, Zachary receives a negative sign, but Mary receives a joyous one. The twin annunciations demonstrate the superiority of Jesus to John.

Luke wastes no time in following up this point. When Mary greets Elizabeth, the child in her womb "leaped for joy," and Elizabeth acknowledges Mary as "the mother of my Lord" (1:41-43). This recognition of Mary's honor leads into one of Luke's poetic masterpieces, the Magnificat (1:46-55). In the Middle Ages, when people read the Bible in Latin, this passage took on the name of its first word, *magnificat,* and scholars still use the name. The poem uses sophisticated Greek and cannot be a translation from the Aramaic. We cannot say for sure how much is Luke's composition and how much came from an existing Christian hymn, but we can see Luke's favorite themes appearing immediately. "[God] has shown strength with his arm; he has scattered the proud in the thoughts of their hearts. He has brought down the powerful from their thrones, and lifted up the lowly; he has filled the hungry with good things, and sent the rich away empty" (1:51-53). And God chose Mary to accomplish this, in spite of "the lowliness of his servant . . . from now on all generations will call me blessed" (1:48).

Two points to note before we go further: first, the conversation between Mary and Elizabeth is the only one between two women in the entire NT; second, note that Matthew (1:29) says the angel gave the announcement of Jesus' birth to Joseph, the man, while Luke says the annunciation went instead to the woman. This is the first of many times that Luke will elevate the status of women in the life of Jesus and thus also for the life of the church.

Elizabeth's pregnancy ends happily because "the Lord had shown his great mercy to her" (1:58), a phrase showing Luke at his best. After John's birth Zachary, again able to speak, proclaims the Benedictus (same reason for the Latin name as the Magnificat), which spells out John's career. He "will be called the prophet of the Most High," but he "will go before the Lord to prepare his ways" (1:76), that is, no matter how great John will be, he will ultimately serve one greater. In his orderly way Luke tells us quickly that John grows up and goes into the desert, where he will announce the coming of the adult Jesus.

Luke now focuses on Jesus and tells the most famous of all Christian stories: "In those days a decree went out from Emperor Augustus that all the world should be registered" (2:1), and we all know the rest. But important Lukan themes appear immediately. Writing after Nero's persecution, Luke works to show the Christians as loyal citizens; Jesus' parents obey the order for the census, just as Jesus and Paul and others would likewise be obedient. Another theme reappears. The angels announce the birth of Jesus to poor, odoriferous shepherds (using the same pattern of annunciation), who believe the angels and rush off to see the newborn Christ. Note that Mary, but not Joseph, ponders all these events in her heart (2:19), maintaining the evangelist's emphasis on her. Obedient to Jewish as well as Roman law, Jesus' parents have him circumcised.

Luke will now shift the drama to the Temple, the scene of later events, but before going there, let us note two things about his infancy narrative. First, where is the famous "Glory to God in the highest, and on earth peace to men of good will" (2:14)? No translation has that because that is not what the Greek says, but the medieval Latin translation, *Gloria in excelsis Deo et in terra pax hominibus bonae voluntatis,* was rendered into English in the familiar verse. Second, and more importantly, note that Mary and Joseph are living in Nazareth of Galilee at the time of the annunciation (1:26), whereas Matthew says they went to Nazareth on their return from Egypt when they were afraid to go back to their home in Judea (2:22-23). This shows that by the 80s some specifics about Jesus' birth had become confused. It also shows that Matthew and Luke did not know one another's writings, or they would have cleared up such an obvious discrepancy.

The Holy Family's visit to the Temple shows Luke's unfamiliarity with Jewish customs. He says "the time came for *their* purification" (2:22), but the Law demanded that only the woman needed purification. Yet we can see Luke's intent: obedience to the Law. In the Temple the Holy Family meets Simeon, a prophet, who, prompted by the Holy Spirit, utters another passage known by its Latin translation, the "Nunc dimittis." Here in the Temple a Jewish prophet proclaims that this child will be "a light for revelation to the Gentiles and for glory to your [God's] people Israel" (2:32). God's special people have a part to play in the new dispensation, but Luke lists the Gentiles first.

Simeon goes on to tell Mary, "A sword will pierce your own soul, too" (2:25), thus linking Mary with Jesus' suffering but also showing the importance of reading the gospels on their own. Many Catholics believe that this reference to the sword piercing Mary's heart means her suffering when she saw Jesus on the cross, but Luke makes no mention of the Blessed Mother in his Passion narrative. The familiar picture of her under the cross comes from John's Gospel, which had not yet been written. Since Luke likes to keep things orderly, he probably means Mary's sufferings in general, starting with her being separated from her son in the Temple, an episode he is about to recount. But before that he tells of the woman prophet Anna, again emphasizing the role of women.

His infancy now over, Jesus disappears from history until his public career, except for an incident unique to Luke. As Jews, Jesus' parents take him to the Temple, but they then lose track of him on the return and need three days to realize that they do not know where he is. No matter how much we try to dress it up, this can never be a flattering portrait of Mary and Joseph if taken completely literally. But Luke partly means the account symbolically: Jesus is gone for three days and then reappears to the first two people to believe in him. Furthermore, here for the first time Jesus himself claims divine paternity, a claim first made by an angel and later, at his baptism, by his Father.

We should also note the compliment Luke pays to a person often forgotten in these accounts, Joseph. The Temple scholars "were amazed at [Jesus'] understanding and his answers [to their questions]" (2:47), clear proof that Joseph has brought up his son to be a good Jew. Now Luke closes this period of Jesus' life by telling us that he "increased in wisdom and in years and in divine and human favor" (2:52).

For the first part of Jesus' public career Luke generally follows Mark, although with his own interests. He sets Jesus' career in an empire-wide setting, mentioning the reign of the emperor Tiberius. He then recounts something of John's preaching but surprisingly goes right into his arrest, which Mark and Matthew put later in their gospels. Luke used the infancy narrative to establish that John goes before Jesus, and now John has literally gone from the scene. Note also that Luke alone of the evangelists says that Jesus prayed after his baptism, which marked the opening of his public life and was thus an appropriate time to ask for God's help.

Next follows a genealogy that simply cannot be matched with that of Matthew (1:1-16), but significantly Luke takes the genealogy back to Adam, the father of all humans, while Matthew took it back to Abraham, father of the Jewish people. It is in little details like this that we see the different emphases of the two evangelists.

Luke's genealogy includes another important passage: "Jesus was about thirty years old when he began his work . . ." (3:23). As we noted in the Introduction, many people drop the word "about" and just assume Jesus was thirty, but Luke does not give an exact age.

Like Matthew, Luke expands on Mark's temptation story, an account so well written that it deserves a longer look because Luke relates it to the ordinary believer (4:1-13). He organizes the sequence of the temptations. First Satan starts with immediate gratification on the physical level: Jesus is hungry. But he does not give in and, like a good Jew, quotes Deuteronomy (8:3) to reject the temptation. Next Satan offers him power and wealth ("all the kingdoms of the world"). Wealth and power are enticing, but Jesus again cites Deuteronomy (6:7) and turns this temptation down. Now Luke's artistry shows. Many of us have done what Jesus did, spurning base physical desires and even an immoral chance for wealth or power. Let's face it, we are really good people! And thus the trap springs: we have fallen into spiritual pride. What harm would it do for Jesus to hurl himself from the Temple and be saved by angels, thus spectacularly demonstrating his power? Cleverly, Satan even quotes Scripture (Psalm 91) to justify this, but Jesus rises above this last, insidious temptation, again citing Deuteronomy (6:16). This sequence works better than Matthew's, as Luke shows Satan deviously starting with the simple temptations and working up to the insidious one. This is Luke at his best.

One other point to consider: Because we believe Jesus to be divine, Catholics often think that Jesus was not really tempted, that Satan just batted his head against a stone wall. Yet all the gospels say that Jesus was tempted, not that Satan wasted his time. But how can this be? Hebrews 4:15 tells us that Jesus was like us in all things except sin, and it is no sin to experience temptation. Let me use an academic example. A student who did not study for the test and is doing badly on it suddenly realizes that he can see someone else's test paper. He is tempted to look at it, which is not a sin. If he gives in to the temptation and cheats, that is sinful. Let us take the gospel writers at their word and see the human Jesus giving us an example of rising above temptation.

Luke next adds to Jesus' rejection at Nazareth (4:16-30), first by telling us that Jesus could read (the only statement that he could), and then showing Jesus citing the story of how the prophet Elijah ministered to Gentiles but not to Jews, which elicits the first attempt by Jewish leaders to kill him, a foreshadowing of the crucifixion.

Jesus continues his ministry but withdrawing "to deserted places" where he prayed (5:16). Jesus is never very far from his true Father.

Luke now follows Mark for a few chapters, but always adding his own concerns. In Mark, when Jesus cures the man with the withered hand the focus is on a possible violation of the Sabbath, but Luke shows the scribes and Pharisees using the occasion to plot against Jesus. More importantly, Luke gives his version of the Beatitudes (6:20-23), which are little known to the general public. "Blessed are *you who are poor* . . . . Blessed are *you who are hungry now* . . . ." Jesus is not Matthew's ethical teacher, but Luke's social reformer. He speaks directly to people, and not in Matthew's third person ("those who are poor in spirit"). Luke's people are poor and not in spirit; they are hungry and not for righteousness; they need money, and they need food, and Jesus calls them blessed. And, in a very stark passage, Jesus pronounces woes upon those who have the goods of this world. We would expect Luke to add "and do not share them," but he does not. These people receive criticism for who they are. Yet Jesus next urges his followers to love their enemies, so even those upon whom woes have been pronounced can be loved. Luke also paradoxically quotes Jesus' saying, "Do not judge, and you will not be judged; do not condemn, and you will not be condemned" (6:37). This evangelist has difficulty being negative for very long.

Addition

Luke again follows Mark and *Q*, but he adds a story unique to him, the raising of the widow's son (7:11-17). Here again we see Jesus' concern for a woman, but Luke also says that the deceased young man was the widow's only son; that is, with no man to care for her she will endure destitution. This is a chance encounter, but Jesus cannot permit this domestic tragedy. Clearly this miracle shows Jesus' power over death, but it simultaneously shows his endless mercy and his concern for women.

After basically repeating Mark's account of John the Baptizer's questions to Jesus, Luke gives another unique story, and again it focuses on a woman in trouble, not from the death of a family member but from her own sins. She repents so sincerely that she can use her copious tears to wash Jesus' feet, which she then dries with her own hair (in those days women did not cut their hair, which often grew down to their waists). The other men at the scene are shocked that Jesus does not send this sinful woman away, but Jesus justifies his conduct and hers: ". . . her sins, which were many, have been forgiven; hence she has shown great love" (7:47). Luke then uses words familiar from Jesus' miracles: "And he said to the woman, 'Your faith has saved you' . . ." (7:50).

Still on the topic of Jesus and women, Luke adds an important historical reference (8:1-3). In addition to the Twelve there were "some women who had been cured of evil spirits and infirmities: Mary, called Magdalene, from whom seven demons had gone out, and Joanna, the wife of Herod's steward, Chuza, and Susanna, and many others, who provided for them out of their resources." One name, of course, stands out. This is the only reference to Mary Magdalene outside the Passion and resurrection narratives, which have her simply appear unannounced at a crucial moment. Luke tells us that she was a follower of Jesus during his ministry and one of several women who provided financial support for him and the other disciples.

Mary's reputation has suffered historically. The gospels say nothing negative about her; on the contrary, they honor her as a witness to the resurrected Christ and, as we shall see, John's Gospel names her the first to see him. Luke says that seven devils were driven from her, but in ancient Jewish demonology a possessed person was a victim, not a sinner. Only in the early Middle Ages did Christian scholars conclude that she was a prostitute, and that was because they assumed that the unnamed woman who washed Jesus' feet was a prostitute who could be identified with Mary Magdalene. This is wrong. She was a good woman who deserves to be known as the gospels actually present her.

But, Magdalene aside, this passage tells us two other important things. First, notice that Joanna is the wife of an official at the Jewish royal court, showing that Jesus' teaching reached the aristocrats as well as the poor. Although the Jewish religious leaders had come to loathe Jesus, the secular leaders initially tolerated him. Second, this passage shows us an important role for women in Jesus' movement. After all, if he and the disciples had given up their professions to evangelize, how did they pay for food and lodging? Luke tells us that women disciples paid for these things. Many religious people play down people like this in favor of those who focus only on the spiritual, as Luke himself does in the story of Martha and Mary (10:38-42), but how could Jesus and the disciples have spread that message without the support these women provided? Spiritual cares may be more important than secular ones, but we should not minimize the role of secular care or the role of the women who provided it.

Luke now goes on (chs. 8–9) to follow Mark about parables and miracles as well as to agree with Matthew in dropping Mark's "other boats" in his account of the storm at sea. Luke does not match Matthew's account of Peter's profession of faith, but neither does he recount Jesus' calling Peter "Satan." He does not like to accentuate the failings of those who would build the church in the Acts of the Apostles. When we recall that the conversation with Peter occurred when Jesus made his first prediction of the Passion, it is significant that only Luke shows Jesus praying at that crucial moment (9:18), a recognition well before Gethsemane that he would need his Father's help to carry out his mission.

Luke now follows Mark on the conditions of discipleship, the transfiguration, and the second prediction of the Passion, probably because he wanted to get to his great contribution to our knowledge of Jesus, a large section (9:51–19:27) virtually unique to Luke and containing some of his greatest writing.

Jesus begins his journey to Jerusalem, to his fate, because "the days drew near for him to be taken up" (9:51). On this journey he will say much about discipleship, tell many parables, and issue warnings about the need to change one's ways. Only Luke has Jesus send out seventy-two disciples, a number corresponding to the Septuagint list of nations in Genesis 10, thus indicating that they minister to the entire world. Combined with this is a warning that at the last judgment things will go better for the pagan cities than the Jewish towns (10:13-15), proof that Luke believes that even Jesus' mercy has limits. When the seventy-two return after a successful ministry Jesus congratulates them and tells one of his immortal parables, the Good Samaritan (10:29-37).

Although this makes Luke's point about the good non-Jew, it also attacks religious hypocrisy. Like Matthew, Luke has his Christian readers in mind. Fearing that the victim of the beating may be dead and thus ritually impure, the priest and Levite walk on. In contrast, the Samaritan, the outcast in Judea, shows mercy to this man cast aside on the road, not just immediately but even after, when he offers to pay the costs of his recovery. Jesus tells this tale to a religious lawyer who has to admit that Jesus is right, that the Samaritan showed mercy, but the lawyer cannot overcome his prejudices. He cannot say the word "Samaritan," but instead uses the circumlocution, "The one who showed him mercy" (10:37). The Samaritan is the true neighbor of the victim; Christian behavior, not ethnic background, shows the true children of God.

Luke's Lord's Prayer, which virtually no one knows, lacks Matthew's sophistication and may reflect an earlier version, yet there is little difference in their spiritual teaching (11:1-4). Note that Luke has Jesus recite this prayer "in a certain place" and not as part of a sermon on a mount.

The rest of chapter 11 parallels Matthew, including attacks on the Pharisees to whom Luke adds religious lawyers, but Luke reworks the story of the sign of Jonah, which for Matthew symbolizes the resurrection. Luke instead focuses on Jonah's ministry to Nineveh, a pagan city, again showing an OT account of the redemption of Gentiles.

The parable of the rich fool shows Luke returning to another theme: the danger of riches. The rich fool "store[s] up treasures for [himself] [but is] not rich toward God" (12:21). This is placed among sayings by Jesus about discipleship and need for total commitment. The account of "the faithful and prudent manager" (12:42) suggests that some disciples, presumably leaders of the community, have a unique task; Luke quickly contrasts this with the lazy servant who did not prepare for the master's return, a symbol of the Last Judgment. Since the evangelist refers to spiritual preparation, what is better than repentance, because "unless you repent, you will all perish . . ." (13:5).

Now Jesus returns to religious hypocrisy, again using the Sabbath (13:10-17). He cures a crippled woman, angering the ruler of a synagogue because he did so on the Sabbath. Mercy counts for more than rules, and Jesus is Lord of the Sabbath—two points well made and appreciated by the people who welcome what Jesus did while their leaders sulk. As always with Luke, the humble prefer Jesus while the proud resent him. Luke next cites a similar Sabbath miracle, this time of a man with dropsy (14:1-6). But after a series of parables and sermons on the strict demands of discipleship and the price for neglecting those, Jesus tells three parables of mercy, the lost sheep, the lost coin, and the lost or "prodigal" son (15:11-32), one of his longest and best parables.

The story is well known. An incredibly rude young man tells his father that he does not want to wait for him to die to get his inheritance; he wants it right away. The father succumbs to the request and the young man squanders his inheritance "in dissolute living" (v. 13).

He falls so low that he must herd pigs. Considering that Jews were not even supposed to touch pigs, we can imagine the revulsion a Jewish audience would have felt at hearing that.

Then he "came to himself" (v. 17) and decided to ask his father for forgiveness, which was readily granted. If the parable ended there it would be a good little story of youthful sin and parental understanding. But Luke turned it into a great parable by adding a third character, the older brother.

We can identify with him. We would never tell our parents, "I don't feel like waiting till you're dead; gimme the money now!" This brother has worked hard and, Luke hints, his father did not appreciate all that he did, not offering him so much as a small lamb for a celebratory dinner with his friends (v. 29). In this way Luke has, so to speak, set a trap for the reader. We understand the older son's resentment. We understand his anger. And we agree with his unwillingness to forgive his brother . . . well, not exactly. Luke has indeed trapped the reader, and he effectively teaches an important lesson. The older brother has the right to be upset, but does he wish to be alienated from his father and brother? Does he wish a life of resentment and rejection? To forgive is not easy, but that is no reason not to forgive. And the unspoken larger lesson is: if an earthly father and brother can forgive, so can God, and in a way we cannot comprehend.

Luke turns again to money, citing words of Jesus about it, including an accusation that the Pharisees love money (16:14), but again a parable gets the lesson across: the rich man and Lazarus. The rich man lived well and paid no attention to the beggar Lazarus who lived at his gate, so weak with hunger that he could not prevent stray dogs from licking the sores on his body. When the two men die the rich man goes to Hades, while Lazarus rests in the bosom of Abraham (the origin of that phrase so well known from the spiritual). The rich man asks for pity, but it is too late. His riches have gotten the better of him. He is not a thoroughly evil man; he cares about his brothers (vv. 27-28), but Luke never backs down on the evil of riches.

The rich man is not alone in ignoring his duties to others. Jesus cures ten lepers (17:11-19) and tells them to show themselves to the priests to get official recognition of their healing. Only one of the ten returns to thank him, and—a typical Lukan touch—that one is a Samaritan, to whom Jesus says, "Your faith has made you well" (v. 19). What the other nine thought, we will never know, but they clearly did not believe that Jesus had performed a miracle for them. Miracles require faith, and only the Samaritan had it.

Jesus now goes from the rich man and the nine ungrateful lepers to a wider canvas: a prediction of the end when those who have neglected their religious duties and their obligations to others will find out it is too late (17:22-37). To keep to the right path makes great demands, and so Jesus tells the parable of the unjust judge and the importunate widow who never relents in pressing her case until she gets her just rights. Jesus links her struggle to those believers who persevere to the end.

Luke's concern for his fellow believers leads him back to familiar topics, religious hypocrisy and universal salvation, here presented in another masterpiece, the parable of the Pharisee and the tax collector (18:9-14).

The Pharisee thanks God that he is not like other people, "thieves, rogues, adulterers," and especially like the tax collector. And the Pharisee indeed differs from those he despises; he fasts twice a week and pays tithes on all he gets. At no point does Luke suggest that the Pharisee is exaggerating, much less lying. He does do all these good things. But his prayer consists of self-congratulation and not the realization that before God even the greatest saints are sinners. The tax collector knows who he really is—and who we all really are—and so he prays simply, "God, be merciful to me, a sinner" (v. 13). His prayer is succinct, direct, and effective, because Jesus tells his audience that the tax collector went home justified while the Pharisee did not. God grants salvation to all who are honest with themselves and with God.

Keeping to familiar themes, Luke next shows Jesus praising the humility of children and warning about the danger of riches. The third prediction of the Passion (18:31-34) reminds us that Jesus will soon give up all that he has for us.

Luke finishes the journey with two meetings at the town of Jericho. Jesus encounters a blind man who knows that he is the Son of David; he cannot see, but he can see the Truth. Jesus praises his faith and then miraculously restores his sight (18:35-43). The other meeting is with the wealthy Zacchaeus, a short man who climbed a tree to get a view of Jesus. The two meet and go to Zacchaeus' house. When he announces that he will give away much of his riches to the poor, Jesus announces, "Today salvation has come to this house" (19:9). The journey ends on the outskirts of Jerusalem where Jesus tells the parable of the pounds, a last admonition to his disciples to use their gifts while there is still time.

But Jesus' own time is running out. He has now entered Jerusalem, and Luke follows Mark in portraying welcoming crowds. The joy does not last long. Jesus knows what this city will do to him, and so he predicts the destruction of the unfaithful city, a destruction Luke's readers knew the Romans carried out (19:41-44).

Luke again follows Mark. Jesus drives out the money changers, and the Jerusalem priests challenge his authority. While the Pharisees try to trick him with the question of tribute to Caesar, the Sadducees with one on the resurrection, and the Pharisees again with one on David's son, we know from Mark and Matthew how all these failed. Jesus then responds vigorously to his attackers and includes a detailed prediction of the destruction of Jerusalem to be followed—at an uncertain but not distant time—by the end of the age. His outraged opponents plot his destruction, but Luke emphasizes that the people responded warmly, so warmly that Jesus can actually preach in the Temple itself during the day and continue to preach in the evening on the Mount of Olives (21:37-38). This would be his last popular triumph.

The Passion

Luke's Passion narrative takes the same approach as the earlier part of the gospel, that is, following Mark and adding his own material and insights. Much on Luke's mind is that the death and resurrection of Jesus will usher in the age of the church, and he occasionally looks forward to that.

Luke 22 starts with the chief priests and also with Satan, who has absented himself from the narrative since the temptation. He "entered into Judas called Iscariot" (22:3). Here Luke mitigates Judas's responsibility, although not his guilt; Luke will soon return to that theme. He is also more orderly in this passage. Having told us that the chief priests feared the crowd (v. 1), he now tells us that Judas sought to betray Jesus "when no crowd was present" (v. 6), a point ignored by Mark and Matthew.

Jesus and the Twelve sit down to the Last Supper; only in Luke does Jesus say he will not eat again until "it [the Passover] is fulfilled in the kingdom of God" (22:16), a point Luke will return to after the resurrection. Luke has slightly changed the account of the Last Supper by having Jesus twice take up the cup (vv. 17, 20), although the second time he does so "after supper." Most likely the first cup was the Passover cup and the second the cup of the Eucharist. Luke also gives a longer account of the supper because he will highlight the importance of the communal meal in the early church in Acts. Parallel to this Luke adds how Jesus praised the disciples for sharing his trials (22:28); unlike his Markan source he wants to emphasize how they will continue Jesus' work. Like the other evangelists, Luke will tell of the disciples' failure to support Jesus in the coming hours, but at the same time he knows they will make up for this after the resurrection. Luke also records positive words to Peter ("I have prayed for you that your own faith may not fail"), even as Jesus predicts Peter's denials of him. The three close disciples accompany Jesus to the Mount of Olives. Unlike Mark and Matthew, Luke does not say that the disciples fell asleep three different times; Jesus awakens them only once.

But Luke's more positive approach to the Passion shows itself most obviously in the account of the arrest. Judas arrives with a crowd. Read what happens next: "He approached Jesus to kiss him; but Jesus said to him, 'Judas, is it with a kiss that you are betraying the Son of Man?' When those who were around him saw what was coming, they asked, 'Lord, should we strike with the sword?' Then one of them struck the slave of the high priest and cut off his right ear. But Jesus said, 'No more of this!' And he touched his ear and healed him" (22:47-51).

Luke follows the same pattern here as in his beatitudes. He does not portray the ethical teacher, but rather the person who deals directly with those who suffer. If you have read the Passion accounts of Mark and Matthew you have probably been wondering why Jesus did not heal the ear of the high priest's slave. That is because Mark and Matthew do not include it (nor would John). Luke realizes that this scene makes Jesus look indifferent to the fate of the slave. To be sure, that would be the normal behavior of a free person in the ancient world. But throughout his gospel Luke has emphasized that Jesus cares for all people—the poor, lepers, Samaritans, women, and even slaves—and Luke will not portray Jesus as indifferent to the fate of a poor man who, as a slave, had to follow the orders his master gave him and go with the group. The slave, not the high priest or the soldiers, will now be maimed for life. Luke wanted his readers to know that Jesus did help the unfortunate victim and cured his ear.

But if we read the passage carefully again, we notice that someone else appears differently than in the other two gospels, and that is Judas, *who never actually kisses Jesus.* Luke says that "he approached Jesus to kiss him," but the kiss never takes place, leaving open the possibility that even Judas would not stoop so low as to turn an affectionate greeting into a means of betrayal. No doubt Mark and Matthew have the actual history here, and Judas did indeed kiss Jesus. But this passage shows how hard Luke works to show the effects of Jesus' life and deeds on all he came in contact with; people remained sinners, but they were better for their encounter with him.

Recall that Satan had entered into Judas. Luke closes the arrest scene with Jesus' pointing out that he had taught in the Temple day by day, that is, in the daylight and in the open, but those who were against him came at night: ". . . this is your hour, and the power of darkness" (22:53), a traditional image of Satan.

Luke moves from one disappointing disciple to another. Mark had placed Peter's denials after the Jewish trial, but Luke locates them before it, heightening the theme of desertion by members of the Twelve and placing it closer to the passage in which Jesus had prayed for Peter to keep the faith. Yet Luke kindly omits the detail that Peter began to curse and to swear that he did not know Jesus (Mark 14:71; Matt 26:74).

The scene now shifts to the Roman trial, which would hold great interest for Luke's Gentile readers. Although today we think of the ancient Romans as persecutors of the Christians, that was not always the case. Luke wrote after Nero's persecution, but that persecution focused only on the city of Rome, did not spread to the provinces, and was not repeated by later emperors until at least the year 95. This means that Luke wrote when Rome was not acting hostilely toward the Christians, so a rapprochement was possible. But one big obstacle stood in the way: Jesus had been put to death as a threat to the state. Think of how this must have sounded in the first century, how potential Roman converts would react when they learned that the Roman empire put Jesus to death as a criminal. Luke needs to establish that Jesus died an undeserved death, and to do so he will focus on the person of Pontius Pilate.

Luke initially follows Mark, but after Pilate asks Jesus just one question he tells the chief priests, "I find no basis for an accusation against this man" (23:4), a passage unique to Luke. The Roman governor should have acted justly and freed Jesus on the spot, but instead he looks to pass the buck. Learning that Jesus is a Galilean, he packs him off to the Jewish puppet king Herod Antipas, the nominal ruler of Galilee and a man Pilate disliked. "When Herod saw Jesus, he was very glad, for he had been wanting to see him for a long time, because he had heard about him and was hoping to see him perform some sign" (23:8). How brilliantly Luke has characterized Herod Antipas: a man's life is at stake, but he wants to see Jesus do a trick. Jesus stands there silent, so Herod mocks him and returns him to Pilate. Their dual complicity in the death of an innocent man now makes friends of the Jewish king and the Roman governor. This is a good touch by Luke. Friendship is a form of community, and Luke has stressed the importance of faith and service as bases for community. No "friendship" based on a mutual crime will last.

But the problem has returned to Pilate, who again tells the Jewish leaders and the crowd, "I have not found this man guilty of any of your charges against him" (23:14), and then he adds that Herod Antipas likewise found no guilt in Jesus. The Roman next says he will have Jesus flogged and then release him. But if he is innocent, why flog him? Because Roman law unofficially presumed that accusations usually had some basis; that is, if you were not guilty of stealing the money this time, you were probably the type to try it some other time. So a flogging would let you know what was in store and make you think twice before you tried something. But, urged on by the high priests, the crowd demands that Pilate release Barabbas and execute Jesus. And here we see Luke's literary abilities in a subtle way.

Mark says that Barabbas committed murder during an insurrection, which Matthew declined to mention. But look at how Luke phrases it: ". . . a man who had been put in prison for an insurrection that had taken place in the city, and for murder" (23:19). Luke has separated the crimes. Barabbas did not commit murder during the chaos of an insurrection; he was both a revolutionary *and* a murderer. Pilate would let this unregenerate criminal go free while he crucified a man he had already twice proclaimed innocent. Just as Peter had denied Jesus three times, so Pilate would proclaim his innocence a third time (23:21). But in spite of this, "He released the man who had been thrown into prison for insurrection and murder, whom they (the crowd) asked for; but Jesus he *delivered up to their will*" (23:25), that is, Pilate did not even order Jesus' execution, but turned him over to the mob (figuratively, of course, since Roman soldiers would perform the deed).

Luke has made a devastating point. Pontius Pilate, a representative of Roman law, three times proclaimed a man innocent; he accepted the verdict of a Roman puppet king that the man was innocent; he instead released a man who committed both revolution and murder (as Luke says twice); he gave in to a mob. We can see Luke's intent. Yes, Jesus had suffered execution at the hands of the Roman state, but that was because a Roman governor did not have the guts to do his job. He tried to pass the buck to Herod; he tried to get the crowd to choose Barabbas; he tried to convince the crowd Jesus was innocent. But none of this worked, and he had to make the right decision. But he could not. He weakly capitulated to a mob, the exact opposite of what a Roman governor was supposed to do. Thus no Gentile should be scandalized by Jesus' "legal" execution, because it was anything but legal.

Luke returns his focus to Jesus, who, beaten and bloodied, must carry his cross to the place of execution. Think of the misery and terror that must have crossed his mind; how could he think of anything else? But he had already accepted this as part of his mission, and Luke wonderfully shows him maintaining another part of his mission, caring for the unfortunate. Luke alone records how Jesus stopped to speak to the women of Jerusalem who lamented and bewailed his fate. Then the compassionate Luke gives way to the orderly Luke. He adds that "two others also, who were criminals, were led away to be put to death with him" (23:32), thus explaining what Mark and Matthew did not, namely, how the other two crucified men got to Golgotha.

Most ancient governments used public executions as a method to deter crime, and Luke had no illusions about the savagery of a crucifixion. But he emphasizes that Jesus remained in control the whole time; even crucifixion would not deter him from his calling. Matthew and Mark recorded only Jesus' cry of dereliction on the cross, but Luke omits it, recording instead three other sayings of Jesus. First, in a remarkable act of mercy he prays, "Father, forgive them; for they do not know what they are doing" (23:34). And can we doubt that God heard this prayer?

The second saying is equally famous. One of the two criminals crucified alongside him berates him, possibly hopefully, by telling him, "Save yourself and us!" But the other criminal, reminiscent of the tax collector in the Temple, knows who he really is and acknowledges, ". . . we are getting what we deserve for our deeds, but this man has done nothing wrong" (23:41). The so-called "good thief" asks Jesus to remember him when he comes into his kingdom, and Jesus responds with the most wonderful promise anyone has ever heard, "Truly I tell you, today you will be with me in Paradise" (23:42).

Jesus' last saying on the cross hearkens, in a sense, back to the twelve-year-old boy in the Temple who went about his Father's business. The adult Jesus has indeed gone about his Father's business, and now, with complete faith, he says, "Father, into your hands I commend my spirit" (v. 46). There is no loud cry at the moment of death as in Mark, just "Having said this, he breathed his last" (v. 47).

Naturally Luke would include Mark's account of the Roman centurion who gave witness to Jesus at this death, but Mark's "Truly this man was God's son" has become in Luke "Certainly this man was innocent" (v. 47)—a bit heavy-handed for the otherwise artistic Luke. And there is another Lukan touch. The people, but not the chief priests, realize what they have done and regret it (v. 48). Luke finishes his account of the

Passion by following Mark on the role of Joseph of Arimathea, although he does not name the women who looked to see where Jesus had been buried.

Luke's resurrection and post-resurrection account differs significantly from those of the other synoptic evangelists; clearly he drew on traditions known only to him. The women go to the tomb at dawn, signaling the end of the power of darkness, but the body is not there. They meet "two men in dazzling clothes" (24:4) who tell them that Jesus has risen from the dead and commission them to tell the eleven. Mark said that the women were too afraid to do that, but Luke says that the women, some of whom he identifies, did tell the apostles, who did not believe them. Actually Luke uses the Greek verb for "proclaimed" to explain how the women told them, thus showing women disciples being the first to proclaim the "good news" of Easter. So all the synoptic evangelists agree that the first witnesses to the Risen Christ were women, a point that should never be overlooked. This does not take away from the special role Jesus accorded to the men of the Twelve, but the women deserve to be as well known as the men who initially ignored their message.

Luke now turns to an account unique to him. Two disciples, disappointed that Jesus did not re-establish the kingdom of Israel (24:21), leave Jerusalem for the town of Emmaus. Jesus draws near to them but makes sure they do not immediately recognize him (v. 16). Amazed that their new traveling companion knows nothing of what has just happened in Jerusalem, the two disciples tell him all about Jesus, including the story of the women, here identifying the two young men the women met as angels (v. 23). They add the detail that some of the male disciples went to the tomb as well (v. 24). Then Jesus begins to explain to them how these events, so initially disturbing to them, fulfilled what had been predicted of the Messiah.

The two disciples hospitably ask their companion to stay with them. When they have food brought, "he [Jesus] took bread, blessed and broke it, and gave it to them. Then their eyes were opened, and they recognized him; and he vanished from their sight" (24:28-31). They recognized him in the breaking of the bread, a sign that the risen Christ would remain with the community in the Eucharist, a point Luke would make again in the Acts of the Apostles.

The two disciples return to Jerusalem and tell the eleven what has happened, and the eleven tell them of an apparition to Simon (Peter), which Luke has not described but which fulfills Jesus' promise to him that he would help him to strengthen his brothers (22:32). The two disciples from the Emmaus road emphasize how they recognized Jesus in the breaking of the bread.

Then Jesus appears suddenly among them, and they are frightened, recalling the reaction of the shepherds of the Nativity when they saw the angelic glory. The disciples fear they may be looking at a false spirit, but for the last time Jesus overcomes their doubts. He tells them, "Touch me and see; for a ghost does not have flesh and bones as you see that I have" (24:39). Luke here insists on the resurrection of the flesh, something that many Gentiles would question. Luke emphasizes the point by recounting how Jesus requested and ate a piece of cooked fish. The risen Christ does not really need food, but he re-establishes table fellowship with his disciples and recalls Luke 22:16 because Jesus is now in the kingdom and is again eating.

Now the risen Christ instructs the disciples: ". . . he opened their minds to understand the scriptures" (24:45), that is, that his suffering, death, and resurrection fit into the divine plan promised so long before in the OT, and all the Scriptures are fulfilled in him. He encourages them to preach to "all nations" (v. 47), continuing a Lukan theme but paralleling Matthew's Gospel in which Jesus also proclaims the obligation to preach to all nations (Matt 28:19). In a Trinitarian scene to be explained fully in the Acts of the Apostles, Jesus, the Son of God, tells his disciples that he sends the promise of his Father upon them, but they must stay in Jerusalem "until you have been clothed with power from on high" (v. 49), referring to the Holy Spirit at Pentecost.

You no doubt noticed that neither Mark nor Matthew refers to the ascension, a widely known event because of the many artistic representations of it. In fact, only Luke mentions this, partly because of his sense of order. He cannot begin to tell the story of the church in the Acts of the Apostles until the story of Jesus has finished completely. (Recall that Matthew finishes with Jesus still on earth, speaking to the disciples.) So he recounts the ascension, now a firm doctrine of Catholic teaching.

But many modern Catholics have a problem with this. Luke has Jesus being carried up into the air, which raises a logical question: if this is so, where did he go? The answer lies in Luke's theological intent and in the cosmology of the ancient world. Luke wants to establish that Jesus, having completed his earthly mission, returned to his Father in heaven. In the ancient world people routinely thought that heaven was above the sky rather than, as we believe today, a state of being perpetually happy with God. If Jesus returned to his Father in heaven and if heaven were above the sky, then Luke had to portray Jesus ascending into the air. As is so often the case, if we understand the Scriptures in terms of the historical circumstances, apparent problems disappear. Exactly how Jesus returned to his Father is a mystery, that is, something we cannot understand, but we can understand Luke's intent. And we can understand its result.

Aware of Jesus' transformation, the disciples worship him (v. 52). Does this mean a full recognition of his divinity? Luke does not say, and we should not push the text too far. But Luke is taking the question very close to that and preparing the way for the recognition of the divine Son in John's Gospel.

"And they . . . returned to Jerusalem with great joy; and they were continually in the temple blessing God" (24:53). Jesus' life began with tidings of great joy (2:10) and with Simeon in the Temple praising God for sending this child (2:27-32). And on this note of joy and fulfillment Luke closes his first book.

In an era when the church extends throughout the globe, embracing people of every geographic region, social status, and ethnicity, we can see why Luke's Gospel retains its popularity. But it has more than universalism in its appeal. A Christ who can forgive his executioners is a Christ who can forgive us; a Christ who can promise paradise to a condemned criminal is a Christ who can promise it to us if, like that criminal, we seek it; a Christ who pays special attention to women is a Christ who can inspire the women who play greater and greater roles in the modern church.

When Luke's christology combines with his literary artistry, a scriptural book of the first rank can be the only result.

Chapter Eleven

The Gospel According to John

I. Prologue (1:1-14)

II. Preparation for Ministry (1:15–4:54)
   - John the Baptist, Cana, cleansing the Temple (1:15–2:25)
   - Nicodemus, early discourses (3)
   - Samaritan woman, return to Galilee (4)

III. Public ministry (5:1–10:39)
   - Discourses and miracles (5:1–6:59)
   - True and false disciples, belief and unbelief (6:60–7:52)
   - Jesus' true identity (8:1–9:41)
   - The Good Shepherd (10:1-39)

IV. End of ministry (10:40–12:50)
   - Conflicts, Lazarus (10:40–12:11)
   - Entry into Jerusalem (12:12-50)

V. Passion (13–19)
   - Last Supper (13)
   - Farewell discourses (14–16)
   - Gethsemane (17:1–18:11)
   - Trials and sentencing (18:12–19:16)
   - Death (19:17-42)

VI. Resurrection narratives (20–21)

Please read chapters 1–4, 6, 8, 10–11, 13–14, 18–21.

For almost two millennia this gospel occupied a unique place in Christian life because it was written by John, not just one of the twelve apostles but also the "disciple whom Jesus loved," who laid his head on Jesus' breast at the Last Supper and cared for Jesus' mother after the crucifixion.

You have probably guessed that none of this is true, and you are right. Two of the objections to John's being the author parallel objections to Matthew. The gospel itself does not name the author, which was provided by a late-second-century Christian writer, and the quality of the Greek points not only to a native Greek speaker rather than a Galilean fisherman but also to someone with a considerable education, since the author uses many literary devices to get his message across. Several other issues further weaken the identification. The gospel never mentions the name John nor does it ever specifically identify the Beloved Disciple, the supposed author, as a member of the Twelve. The final chapter of the gospel speaks about the Beloved Disciple as already dead, which makes it impossible for him to have written the entire gospel. In fact, many scholars have found more than one hand at work in its composition. Scholars have also discerned how this gospel grew in relation to the difficulties the gospel's community had with the local Jewish community; that is, this is not a straightforward account of Jesus' ministry but a document much influenced by events that occurred much later.

To these can be added the contradictions between this gospel and the Synoptics, especially on the point of John's being underneath the cross. The other three portray the Twelve (except, of course, for Judas) as having fled and being nowhere near Calvary. Why would they have said that if John were there? To say that they did not know cannot answer the question because they knew of Judas' betrayal and Peter's denials and the women standing nearby and Joseph of Arimathea's request for Jesus' body. How could they not have known about one of the Twelve being under the cross?

So, who was "John"? As usual, we can only say what the gospel tells us about him. He was well educated. His concern for the community's difficulty with the Jews suggests that he was Jewish himself, to which can be added his knowledge of Palestinian geography and of Jewish feasts and customs. Ancient Christian tradition claimed that John the "apostle" (a word never used in the gospel) had migrated to Ephesus in western Asia Minor after the resurrection. Possibly that tradition evolved because the Christians knew the gospel came from that area, but the gospel's location likewise eludes identification. Most scholars are comfortable with a location somewhere in Asia Minor, which would make the author a Diaspora Jew like Paul, but that cannot be proved. As for when he wrote, the end of the first century seems most likely. Although we cannot be sure whether the author knew the written Synoptic Gospels, he certainly knew traditions preserved by the Synoptics. Furthermore, his christology has advanced well beyond that of the Synoptics and also Paul because it has a strong emphasis on the divinity of Christ, a doctrine now accepted by Catholics but one not enunciated in the early NT literature. In fact, John's Gospel provided the best basis for this doctrine. That the gospel cannot be much later than the year 100 C.E. is certain because the earliest manuscript evidence of the NT, a fragment dated *ca.* 120, is of John's Gospel, an irrefutable proof of its existence.

As with the Synoptics, we will use the author's traditional name, and we will treat the gospel in its final form, that is, speaking of John as the author even when scholars believe another hand was at work at particular points. We are not minimizing the importance of these scholarly insights, but an introductory book must deal with the gospel as it exists.

And when we do read it, this gospel has lots of surprises, mostly of omission: no infancy narrative, no exorcisms, a limited number of miracles, few parables, no list of the Twelve, no betrayals by Peter at the Passion, only two references to Jesus' mother but without mention of her name, a stay in Jerusalem (including the Passion narrative) that takes up forty percent of the gospel, no commissioning of the disciples to evangelize the world, and a major figure, the Beloved Disciple, who literally appears nowhere else in the NT. We also find many literary devices, which only a detailed commentary could highlight effectively, but to mention just a few we see irony, a play on light and darkness, and an extensive use of words or phrases that have a double meaning. Some of the surprises are historical, and one comes up very early. In the Synoptic Gospels Jesus tries to keep his messianic identity hidden until at least his closest disciples recognize that he is a different kind of Messiah. But in this gospel John the Baptist gives witness to Jesus right at the beginning. Jesus does not deny it, and in the next episode he promises some new disciples that they "will see heaven opened and the angels of God ascending and descending upon the Son of Man" (1:51). In this gospel Jesus repeatedly manifests who he is. The question is not whether he is the one sent from God but whether people can bring themselves to acknowledge this and change their lives accordingly.

Also note that this evangelist and his community had suffered a break with the local synagogue, and he often refers to the Jews in a negative—sometimes very harsh—way (cf. 8:44). He often separates Jesus from his people: for example, Jesus says to the Jews, "*Your* ancestors ate the manna in the wilderness" (6:49) and "In *your* law it is written . . ." (8:17), not, as we would expect, "*our* ancestors" or "*our* law." We can only say that this is unfortunate, that it does not justify any anti-Jewish attitudes, and that we cannot change history. We will look at the reason for John's stance when we get into the gospel.

Finally, John presumes that his readers already know a good deal about Jesus, possibly from the other gospels, possibly from oral tradition, and probably from a combination. He speaks of John the Baptizer's being in prison (3:24) but never mentions his arrest or execution. The crowd says the Messiah should come from Bethlehem, which they think Jesus does not (7:42), an irony that makes no sense unless the Christian reader knew that Jesus was born there. Clearly John had other concerns and a different christology to present, and so he did not cover everything he thought his readers might know.

Matthew and Luke wrote prologues to their gospels, what we call the Infancy Narratives. John's Gospel also has one, almost in poetic form, speaking of the Word who is God. Older Catholics will remember that this used to finish the old Mass when the priest read it in Latin. Not just the language of the Prologue but also its content present problems because this image of the "Word" never appears elsewhere in the gospel. A later editor or a literate member of the community added it to the basic account.

The Greek word for "word" is *logos,* and it means a statement or representation of the mind, in this case the divine mind. In ancient philosophy God governs and orders the world through the divine *logos,* and from earliest Christianity theologians believed the term had a philosophical background. In fact, this led to John's Gospel becoming a major source for the early Christian theologies of the Trinity and Incarnation because the early theologians were all educated in Greek philosophy and saw in the word *logos* a technical term they could use to explain such difficult notions as how one divine being could subsist in three person or how one person could unite in himself both human and divine natures. Although the early Christian theology of the Trinity and Incarnation represents the greatest intellectual achievement of the church, modern exegetes point out that this later development does not help us to understand the gospel.

Although the author of the prologue might have had some Greek education, we do better to look for Jewish rather than pagan sources. In Jewish tradition God created the world with the aid of *Sophia*, divine wisdom, who was often personified (see Sirach 24). Furthermore, the prologue's emphasis on light and dark parallels elements in the Dead Sea Scrolls. So, as with the other gospels, we look primarily at a Jewish environment for John as well.

The opening verse is a theological bombshell. ". . . the Word was God." Although the bulk of the gospel points undeniably to Christ's divinity, the prologue starts with it. We do not need a Roman centurion under the cross to tell us that Jesus was not an ordinary man; here we know it from the beginning. And from the creation the Word interacted with us because "all things came into being through him" (1:3), and not just inanimate objects: "What has come into being in him was life, and the life was the light of all people. The light shines in the darkness, and the darkness did not overcome it" (1:4-5).

Stepping back a bit, the author turns to tradition, citing John the Baptizer as a witness to the light. Furthermore, "he [the Word] came to what was his own, and his own people did not accept him" (1:11), but those who did accept him (Jews and Gentiles) became children of God, another familiar theme. "And the Word became flesh and lived among us, and we have seen his glory, the glory as of a father's only son, full of grace and truth" (1:14). The prologue focuses John's christology: a divine being came down from heaven, took on humanity, and offered us salvation. Now we can understand the gospel better, the author believes, because we know who Jesus really is and why he does what he does, the same approach Mark used, but here on a higher level.

For generations scholars have divided John's account of Jesus' ministry into two parts, a Book of Signs (1:19–12:50) and a Book of Glory (13:1–20:31). These can be further broken down: for example, from 1:19 to 4:51 Jesus' signs win over people to him, while subsequent signs provoke controversy and unrelenting opposition. While we do have some historical accounts here, clearly John has arranged the material to make a theological point: accepting Jesus may be easy for some but difficult for others. Accepting Jesus may not initially make great demands, but the better one recognizes the nature of those demands the more stringent they become, too stringent for many people.

Although John has a traditional beginning with John the Baptizer, he has altered the story considerably. If we look carefully (1:19-34), *John the*

Baptizer does not actually baptize Jesus. Furthermore, he becomes a witness to Jesus; he sees the Spirit in the form of a dove, and the Baptizer, not a voice from heaven, proclaims Jesus to be the chosen one of God. He repeats this next day, telling two of his disciples that Jesus is the lamb of God. The disciples leave John to follow Jesus, a symbol that John's time is fast disappearing. One disciple is Andrew; the other remains unnamed. Andrew gets his brother Peter to join them, and Jesus renames him Cephas or "Rock." But the evangelist provides no list of the Twelve, and he includes in this passage someone name Nathanael who is not found in the Synoptics. Presumably Nathanael was another name for someone who belonged to the Twelve, since he is among the members of the Twelve to whom Jesus appears after the resurrection (21:1-2).

John the Baptizer will reappear in 3:22-36 to again bear witness to Jesus. This chapter contains a paragraph (after John's speech, but supplied by the narrator) with a very advanced christology: "The one who comes from above is above all. . . . The Father loves the Son and has placed all things in his hands." John's last recorded words in this gospel are "He must increase, but I must decrease." John then disappears from the gospel. Jesus and others will refer to him a few times, but aside from a reference to his having been in prison (3:24), the gospel gives no account of John's arrest or death or sending disciples to Jesus. No other person will distract from the account of Jesus.

"On the third day" (2:1) of what was proving to be a very busy week Jesus attends a wedding at Cana, where he performs what John the evangelist calls the first of his signs (2:11). This is why many standard accounts of Jesus' ministry list this miracle first, but John prefers the word "sign" to miracle. He presumes that his readers know Jesus performed miracles. The word "sign" means that the miracles point to something more, in this case to the nature of the one performing the sign. Jesus' mother, unnamed, asks him to help out when the wine runs short. He declines, but his mother persists, symbolizing the Christian whose faith must weather disappointments. She is not disappointed now; he turns six jars of water into wine. The family and the president of the feast do not know what happened, but the servants do. Significantly, Jesus does not bind the servants to silence. This is not the Gospel of Mark.

Jesus follows this act with a blatantly public one, driving the money changers from the Temple, which the Synoptics place at the end of his ministry. Here we see for the first time John's literary device of having Jesus' words understood on one level while their meaning lies on a higher one. When he tells the authorities, "Destroy this Temple, and in three days I will raise it up" (2:19), his opponents think he means the building, but John tells us "he was speaking of the temple of his body" (2:22). God can no longer be encountered in the Temple (which by the time of this writing had been destroyed) but can be met in the person of his Son, something his disciples realize after the resurrection.

Jesus' meeting with Nicodemus illustrates the dark-light theme. The Pharisee comes to Jesus at night to ask him questions about religion. Jesus will enlighten him. But John quickly mixes in another element. Jesus tells Nicodemus that no one can be saved without being "born again" *or* being "born from above" since the Greek could mean either and the context would determine the meaning. Jesus means "above," but Nicodemus assumes he means "again" because he asks, "How can anyone be born after having grown old? Can one enter a second time into the mother's womb and be born?" (3:4). This allows Jesus to take the question out of the physical realm, telling him that one must be born again in the Spirit, an allusion to recognizing who Jesus is but also likely to baptism since that is where John's readers had themselves met Jesus sacramentally. Nicodemus asks another question, and then the dialogue becomes a monologue.

Jesus informs Nicodemus that "no one has ascended into heaven except the one who descended from heaven . . . as Moses lifted up the serpent in the wilderness, so must the Son of Man be lifted up" (3:13). "Lifted up" can mean both honorary exaltation and physically being lifted up, a reference to the cross. God sent his only Son to save the world, but "the light has come into the world, and people loved darkness rather than light" (3:19). Here John explains the Incarnation, implied in the Prologue. God's Son had to enter the world in order to save it, with the consequence that "everyone who believes in him may . . . have eternal life" (3:16), but there are many who do not wish to see the light. John closes the account by saying simply, "After this Jesus and his disciples went into the Judean countryside . . ." (3:22), with no mention of how Nicodemus responded to all this. But this truth-seeking Pharisee appears twice more, once in defense of Jesus (7:50) and then joining Joseph of Arimathea in burying him (19:39).

Jesus' encounter with the Samaritan woman uses some similar devices (4:1-42). She comes to the well to draw water. Jesus asks her for a drink and then speaks of living water. She notices that he has no bucket and so asks him where he will get this living water. He replies that whoever drinks this water will never thirst again. By now we would expect the woman to realize something was up, but she insists on giving the water a physical interpretation, a symbol of those who hear the word but cannot bring themselves to believe it. Jesus persists and shows his more than human knowledge by telling her that he knows she has had five husbands. Still uncertain of his meaning, she points out that he, as a Jew, sees Jerusalem as the place of worship.

Now Jesus speaks at some length, acknowledging that "salvation is from the Jews," but "the hour is coming, and is now here, when the true worshipers will worship the Father in spirit and truth" (4:20, 23). Abandoning her interest in the well, the woman says that when the Messiah comes, "he will proclaim all things to us." Jesus replies, "*I am* he" (4:26). In a literary context this recalls Jesus' answer to the high priest's question in Mark's Passion narrative (14:61-62). This phrase in a religious context means a self-identification of Jesus with YHWH speaking to Moses (Exod 3:14), but whereas Mark did not make a claim of divinity for Jesus, John's Gospel did so in the Prologue and will do so several more times in the body of the gospel. Jesus makes quite a demand on the Samaritan woman, and she accepts it as best she can. Just as Jesus' disciples wonder why he is talking with her, so she, as she tells her neighbors about Jesus, wonders, "He cannot be the Messiah, can he?" (4:29) When she returns to Jesus with a crowd of townspeople, the Samaritans accept Jesus. Here John makes an unspoken but necessary contrast with the Jews, from whom salvation was to come but who have not accepted it. The Samaritans respond to the message that true worshipers "worship [the Father] in spirit and truth," and not in the Jerusalem Temple.

The message may be historical as well as theological. Possibly some Samaritans had joined John's community—his is the only gospel that reports conversion among them—which would have caused resentment among the neighboring Jews. Another possibility is that a woman disciple preached the good news to the Samaritans, and this episode remembers her work.

John finishes the first part of the Book of Signs with the healing of a royal official's child. Like Jesus' mother at Cana, the official does not receive an affirmative answer when he requests Jesus' help, but he too persists because his faith is strong, and so that faith is rewarded.

Starting in chapter five Jesus encounters opposition to his good works. He cures a crippled man at the pool of Beth-zatha (or Bethesda). When the cured man carries his mat, "the Jews" (5:10)—note, not the Pharisees, just "the Jews"—tell him he should not do so on the Sabbath.

He replies that the man who cured him told him to do so, the implication being that a man with such power can say things like that, even on the Sabbath. "The Jews" are further incensed by Jesus' apparently equating himself with God by speaking of God as his Father. They then plot to kill him, something that occurs later in his career in the Synoptic Gospels.

Yet this fits John's theology. Jesus makes demands, and those who refuse them often find themselves morally and spiritually adrift, having refused a chance at redemption. Jesus responds to the charge of blasphemy by insisting that "the Son can do nothing on his own, but only what he sees the Father doing" (5:19), but the Father "has given all judgment to the Son" (5:22), that is, the Son can act on earth in place of the Father. This is a huge statement to make, but Jesus supports it by citing five witnesses: God ("another who testifies on my behalf," 5:32), John the Baptizer, "the works that the Father has given me to complete" (5:36), the Scriptures, and Moses. How different from the Markan Jesus, who moves ever so carefully to reveal who he is!

Chapter six contains the famous discourse on the bread of life, and we Catholics naturally and rightly think of the Eucharist, but it has another meaning. The chapter begins with the feeding of the multitude, the only miracle recounted in all four gospels, to which John then joins the walking on water. Miraculous feeding and power over water would recall for Jewish Christians the figure of Moses, and God's parting the Red Sea and feeding the people with manna. All the evangelists emphasized Jesus' relation to the OT.

But the gospel focuses on Jesus, who identifies himself—again using the "I am" formula—as the bread of life (6:35), here meaning not the Eucharist but Jesus himself, a statement reinforced by his saying that "all who see the Son and believe in him . . . have eternal life" (6:40). But John is writing six decades after the crucifixion, and he knows the body of Jesus now has a different meaning for his readers (6:51-56): "I am the living bread that came down from heaven . . . the bread that I will give for the life of the world is my flesh . . . unless you eat the flesh of the Son of Man and drink his blood, you have no life in you. Those who eat my flesh and drink my blood have eternal life . . . for my flesh is true food and my blood is true drink. Those who eat my flesh and drink my blood abide in me, and I in them."

This famous account reflects John's understanding of the Eucharist. He does not emphasize its communal nature but rather emphasizes the individual encounter with Jesus in the Eucharist. John adds that these words drove away many of Jesus' disciples, apparently disturbed by the seemingly cannibalistic nature of the discourse, but the Twelve stand fast, realizing that Jesus often intended more than the surface meaning of his words. Peter speaks for the group, and this passage (6:67-69) is John's version of Peter's confession (Mark 8:27-30; Matt 16:13-20). John knows of the tradition that Jesus called Peter a Satan, but he drops it. Instead Jesus says: "one of you is a devil" (6:70), and John identifies this person as Judas.

Jesus' brothers, that is, his male relatives, enter the scene, telling him to go to Jerusalem for the festival of Booths. Jesus declines, mostly because "not even his brothers believed in him" (7:5), but also because Jesus does what his Father wills, not what humans want him to do. In fact, when his brothers leave he does go to Jerusalem. There he encounters both resentment and questions, the latter mostly on the identification of the Messiah. John uses the omniscient reader to ironic effect. The people say that no one knows from where the Messiah comes, but they know where Jesus comes from (7:27); then they point out the Messiah must come from Bethlehem (7:42), an irony lost on the crowd but no doubt enjoyed by John's audience. We also see Jesus again using phrases with more than one meaning (7:33-34). Predicting his resurrection with "I am going to him who sent me," he adds, "where I am, you cannot come." The Jews think he is going to Gentile territory.

John also adds an unusual point for him. The Pharisees send the Temple police to arrest Jesus, but they refuse to do it because "Never has anyone spoken like this" (7:46). These good Jews do not recognize exactly who Jesus is, but they know man sent by God when they see him.

The story of the woman caught in adultery whom Jesus saves from stoning is one of the most famous NT passages, yet most scholars do not consider it part of the original gospel but rather a later addition. The passage sounds more like Luke than John, and some ancient manuscripts have the story in Luke's Gospel. Jesus saves the woman by asking the men about to kill her if they are sinless; that is, do they have the right to play God and take this woman's life? Also Lukan is the implied reproach, which feminist scholars often point out—it takes two people to commit adultery, yet only the woman is being put to death.

Most of chapter eight focuses on conflicts between Jesus and his opponents in Jerusalem. Jesus announces (8:12) that he is the light of the world, darkness opposes him, and the light brings life, themes we saw in the prologue. The Pharisees oppose him, but Jesus, citing "your law," identifies himself and his Father as witnesses to who he is. When the

Pharisees ask where his father is, Jesus replies that to know him is to know his Father—again the notion that people encountering Jesus must respond faithfully to him, which his opponents cannot do.

Possibly reflecting conflicts between the Johannine community and the local synagogue, John attributes a harsh saying to Jesus. He is from above and not of this world, whereas his opponents are from below and of this world (8:23). He then switches into ambiguous language, saying that he will be recognized only when he has been lifted up, that is, either exaltation or physically being lifted up. If these skeptics could only accept the truth, "the truth will make you free" (8:32). Annoyed at his references to his Father, Jesus' opponents insist they are right because Abraham is their father. Jesus turns this upside down, telling his opponents that their true father is the devil (8:44), a very blunt statement that denies any hint of goodness in his opponents. Again we may see here echoes of a conflict John's community experienced.

"The Jews" respond in kind, saying Jesus is possessed; he insists he is not and goes on to say that "whoever keeps my word will never see death" (8:51), proof to the Jews that he is possessed since even the great Abraham died. In his strongest claim to divinity, Jesus replies, "*Your* ancestor Abraham rejoiced that he would see my day." When the Jews reply that Jesus could never have known the long-deceased patriarch, Jesus asserts, "before Abraham was, I am" (8:58). This is not a man who was born three decades ago; this is a divine person who knew Abraham. So provoked are the Jews that they try to kill Jesus, who escapes unharmed.

After facing the blindness of his opponents, Jesus now encounters a man born physically blind. Again John makes a play on words as Jesus, who will give the blind man the light of sight, identifies himself as the light of the world. He cures the man but does so on a Sabbath. This enrages the Pharisees, who turn on the man and his parents, that is, not on Jesus himself but on those who accept him, like John's readers. The parents avoid a decision in order to avoid expulsion from the synagogue, but the cured man stands up for Jesus and even tries to win the Pharisees over. Furious, they eject him from the synagogue. Jesus meets the man, who tells him, "Lord, I believe," and then worships Jesus, a reverence usually reserved for God. The narrative closes with Jesus telling the Pharisees that they are blind. Since they refuse to see, they are guilty for what they do.

Although John has little interest in parables, he recounts a brief one about a good shepherd (10:1-6). But this is an introduction to yet another monologue. This image has strong OT overtones; David was a shepherd, and Psalm 23 says "The LORD is my shepherd." Jesus predicts his Passion when he says that "the good shepherd lays down his life for the sheep" (10:11). He compares himself to his Father; as his Father knows him, so he knows his sheep. But he tells his Jewish audience, "I have other sheep that do not belong to this fold. I must bring them also . . . there will be one flock, one shepherd" (10:16). The message would go to the Gentiles, but the Jews would be welcome. Jesus closes this by addressing an often troubling point: why would a loving father ask his son to die? The synoptic evangelists made it clear that redemptive suffering was necessary for us, and so Jesus had to accept this. But John has emphasized Jesus' divinity and his oneness with the Father, and here Jesus says, "I lay it [my life] down of my own accord. I have power to lay it down, and I have power to take it up again. I have received this command from my Father" (10:18). John maintains the Synoptic tradition of Jesus doing the Father's will, but he follows the Father's will by his own free will. The Father and Jesus are so united that they can never be of different minds. The "lifting up" of Jesus is what both have concluded must be done.

After this dramatic assertion of divinity John takes us, for the last time, into the nitty-gritty of Jesus' dealings with his Jerusalem opponents, who again want to arrest him. Jesus eludes them and, no doubt with some relief, goes to the Jordan River district where people remember what John the Baptizer said about him, and "many believed in him" (10:42), a far cry from his Jerusalem experiences.

But the rest does not last long. Jesus' friend Lazarus is ill, and his sisters Martha and Mary notify Jesus, who deliberately waits until he dies before going to their home in Bethany, which his disciples point out is uncomfortably close to Jerusalem, the home of his enemies. Jesus goes anyway, and Thomas, one of the Twelve, says to the others, "Let us also go, that we may die with him" (11:16), a good piece of Johannine irony. In the gospels the Twelve will flee, but John knew that some of them would indeed die for Jesus after his resurrection.

The sisters believe in Jesus, and Martha tells him, "Lord" (note the same title the cured blind man used), "if you had been here, my brother would not have died" (11:21). Martha believes in the resurrection, but Jesus says, "I am the resurrection and the life" (11:25), thus linking his resurrection, yet to come, with the giving of life. Jesus then goes to Lazarus' tomb. In a gospel that emphasizes Jesus' divinity, John shows his humanity: "Jesus began to weep" (11:35). He then performs a miracle, another sign, telling his Father it is "for the sake of the crowd standing here, so that they may believe that you sent me" (11:42), a significant departure from the Synoptic insistence that people had to have faith before Jesus would effect a miracle. This, however, follows John's practice of showing how Jesus must labor to win people over. The rejections of his ministry have been so strong that he cannot presume that people have the faith so evident in the Synoptics. John finishes the account by describing Lazarus' funereal bindings, a reminder that he will die again, contrasting this with Jesus' resurrection, when the burial clothes are neatly left in the tomb (20:5-7), a point made only by John.

A miracle of this magnitude will surely win Jesus many followers, and his opponents now justify their opposition by claiming fears that the Romans will move against him and harm the holy places in the process. There is more irony here: the high priest Caiaphas says shrewdly to the crowd that "it is better for you to have one man die for the people than to have the whole nation destroyed" (11:50). John's readers knew what happened when the nation revolted against Rome.

The Sanhedrin leaders decide to put Jesus to death, and they quickly find the instrument to use, Judas, who John says "kept the common purse" and was a thief (12:6), thus providing a solid reason—greed—for the betrayal where the Synoptics are unclear.

But Jesus has a last moment of triumph in Jerusalem. He enters the city, and a great crowd of people welcome him, carrying "branches of palm trees," mentioned only by John and becoming the basis for Palm Sunday. But the people's welcome does not mean acceptance by the authorities, and the first individuals Jesus encounters in Jerusalem are not Jews but Gentiles, Greeks who politely tell a disciple, "Sir, we wish to see Jesus" (12:21). Jesus replies to this request by enumerating some qualities of discipleship that are open to all, using words like "anyone" and "whoever." But then Jesus realizes what price his discipleship to his Father will exact, and he asks again, quite humanly and plaintively, "And what should I say—'Father, save me from this hour'? No, it is for this reason that I have come to this hour. Father, glorify your name" (12:27-28). (This echoes Matthew's Lord Prayer, "hallowed be thy name.") Clearly rejecting Mark's portrayal of a Jesus who must face his trial alone, John tells of a voice from heaven, answering Jesus' prayer. In this gospel Father and Son are united, and Jesus cannot and will not be alone.

The crowd misunderstands what they have heard, thinking it a clap of thunder or the voice of an angel. Jesus responds to their misunderstanding

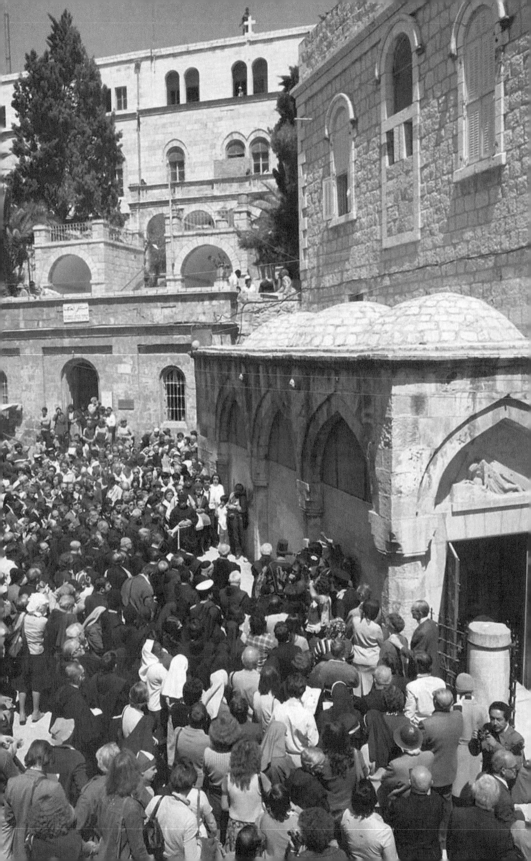

by predicting the defeat of the devil "when I am lifted up from the earth" (12:32), again the double meaning. The Book of Signs finishes with the Jews not accepting the signs, some out of fear (12:42), while Jesus proclaims his message to them of light, life, and unity with the Father one last time. The public ministry is now over, and the Passion has begun.

One of the odd things about this twenty-one-chapter gospel is that the last week of Jesus' life plus the resurrection appearances occupy nine full chapters, or more than forty-two percent of the work, versus thirty-five percent for Mark and twenty-five percent for Luke and Matthew. This is largely due to a major insertion in the gospel. At the end of chapter 14 Jesus tells the disciples, "Rise, let us be on our way," but at 15:1 he starts speaking again and continues until 18:1 when "he went out with his disciples . . . ." Many scholars suggest that another Last Supper discourse had been circulating orally and the final editor of this gospel did not want it to become lost and so added it.

Catholics may be surprised that John does not include the institution of the Eucharist in his account of the Last Supper, instead telling of Jesus' washing the disciples' feet. Possibly John thought the bread of life discourse was sufficient. The washing of the feet is an act of considerable humility, so much so that Peter objects to it, but Jesus has a point to make: in his community leaders lead by serving others, which he does by performing a service usually done by a slave.

They all then sit down to the Passover meal and, with no advance notice, we meet a new, unnamed person, "the [disciple] whom Jesus loved" (13:23), who rapidly becomes a major figure in the gospel and later on will be cited as its source. The gospel provides no identification of this person, not even saying that he was one of the Twelve. When Jesus announces that one of them will betray him, Peter asks this disciple to ask Jesus who he means, so the traditional leader of the Twelve must get assistance on this crucial matter. The Beloved Disciple leans his head on Jesus' chest to ask the question, the origin of the familiar image of John the apostle. Jesus does not provide the traitor's name, and even the Twelve do not know it is Judas, who leaves the meal *at night* (13:30), the time of darkness and contrasted by John to the light that is Christ.

The narrative now ends, and Jesus begins four chapters of a farewell discourse, a common device in the literature of the ancient world whereby a great figure bids farewell, gives advice, and often makes prophecies to his family or disciples, paralleling the patriarch Jacob's farewell to his twelve sons (Genesis 49). The discourse is long and often

The Way of the Cross (via Sacra), Jerusalem

repetitive of what Jesus has said before, but it includes some of his most famous words and has some originality.

Jesus urges the disciples to love one another as he loves them (13:34); he stresses his unity with the Father ("I am the way, and the truth, and the life. No one comes to the Father except through me," 14:6). He emphasizes his imminent departure (14:30) but adds an important new note. When he returns to heaven his Father will send the Paraclete to the disciples "to be with you forever. This is the Spirit of truth, whom the world cannot receive . . . . You know him, because he abides with you, and he will be in you" (14:16-17). Like Jesus himself, the Paraclete (often translated as "advocate") is not of the world but is in the world and will never leave the disciples. The Paraclete will teach the disciples and be a constant reminder to them of Jesus (14:26). In an upbeat note, despite the impending Passion, Jesus assures the disciples, "Peace I leave with you; my peace I give to you" (14:27). Abruptly he tells the disciples, "Rise, let us be on our way."

But he does not go anywhere. Instead, he launches into a very long discourse (chs. 15–17), the section that most scholars believe a later editor added. It contains few new ideas but adds a new image: "I am the vine, you are the branches" (15:5), part of an extensive allegory. Jesus is the vine, the Father the vinedresser, Christians the branches, and those who reject him are the dead branches. It may be tempting to see here the eucharistic wine, but Jesus speaks only of the vine. This image shows the organic relationship between Jesus and those who believe in him.

Now Jesus turns to his disciples and their relationship with the world. Sometimes in this gospel the world means those in it, as when Jesus came to save the world. Other times, such as here, it means those who follow worldly values or those values themselves. Jesus tells the disciples that the world hates them: "If they persecuted me, they will persecute you" (15:20). Here "the world" means the Jews, because the worldly have "their Law" (15:24). So vicious will the persecution become that "those who kill you will think that by doing so they are offering worship to God" (16:2), yet more evidence that John's community was in conflict with the local Jews. The Paraclete will witness to Jesus, but "the world" will not listen.

The Paraclete will benefit the community, so much so that Jesus must depart for the good of the disciples "for if I do not go away, the Paraclete will not come to you" (16:7). But Jesus will return in time: "The hour is coming when I will no longer speak to you in figures but will tell you plainly of the Father" (16:25), because then they will understand. Jesus finishes the discourse with a long prayer (ch. 17) for himself (vv. 1-5), his disciples (vv. 6-19), and future Christians (vv. 20-23): "I ask . . . also on behalf of those who will believe in me . . . ." Jesus concludes the prayer with a request to the Father always to be with his disciples (vv. 24-26). Then picking up where 14:31 had left off, 18:1 tells us that Jesus left with his disciples and went to a garden, here not identified as Gethsemane.

By the time John wrote, the Passion narrative was well established— the arrest, the Jewish and Roman trials, Peter's denials, Pilate's proclamation of Jesus' innocence—and although John does little to alter the narrative, he does include his own touches.

John has already told us that Jesus made the decision to lay down his own life (10:18), and so he will emphasize that Jesus is not a victim, but one who controls the situation. Judas leads the arresting party to the garden, where Jesus comes out to meet them, relegating Judas to just finding the garden and no more. Jesus asks whom they seek. They reply, "Jesus of Nazareth," to which he answers, "I am he," another "I am" saying and one that literally floors the guards (18:6). If Jesus could knock armed men to the ground with just a word, clearly he could prevent them from arresting him. Although he asks the guards to let his companions go, Peter draws a sword and strikes off the ear of Malchus, slave of the high priest; John alone identifies both the sword wielder and the victim. Jesus reproves Peter with the words, "Am I not to drink the cup that the Father has given me?" (18:11).

For John the Jewish trial has become a kangaroo court. Mark has Jesus before the Sanhedrin, but in John the "trial" occurs in the house of Annas, not a high priest but the father-in-law of the current high priest and a power behind the scenes. John says little about the questions asked of Jesus and mentions an instance of abuse (18:22). The evangelist also weakens Peter's prominence in the account, because an anonymous second disciple (the Beloved Disciple?) has accompanied Peter. This disciple knows the high priest and arranges for Peter to go into the courtyard of Annas' home. Thus the anonymous disciple makes the denials possible.

When Annas has finished with Jesus he sends him bound to Caiaphas, as in the Synoptics, but John gives no account of what happened, moving on quickly to the high priest's decision to send Jesus to Pontius Pilate, which occurs in the morning. Thus John shows Jesus being arrested at night, when the powers of darkness temporarily overpower him, and then being lifted up in the day, when the light will bring life to the world.

John shows Pilate being sensitive to the Jews' reluctance to enter the Praetorium, a Gentile building, and so he goes out to them, starting a pattern of inside-outside events (18:28-32, 33-38, 38-40; 19:1-3, 4-8, 9-12, 13-16), creating a sense of constant motion and even some confusion as events run ahead of Pilate. He tries to get the Jews to take responsibility, but they shift it back to him. John recounts two conversations between Pilate and Jesus, and the evangelist uses irony effectively. Pilate tries to avoid using his power, while Jesus tells him that "you would have no power over me unless it had been given you from above" (19:11). This is reminiscent of the conversations with Nicodemus and the Samaritan woman. At one point Pilate tries to get things straight on the human level: "So you are a king?" The reader by now knows what will happen! Jesus replies, "You say that I am a king" and then goes on: "For this I was born, and for this I came into the world, to testify to the truth" (18:37). This provokes the world-weary governor to utter cynically one of the gospel's most famous passages, "What is truth?" The answer, of course, is that incarnate truth is standing in front of him.

John abbreviates what the other evangelists had portrayed in some detail, such as the Barabbas incident, Pilate's insistence on Jesus' innocence, and the scourging, although he again uses irony as the Roman soldiers hail Jesus as a king at the very moment when, thanks to the beating, he is barely recognizable as human (19:3). John adds two new details. Pilate presents the beaten and bloodied prisoner to the crowd, perhaps hoping to encourage their mercy toward him ("Here is the man!"). When Pilate still proves reluctant, the crowd claims that the governor is defying the emperor. Pilate knows he cannot win, but he pulls a quick one on the priests. "'Shall I crucify your King?' The chief priests answered, 'We have no king but the emperor'" (19:15), a public admission of the emperor's lawful rule. But this small Roman victory does nothing for Jesus, who will now be crucified.

When this dramatic passage ends we also discover something else. John has used another favorite literary device, adding Pilate to the list of people who encounter Jesus but cannot accept the challenge he gives them.

John introduces some new elements to the Passion narrative. Chagrined at his own weakness and at having been outmaneuvered by the Temple priests, Pilate scores some petty points by placing on the cross the inscription "Jesus of Nazareth, King of the Jews," infuriating the Jewish leaders who try unsuccessfully to get him to change it. Pilate's stubbornness reflects his belated awareness of who Jesus really is; the three languages announce Jesus' kingship to the entire Roman world, an effective and ironic Johannine touch.

John alone of the evangelists places Jesus' mother under the cross, although she is not the only woman there, which is how artists have almost universally portrayed her. Two or three others, his mother's sister, Mary the wife of Clopas (it is not clear whether this is one person or two), and Mary Magdalene, accompany her (19:25). The Beloved Disciple is also present. From the cross Jesus speaks to his mother and the disciple, entrusting each to the care of the other. In the days when Christians believed John the apostle wrote this gospel, this verse (19:27) was taken historically, that is, Mary went to live with John whom she knew from Jesus' ministry. But with the Beloved Disciple no longer considered to be John, many Catholic scholars understand these verses symbolically. Raymond Brown suggests (*Introduction to the New Testament*, 358) "Jesus brings them (Mary and the Beloved Disciple) into a mother-son relationship and thus constitutes a community of disciples who are mother and brother to him—the community that preserved this Gospel." Pheme Perkins (*NJBC*, 981–82) acknowledges, "It is impossible to decide what the relationship is between this tradition that she (Mary) comes under the care of the Beloved Disciple and that in Acts (1:14), which places her and the brothers of Jesus in the circle gathered around the Twelve. Nor is it entirely clear how much symbolism should be attached to the figure of the mother of Jesus. Clearly, entrusting the Beloved Disciple and his mother to each other shows that Jesus' mission is completed in the care and provision that Jesus had made for 'his own.'"

John's Passion narrative also shows Jesus "in charge," so to speak, of his own death. He announces, "It is finished," and then he dies. What is finished is his mission from his Father, which Jesus alluded to many times (8:29; 14:31; and especially 17:4). No Markan cry of dereliction here; Jesus dies quietly and with dignity: "Then he bowed his head and gave up his spirit" (19:30).

But John has not finished. He adds yet another detail. As in the Synoptics, a Roman under the cross will recognize Jesus, but here in a different way: ". . . one of the soldiers pierced his side with a spear, and at once blood and water came out" (19:34). This should be understood symbolically, with the water representing life (Moses striking the rock in the desert in Exodus 15 and 17, to cite one of many possible examples) and the blood recalling the sacrifice of the Passover lamb. But John writes well after the crucifixion when the church has established itself, so we can also see here symbols of the blood of Christ in the Eucharist and the water of life in baptism flowing from the body of Christ, that is, the Church.

Nicodemus reappears to join Joseph of Arimathea to bury Jesus; John adds the detail that the new tomb was in a garden. John has now finished his Passion narrative.

As he has done throughout his gospel, John wrote a resurrection narrative that combined some synoptic elements with his own significant additions. Only one woman, Mary Magdalene, goes to the tomb. She does not see any angel, but she goes to "Simon Peter and the other disciples" to tell them that "they" (unspecified) "have taken the Lord out of the tomb." Peter and the Beloved Disciple, and only those two, set off for the tomb. The disciple gets to the tomb first but does not go in, although he can see that the linen around Jesus' body has been wrapped carefully and left behind—something that thieves would not do. Peter goes into the tomb but draws no conclusions. The other disciple "saw and believed" (20:8). Scholars have pondered the symbolism here. Most likely the evangelist shows the Beloved Disciple coming to faith before Peter, an institutional symbol for John, yet the disciple's yielding to Peter the first place of actually going inside the tomb may reflect a situation in which the Johannine community had to defer to a more institutional community.

The resurrection now enables the disciples to understand what Jesus had been pointing to during his life (20:9).

John now recounts Jesus' first apparition, a private one to Mary Magdalene. How significant that the only private apparition is to a woman! All the other apparitions in the gospels are to disciples in groups, including the two disciples on the Emmaus road. We do not know what role Mary Magdalene played in or symbolized for the Johannine community that it should render her such honor. Mary first encounters not Jesus but two angels who do not alleviate her sorrow but merely ask her why she weeps. She then turns and sees Jesus, whom she does not recognize, thinking he is the gardener. He calls her by her name. She knows him and seeks to touch him, but he pulls away, telling her, "Do not cling to me because I have not yet ascended to my Father" (20:17). What does he mean? Is his resurrection incomplete until he returns to his Father? Is Mary attempting to cling to the Jesus of this world when his body is now transformed? To quote George MacRae, S.J., "To cling to the earthly Jesus would be tantamount to a faith based merely on signs, and that is not enough" (*Invitation to the Gospels*, 400).

Next Jesus appears twice to all his disciples in the best known of all post-resurrection narratives. He says, "Peace be with you" and shows them his wounds so that they will know it is really he. He now involves them in his mission: "As the Father has sent me, so I send you" (20:21). Although John does not tell of Pentecost, Jesus next tells the disciples, "Receive the Holy Spirit," making it clear that the Spirit will be with them in their mission. But the disciple Thomas is absent. When the others tell him what happened, he refuses to believe, forever making him known as Doubting Thomas. He utters starkly cynical words: "Unless I see the mark of the nails in his hands, and put my finger in the mark of the nails and my hand in his side, I will not believe" (20:25). The contrast with the faith of the Beloved Disciple (20:8) could hardly be stronger.

Jesus appears to the disciples a second time when Thomas is there. He asks Thomas to do what he said he wished to do, but Thomas replies simply, "My Lord and my God," an unambiguous affirmation of Jesus' divinity in this gospel. Jesus replies, "Blessed are those who have not seen and yet have come to believe" (20:29), an obvious reference to all later disciples, including us, who have not seen the earthly Jesus and yet believe.

The gospel closes by acknowledging that "Jesus did many other signs in the presence of his disciples, which are not written in this book" (20:30), proof that the gospels do not contain all that the first Christians knew about Jesus.

I just said that the gospel closes at chapter 20, but there is also chapter 21. Catholic scholars such as Raymond Brown and George McRae believe that chapter 21 is an epilogue, added after the gospel had been written; the chapter goes by that name in the Jerusalem Bible. This chapter is, of course, part of the canonical gospel and thus a vehicle of divine revelation, but note that in verse 24 the author uses the first person plural, asserting that "we know that his [the Beloved Disciple's] testimony is true," proof that the disciple, the supposed author of the first twenty chapters, did not write this one. Remember also that most scholars believe the Prologue and chapters 15 to 17 were added, so this gospel did not come to us untouched from the hand of the Beloved Disciple. Most scholars believe that a later writer added oral traditions stemming back to the Beloved Disciple.

This epilogue contains another apparition story, this time to disciples who are fishing unsuccessfully. From the shore Jesus, as yet unrecognized, urges them to fish differently, they catch hordes of fish, and the Beloved Disciple recognizes Jesus and identifies him for Peter—again the man of faith comes before the group leader. Peter goes to Jesus while the other disciples land the boat. They eat breakfast with Jesus and, as in

Luke's account of Emmaus, all the disciples recognize Jesus in a meal, a foreshadowing of the communal eucharistic meals of the early liturgy.

Jesus now gives special recognition to two disciples. He commissions Peter three times, paralleling his three denials, and then he predicts Peter's martyrdom (21:18), although not its form. The tradition that Peter was crucified upside down does not appear until the end of the second century. Fittingly for this gospel, Jesus concludes with the Beloved Disciple, saying rather bluntly to Peter, "If it is my will that he remain until I come, what is that to you?" (21:22). Jesus has a special mission for the disciple, one unspecified although not necessarily better than the one for Peter. Apparently the Beloved Disciple lived so long that a "rumor spread in the community that this disciple would not die," an observation that makes sense only if he was dead when the gospel was written. This finishes the gospel's account of Jesus.

The author closes by saying that "this is the disciple who is testifying to these things . . . and we know that his testimony is true" (21:24), a mildly defensive assertion by a community that has clearly gone its own way on some issues. The last line informs the reader that Jesus had done so much that if all of it were recorded, the world itself could not hold all the books that would need to be written, another proof that the gospels used material about Jesus selectively, but also a testimony to the community's faith in the continuing work of the Risen Christ among them, through the Spirit.

This is a remarkable gospel. As noted earlier, because Christians believed that John of the Twelve wrote it, it enjoyed immense influence in Christian tradition. Modern scholarship has changed its status a bit, not by criticizing John but rather by emphasizing the great value of the Synoptic Gospels, formerly thought to be of less value than this gospel. Furthermore, modern Catholics reject its bitter criticism of "the Jews" and look for a more nuanced approach that separates the Jewish leaders from the entire people. But this should not diminish our appreciation of this gospel's achievement.

John demonstrates how christology has developed well beyond the Synoptics, especially with its emphasis on Jesus' divinity. This represents a major doctrinal development and points the way toward much future christology. We can also see how the evangelist anticipates the growing church with its emphasis of the role of the Eucharist and the communal meal. This gospel must be balanced with the Synoptics, but it is still an extraordinary document that rewards careful reading.

Chapter Twelve

The Acts of the Apostles

Please read chapters 1–2, 4–10, 13–15, 17–18, 21–25, 27–28.

The first thing the reader notices about this book is that it is not about the acts of the apostles. We think we are going to find out what happened to the twelve apostles after Jesus' death and resurrection, but the book focuses first on the Jerusalem community, then on the spread of the faith in Judea (where Peter plays a role), and then on the career of the apostle Paul, whose life we looked at in an earlier chapter. But, misleading title or not, this book plays a great role in our understanding of the earliest Christians.

No one questions that the author of Luke's Gospel wrote this book. So close are the two that scholars use the phrase "Luke-Acts," not just to indicate their similarities but to stress that one cannot understand either book without knowing the other. Since it continues the story of Luke's Gospel, it came after that gospel, but not by much since scholars believe that Luke intended a two-volume work right from the beginning. Like the gospel, Acts dates between 80 and 90. Luke probably wrote it somewhere in the eastern Mediterranean.

Why did Luke write Acts? After all, the other three evangelists contented themselves with gospels. A combination of history and theology provides the answer. By the 80s, Jesus had been dead for a half century. Many Christians still believed in an imminent end of the world, but others had begun to conclude that the church would be in the world for an undetermined time. Luke too believed that history would continue and that Christians should have some sense of their place in the world, a sense they would never get without being conscious of their own history. As one of my professors said of the need for history, "If you don't know where you came from, you don't know where you are. And if you don't know where you are, you don't know where you're going."

But the historical realization led to a theological one. For Luke the church meant more than a collection of believers providing mutual encouragement while awaiting the end. He saw the church as a positive force in the world, as a continuation of the People of Israel through whom God worked historically and a continuation of the ministry of Jesus.

This makes the book sound very wide-ranging, but in fact it provides a limited history. For example, when Paul arrives in Italy (Acts 28) some local Christians come to greet him. Who are they? Who founded the community to which they belong? And when Barnabas and Mark depart from Paul and go to Cyprus (Acts 15:39), what do they do there? We simply do not know because the focus of Acts lies elsewhere. Only a few of the missionaries, heroes, and saints who spread the faith appear in Acts.

Yet this should not lessen its importance because it focuses on the key figures, particularly Peter and Paul—and God. Luke makes it clear who really is spreading the faith, and time and again he attributes an action specifically to divine initiative. We might think it obvious that God was involved, but Luke must establish for people who thought the world would end soon that the continued existence of the community served a divine purpose.

Looking at Acts, the modern mind raises an immediate question: how accurate historically is this book? Here we must refer back to our earlier discussion of how ancient people wrote history. Although we can be comfortable with Luke's overall narrative, clearly he uses some literary devices.

Almost twenty-five percent of the book consists of speeches, including some that Luke could not possibly have heard (1:14-36). Luke uses the speeches to set certain themes: for example, Peter assuring a Jewish audience that the life and work of Jesus fulfilled the Scriptures (that is, the Old Testament). Then Luke shows the apostles establishing the new People of God.

Since Luke wants to establish continuity between Jesus and the earliest disciples he gives parallel accounts of their activities. Bart Ehrman sums up this approach: "In Luke (the gospel), Jesus heals the sick, casts out demons, and raises the dead; in Acts, the apostles heal the sick, cast out demons, and raise the dead. The Jewish authorities in Jerusalem confront Jesus in Luke; the same authorities confront the apostles in Acts. Jesus is imprisoned, condemned, and executed in Luke; some of his followers are imprisoned, condemned, and executed in Acts" (*Historical Introduction*, 128). As Ehrman suggests, examples abound, but let me cite just two. First, when the women arrive at Jesus' empty tomb in the gospel they meet "two men in dazzling clothes" (24:4) who explain that Jesus is risen. When Jesus ascends into heaven in Acts, "suddenly two men" appear and explain to the disciples that Jesus has ascended to heaven (1:10-11). Second, as the Christian protomartyr Stephen is being stoned, he prays, "Lord, do not hold this sin against them" (7:60), echoing Luke 23:34: "Father, forgive them; for they do not know what they are doing." Recall that only Luke preserves this saying of Jesus from the cross. Luke was not in Jerusalem to hear Stephen's prayer, but for him Stephen's death recalled how Jesus died for the faith. Luke uses this image more than once. Speaking of Jesus' crucifixion, Peter tells a Jewish crowd, "And now, friends, I know that you acted in ignorance, as did also your rulers" (3:17).

In the earliest church Peter enjoyed great prestige as the leader of the Twelve, but Paul tells us in Galatians that he and Peter did not always get along. Writing two decades after the martyrdoms of both men, Luke realized that their work and suffering for the faith united them more than any disagreement could separate them. Thus in Acts he leaves out any references to conflict and actually sets up parallels between them, such as their speeches (3:11-26, Peter's address to the people at the Temple, and 13:17-43, Paul's address to the Jews of Cyprus). Both apostles escape miraculously from prison (12:1-11 for Peter, 16:19-34 for Paul).

Luke has other things in mind. Since he wrote in the 80s and both Peter and Paul died in the 60s, why does he not mention their deaths? As we saw in the gospel, Luke believes that the Christian message should go to all people, and he does not wish to make Christianity into an opponent of Rome by recounting that the Roman state executed the two great leaders of the early church in addition to Jesus himself.

Because more than half of Acts deals with Paul, scholars have focused much on Luke's portrayal of the great apostle. As we saw earlier, scholars decided to rely primarily on Paul's letters to recreate his life and to use Acts only to verify or support what the epistles say. Most Catholic scholars accept that basic approach but on occasion are willing to give Luke the benefit of the doubt. For example, in 2 Cor 11:25, Paul says, "Three times I was beaten with rods. Once I received a stoning. Three times I was shipwrecked," but he does not provide specifics. Acts 14:19 reports a stoning at Iconium; Acts 16:23 reports a beating at Philippi; Acts 27:27-44 reports a shipwreck off Malta. While we cannot say with finality that Paul refers to these, they certainly fit Paul's description of his mishaps. And if Luke were making these up to match Paul's own words and give Acts more authenticity, then why did he not make up three beatings and three shipwrecks? If we bear in mind that ancient historians did not write as modern ones do, we can use Acts safely and well.

But Acts seems to offer something that many other ancient histories do not: eyewitness accounts. These are the "we passages," that is, four sections where Luke's narrative employs the first person plural (Acts 16:10-17; 20:5-16; 21:1-19; 27:1–28:16), all of which occur during Paul's travels. At first glance these passages settle the question of Luke's reliability. If he was a companion of Paul, of course he knew what he was writing about. But nothing is ever simple in modern biblical study.

The passages suggest that the author met Paul after he had become the apostle to the Gentiles, which in turn suggests that the author was a Gentile whom the apostle converted. Paul and a number of post-Pauline epistles mention several Gentiles whom the apostle converted.

Tradition settled upon Luke, although the NT provides no evidence that he was the author of this text any more than he was the author of the gospel. Since scholars have found discrepancies, albeit minor ones, in the Acts account of Paul and in his own letters, many, even the majority today, think the "we passages" do not come from the pen of one of his companions but from a travel diary of a now unknown Christian.

This rather surprising contention—that the author stuck someone else's first-hand account into a text without warning—is helped by the "we passages" themselves. They begin abruptly. The author does not say, "At this point, I, Luke, joined the mission . . . ." Nor does any passage conclude with, "And now Paul went to (wherever) and I stayed here." Furthermore, the first "we passage" starts in Iconium but does not finish the account of what happened to Paul there; that is, the beginning of the Iconium narrative is given in the first person but the end returns to the third person—odd that the author would have departed so abruptly but still have a claim to know the end of the account.

On the other hand, it is difficult to believe that a skilled author like Luke would have simply begun to copy out someone else's travel diary. Scholars who support the "borrowing" theory appeal to some ancient texts, but they do not explain why ancient Christian writers who should have known this literary device believed the "we passages" came from Luke. Scholars remain divided on this; Bart Ehrman leans to the travel diary theory while Raymond E. Brown concedes "it is not impossible" (*Introduction to the New Testament*, 326) that the author of Acts traveled with Paul. Personally I find the travel diary theory unconvincing and the companion theory plausible but unprovable.

But the identity of the author does not determine the value of the book, so let us turn to it now.

The Acts of the Apostles presents a problem for this book. It is a long text. Of all the NT books, only Matthew, Luke, and John are longer. But, thanks to liturgical readings, most of us know the gospel accounts, and so it is easy to make general remarks about the narrative and then get into the meaning of the text. Acts, however, contains many unfamiliar narratives that would take a long time to recount, much less discuss. Furthermore, it has more than one hundred proper names of people, and there are also proper names of places. To these can be added unnamed figures (a centurion, a beggar). Some, like the apostles, are familiar, but others are not and appear just once, such as Damaris (17:34) and Sopater (20:4). Therefore we will outline some passages and discuss their significance, in the hope that the reader will find Acts to be a readable narrative without detailed commentary. As always, the reader can consult one of the many good, detailed commentaries available, some of which are listed in the bibliography at the end of the book.

Prologue and Ascension (1:1-11)

"In the first book, Theophilus, I wrote about all that Jesus did and taught from the beginning until the day when he was taken up to heaven, after giving instructions through the Holy Spirit to the apostles whom he had chosen" (1:1). Here we again meet Theophilus, Luke's patron, and the evangelist uses terms of finality regarding Jesus' mission: he did what he came to do and now he would return to heaven. But he does not depart abruptly; ". . . he presented himself alive to them . . . appearing to them during forty days . . ." (1:3) and promising them the Holy Spirit. Some still do not understand his work, asking him, "Lord, is this the time when you will restore the kingdom to Israel?" (1:5). He replies, ". . . you will be my witnesses in Jerusalem, in all Judea and Samaria, and to the ends of the earth" (1:8), that is, Israel will be included in their work, but—in good Lukan fashion—it will go far beyond the borders of the old kingdom. Then Jesus ascends into the sky, and two men in white suddenly appear beside the apostles and assure them, "This Jesus, who has been taken up from you into heaven, will come in the same way as you saw him go into heaven " (1:11), a reference to the Second Coming or Parousia, although Luke carefully avoids saying that the end is near.

The Church in Jerusalem (1:12–5:42)

Luke recounts how the apostles returned to Jerusalem and to the upper room where they prayed, "together with certain women, including Mary the mother of Jesus" (1:14), the only mention of her outside the gospels. Luke's devotion to Mary has not abated since the Infancy Narrative, and he uses her here to demonstrate continuity: she played a role before Jesus' birth, during his ministry, and after his ascension. This also shows that the "disciples," a broader term than "apostles," included women.

Led by Peter, the apostles decide to replace Judas, whose death in Acts differs from that given in Matthew, who says that Judas hanged himself. Here he "burst open in the middle and all his bowels gushed out. This became known to all the residents of Jerusalem . . ." (1:18-19). There is no way to decide which account is accurate. We can only say that Judas died a violent death that became well known locally. Replacing Judas does not seem practically important because the person chosen, Matthias, disappears immediately, never to be mentioned again in Acts or any other NT book, but Matthias' significance lies in the symbolism of the number twelve. Just as Jesus chose twelve apostles to dramatize that his work continued God's work through the twelve tribes, so the eleven apostles want to maintain that symbolism.

Now occurs one of the NT's most decisive events. At the Jewish feast of Pentecost "from heaven there came a sound like the rush of a violent wind, and it filled the entire house where they were sitting. Divided tongues, as of fire, appeared among them, and a tongue rested on each of them. All of them were filled with the Holy Spirit . . ." (2:2-4). The Spirit manifests itself by allowing them "to speak in other languages," which they do, to the amazement of visiting Jews from a variety of countries and provinces.

As we will see, Paul is Luke's hero, and here Luke uses a Pauline theme, Christ as the New Adam, by making parallels to Genesis. In the beginning the Spirit of God moved over the waters (1:2), but some translations call it "a wind from God." That is because in Hebrew and Greek the words for "spirit" could also mean "wind" or "breath." For Luke a new world had come into being when the Spirit descended on the apostles. Yet every reader of Genesis knew that the summit of creation, humans made in the divine image and likeness, sinned and became steadily worse, culminating in the Genesis creation narrative with the Tower of Babel. But notice that the Spirit's first gift to the apostles is the ability *to speak a variety of languages and be understood by everyone,* that is, the coming of the Spirit has reversed the Tower of Babel.

But some people who hear the apostles think they are drunk, which sets up Peter's speech (2:11-26) in which he assures the listening Jews that the history of the OT led up to Jesus. Peter interprets prophecies, especially from David, that prove this point. "Now when they heard this, they were cut to the heart and said to Peter and to the other apostles, 'Brothers, what should we do?' Peter said to them, 'Repent, and be baptized every one of you in the name of Jesus Christ . . . and you will receive the gift of the Holy Spirit'" (2:37-38). Luke says, "that day about three thousand persons were added" (2:41), an impossibly high number since Jerusalem's population at the time was only around twenty thousand. But biblical numbers often exaggerate (three million people on the

Exodus!), and Luke simply means that a surprisingly large number of people joined the church, which he considers the work of the Holy Spirit.

Yet the numbers should not distract us from the key point: to become Christians, people had to be baptized in Jesus' name, at which point they would receive the Holy Spirit—a common and modern practice that goes back literally to the first days of the church.

Luke then describes the Jerusalem Christians: "They devoted them-selves to the apostles' teaching and fellowship, to the breaking of bread and the prayers" (2:42). How might we interpret this? The first com-munity had an authority structure, although not yet an ordained one; the apostles' authority derived from their personal contact with Jesus. Fellowship is obvious. The "breaking of bread" could mean the bread of a Jewish meal, but Luke is writing in the 80s and for Gentiles, so we should see the Eucharist here. Prayers meant communal prayer, that is, a liturgical event of some sort.

Luke also says that "all who believed were together and had all things in common" (2:44). But modern scholars think that Luke may have been idealizing the community here; that is, they did not live a strict communitarian life but rather were willing to share with others, even to the point of giving up their own goods. He also gives another valuable insight into their life: "Day by day, as they spent much time together in the Temple, they broke bread at home and ate their food with glad and generous hearts" (2:46). The first Christians have not cut themselves off from Judaism; they still feel at home in the Temple. But they already recognize that their community differs from the larger Jewish one, and thus they meet in people's houses to "break bread." In fact, archaeologists can point to no Christian church building earlier than the middle of the third century, and Christians continued to meet in people's houses (the common title is "house church") for centuries.

In the gospels Jesus' miracles make the strongest impression on the people. As a sign of God's presence in the community, the apostles also do miracles (2:43). Luke describes one in particular, Peter's cure of a lame man (3:1-10). A crowd collects in response to this, so Peter gives another speech, again stressing that Jesus' life and career fulfilled the OT prophecies. While the crowd may listen appreciatively, others hear a different, threatening message. The Jerusalem leaders, including An-nas and Caiaphas (4:6), have Peter and John arrested. The apostles de-fend themselves to the Jerusalem leaders, who decide not to harm them but to give them a stern warning "to speak no more to anyone in this name" (4:17).

Luke says the leaders' fears have justification; the number of Christians in Jerusalem has now risen to five thousand (4:4).

Peter and John return to the community, give thanks to God, and recognize that this arrest marks only the beginning of a difficult and dangerous ministry. But they trust God, and "When they had prayed, the place in which they were gathered together was shaken" (4:31), a wonderfully vivid image of the intensity of their prayer. Luke again speaks of their communitarianism and mentions the particular generosity of a Levite from Cyprus named Barnabas, who will play a great role in Acts (4:32-37).

In contrast to the generous Barnabas, Luke tells the story of Ananias and Sapphira, a husband and wife who both withhold part of their property from the community. Peter accuses them of lying to the Holy Spirit (5:3) and strikes them both dead. What disturbs the modern believer is the unmerciful denial of a chance to repent, seemingly uncharacteristic of the evangelist who stresses divine mercy and forgiveness. But even Luke acknowledges God's judgment (Luke 21:8-36). Furthermore, he reports that the apostles "will sit on thrones judging the twelve tribes of Israel" (Luke 22:30); in this case Peter acts the judge.

Luke turns to the positive, praising the "signs and wonders" wrought by the apostles. When the high priest has them locked up in prison, an angel opens the gates for them. Miracles and angelic intervention prove this is a movement backed by God!

But the high priest, furious at the escape, has the apostles re-arrested and brought before the Sanhedrin, the grand council of Jerusalem. Again Peter acts as spokesman, and again their enemies back off, even though they want to execute the apostles. This time a famous rabbi named Gamaliel prudently suggests caution: "If this plan or this undertaking is of human origin, it will fail; but if it is of God, you will not be able to overthrow them" (5:38). The high priest accepts the advice, orders the apostles to be flogged, and then releases them. They rejoice that they have suffered for the name of Jesus.

The Earliest Missions (6:1–12:25)

Up to now Luke has presented a picture of universal harmony among the believers, but suddenly he switches, announcing that "the Hellenists complained against the Hebrews because their widows were being neglected in the daily distribution of food" (6:1). Who are these Hellenists and Hebrews? Barrels of ink have been spilled trying to decipher these vague terms; here is the consensus. Scholars believe the "Hellenists" were Greek-speaking Jews, probably mostly from the Diaspora, who heard the apostles preach, converted, and then remained in Jerusalem. They would have accommodated themselves to much of the Greco-Roman culture in which they lived. The "Hebrews," by contrast, were Aramaic-speaking Jews, mostly from Judea itself. These tensions arose in the Christian community but had existed long before it. It was impossible that they would simply dissipate with conversion to Christianity.

But the differences included more than culture. The only Hellenist whose views we know is Stephen, who makes a long speech to the Jerusalem Jews before his execution. Stephen speaks patronizingly of the Temple (". . . the Most High does not dwell in houses made with human hands"—7:48), but the Christians resident in Jerusalem routinely went to the Temple.

Although Luke now presents a more real situation than one of universal harmony, the goal of community remains. The Twelve meet with the disciples as a whole. They decide that the assembly will choose seven men of their own to serve the widows, men "of good standing" and "full of the Spirit" (6:3). This admirable approach preserves the sense of community by recognizing that there will be differences among Christians, but as long as those differences do not challenge the basics of the faith, church leaders should respect and work with them. "What they said pleased the whole community, and they chose [seven names follow] . . . " (6:5). Note the trust that the Twelve put in the people, since Luke says that the assembly chose the men. The seven all have Greek names. Luke singles out one, Nicolaus of Antioch, as a convert to Judaism, so the other six also would have been Greek-speaking Jews.

One note about this: for centuries the choosing of seven to serve the widows was thought to be the establishment of the diaconate, since the word "deacon" *(diákonos)* comes from the Greek word to serve. But the word "deacon" does not appear here, and when it does appear in the NT the deacon is usually working with an *epískopos*. Modern Catholic exegetes do not equate the choice of the seven with the diaconate.

As he often does before heading into a big new topic, Luke provides a summary of the church's growth, this time including the startling information that "a great many of the priests" also converted (6:7).

Luke's new topic is the fate of Stephen (6:8–7:60), whose "great wonders and signs among the people" won many converts, especially among Diaspora Jews. But some turn against him and have him arrested and brought before the Sanhedrin. The charge? "This man never stops saying things against this holy place [the Temple] and the law" (6:13). But the case is shaky, so "they set up false witnesses" against him. This scene sounds a bit familiar, and it should. In his Passion narrative Mark, Luke's chief source, says that his opponents accused Jesus of speaking against the Temple and that they brought false witnesses against him (Mark 14:57-58). The trial of Stephen, Christianity's protomartyr, parallels that of his Lord in several ways, although Jesus remains silent, while Stephen gives a long speech. It recalls Peter's speeches, tracing the history of Israel to prove that Jesus fulfilled the prophecies of the OT.

Both trials end the same way, although Luke here shows the lawlessness of the Sanhedrin members. They do not take Stephen to the Roman governor; they do not even convict him. Enraged by his words and by his calm demeanor, they grind their teeth, rush at him, drag him "out of the city," and stone him to death. This is a lynching. Luke concludes the story with the peaceful Stephen asking God to have mercy on his infuriated killers.

Cleverly Luke uses a minor detail to introduce a major character. To throw stones at Stephen, the Sanhedrin members must take off their cloaks. They pile them at the feet of a young Diaspora Jew from Tarsus in Asia Minor named Saul (7:58), who "approved of their killing him" (8:1). A few verses later Luke adds that Saul became a persecutor (8:3). These details rouse the reader's interest because by the time Luke wrote, Christians remembered Saul (Paul) as one of the great heroes of the faith. But Luke is just foreshadowing here, and he returns immediately to the Hellenists.

"That day a severe persecution began against the church in Jerusalem, and all except the apostles were scattered throughout the countryside of Judea and Samaria" (8:1). In spite of "all" scattering, Luke discusses only one person, the Hellenist Philip, one of the seven. Philip flees to Samaria, where he preaches and works miracles. Some people convert, and now Luke initiates the main thrust of Acts: the extension of Christianity to non-Jews. Note that this movement was not planned by the Twelve in Jerusalem. It happened because Philip had to flee a persecution. On the historical level the extension of Christianity to non-Jews was a sort of accident, but Luke does not see it that way. Philip can work miracles, and the Samaritans receive the Holy Spirit. This was no historical accident; God was behind this movement.

Word of Philip's successful evangelization among the Samaritans reaches Jerusalem. The apostles, acting like a modern mission board, send Peter and John to see what has happened. Significantly, these two prominent members of the Twelve approve what Philip has done. These two Palestinian Jews welcome the Samaritans: "Peter and John laid their hands on them [the Samaritans], and they received the Holy Spirit" (8:17).

This episode has a curious sidebar. A magician named Simon (often called Simon Magus, "magus" meaning magician) saw the disciples work miracles in the name of the Holy Spirit. Wanting to add these "tricks" to his professional repertoire, Simon offers to buy the power of the Holy Spirit from Peter, who furiously refuses but also urges Simon to repent (8:14-24). From this account comes the word "simony," which means the attempted purchase of spiritual power or ecclesiastical offices.

Philip keeps up his evangelizing, next converting an Ethiopian Jew who had made a pilgrimage to Jerusalem and was returning home. This man was a court official, serving the *kandakē* or queen of Ethiopia (from which comes the name "Candace"). Note that Philip "*heard* him reading the prophet Isaiah" (8:30); that is because in the ancient world people read books out loud. (In his *Confessions*, St. Augustine is surprised to learn that St. Ambrose reads silently.) The Ethiopian finds a passage from Isaiah confusing—no surprise there—and so Philip interprets the passage with an application to Christ. The Ethiopian requests and receives baptism. Since the Ethiopian is a Jew, this is technically not an extension of Christianity to non-Jews, but the symbol of the faith going to a man from Ethiopia, a country beyond Rome's frontiers, is very strong.

Now Luke satisfies the reader's curiosity about Saul. He has been persecuting Christians, some of whom had fled to Damascus. Saul decides to pursue them there. On the road to Damascus "suddenly a light from heaven flashed around him. He fell to the ground and heard a voice saying to him, 'Saul, Saul, why do you persecute me?'" (9:3-4). Perhaps conscious of Paul's still controversial reputation at the time he wrote, Luke effectively contrasts the Ethiopian who is converted by Philip with Saul who is converted by Jesus himself. Luke considers this so important that he tells the story three times (9:1-9; 22:1-11; 26:12-18) and not always consistently, as we shall see. This dramatic conversion changed the history of Christianity.

Saul rises from the ground to find himself blind. His companions take him to Damascus, where the Lord directs a disciple named Ananias to cure him. Not surprisingly, Ananias fears to go anywhere near Saul, but he follows the Lord's command. After his sight is restored Saul begins to preach so effectively that he "confounded the Jews who lived in Damascus" (9:22). Some local Jews plan to assassinate him, but Paul escapes by being lowered in a basket from the city walls. He then goes to Jerusalem, where the disciples suspect his conversion is a trick, but Barnabas, the generous Cypriot Jew, stands up for him. Paul preaches but gets into an argument with "the Hellenists" (9:29) who plot to kill him. Luke does not identify the Hellenists, but they are not the Hellenists of chapter 6 who served the widows. Most likely they were Diaspora, Greek-speaking Jews who resented one of their own who had become a Christian. The Jerusalem brothers spirit him away to Caesarea (first mention of Christianity there) and then to Tarsus, his home.

Luke will return to Paul soon, but again he puts in a summary: the churches are now at peace and are continuing to grow.

Peter now takes center stage. He has gone to Joppa, a Gentile city where there are already some disciples. He raises from the dead a woman named Tabitha or Dorcas, famous for the clothing she made for the community members, and while he was in Joppa, Peter received messengers from a Roman centurion named Cornelius.

Although a Gentile, "He was a devout man who feared God with all his household; he gave alms generously to the people and prayed constantly to God" (10:2). Luke implies that Cornelius has accepted basic Jewish teachings, but he has not become a Jew. An angel tells this good man that his prayers have been heard—presumably to find the true God—and Cornelius is to "send men to Joppa for a certain Simon, who is called Peter" (10:5). Like an observant Jew, Peter refuses to enter the house of a Gentile. But in a triple dream the Lord tells the stubborn Peter that "What God has made clean, you must not call profane" (10:15). Peter listens, goes with Cornelius' men, and converts the centurion and his family. Thus Luke shows the leader of the Twelve supportive of the movement of Christianity into the non-Jewish world. Indeed, Peter converts a member of the occupying Roman army, the kind of person most patriotic Jews would loathe and distrust. As so often in both the OT and NT, the ways of God are not the ways of humans. Peter accepts this.

Peter addresses his imminent converts. "While Peter was still speaking, the Holy Spirit fell upon all who heard the word. The circumcised believers [that is, Jewish Christian men] who had come with Peter were astounded that the gift of the Holy Spirit had been poured out even on the Gentiles, for they heard them *speaking in tongues* and extolling God" (10:44-46). "Speaking in tongues" points the reader back to the descent of the Holy Spirit on the apostles at Pentecost (1:4). Luke makes his point well with this narrative.

But what pleases Luke would not necessarily please the Jerusalem Christians, and Peter, in spite of his prestige, must explain himself to them: ". . . when Peter went up to Jerusalem, the circumcised believers criticized him, saying, 'Why did you go to uncircumcised men and eat with them?'" (a serious violation of Jewish law) (11:2-3). But Peter meets their objections by recounting what had happened, and "when they heard this, they were silenced. And they praised God, saying, 'Then God has given even to the Gentiles the repentance that leads to life'" (11:18).

The Jerusalem church now learns that the faith has reached Antioch, so the leaders send Barnabas there to confirm this. He makes a side trip to Tarsus and brings Paul back to Antioch with him. The two of them work there for a year and, Luke tells us, "it was in Antioch that the disciples were first called 'Christians'" (11:26). Why? Because the Greek word *christos* means the "anointed one" or "Messiah." The Christians in Jerusalem, realizing the term had strong political overtones, may have used it sparingly, but it had no such overtones in Antioch. Thus the Antiochenes spoke of "those of the *Christos*" or "Christians."

Antioch would become the second great Christian community, but the first still dominates things. A prophet named Agabus came from Jerusalem and predicted a famine, which occurred during the reign of Claudius. The Antiochene community entrusted Saul and Barnabas with a financial contribution for the Jerusalem community.

Two items of note: first, the early church had prophets, although they were few and we know little about them; second, Luke is the only writer to mention any Roman emperors, citing Augustus in his Infancy Narrative (Luke 2:1) and Tiberius at the beginning of Jesus' career (3:1). (Some wits might add a third note: here we see the first collection!)

The next episode jolts the reader. Herod Agrippa I, the Roman puppet king of Judea, "laid violent hands upon some who belonged to the church. He had James, the brother of John, killed with the sword" (12:1-2), and so James became the first of the Twelve to die as well as to be martyred. Later traditions made martyrs of all the apostles, but historically we know that only James and Peter died as martyrs.

Luke gives no reason for Herod's action. Many Jews resented the Romanized king, and possibly Herod wanted to impress the Sanhedrin. Whatever his reason, it worked. "After he saw that it [James' execution] pleased the Jews, he proceeded to arrest Peter also" (12:3). For the first time Luke suggests that not just the Jerusalem aristocracy but "the

Jews" as a larger group now oppose the Christians, a foreshadowing of the hostility Paul would encounter. But just as an angel enabled all the apostles to escape from prison (5:17-21), so again an angel rescues Peter. After his escape Peter "went to the house of Mary, the mother of John whose other name was Mark, where many had gathered and were praying" (12:12), which might mean a liturgy, or possibly they were praying for Peter's deliverance. (Tradition would later identify John Mark as the author of the Gospel of Mark.)

The group welcomes Peter, who decides to leave Jerusalem. He asks the others to "tell this to James and to the believers, " the first mention of James "the brother of the Lord," who headed the Jerusalem community and to whom the leader of the Twelve, a man of a very different calling, shows respect. "Then he [Peter] left and went to another place" (12:17). For centuries believers identified this with Rome, but that is impossible because Peter reappears in Jerusalem in Acts 15, and after that Paul met him in Antioch (Galatians 2). Luke probably meant that Peter went into temporary hiding for his safety. Luke finishes this account in good OT fashion by describing the sudden and miserable death of Herod Agrippa I.

As usual, Luke has a transition passage: "Then after completing their mission Barnabas and Saul returned to Jerusalem and brought with them John, whose other name was Mark" (12:24). Now the "Acts of the Apostles" will become the "Acts of the Apostle" as Luke presents, historically and theologically, the missionary career of Paul.

Paul's First Missionary Journey and the Council of Jerusalem (13:1–15:35)

Ever the organizer, Luke has divided Paul's missionary activity into three journeys (13:1–14:28; 15:36–18:22; 18:23–21:16). Luke has established his basic points: that the church continues the work of Christ under the guidance of the Holy Spirit and that God intended Christianity to go to all people, not just the Jews. He will now show this happening in the career of Paul, which we will outline, focusing only on some central points.

The church at Antioch sends Saul and Barnabas, accompanied by John Mark, to Cyprus. The missionaries preach first to the resident Jews and then to the proconsul Sergius Paulus. A magician named Elymas challenges Saul, who strikes him blind as proof of God's power. The proconsul promptly converts, although Luke insists he was "astonished at the teaching about the Lord" (13:12) rather than by fear.

This brief passage has five important elements. First, we see what would become a standard approach, preaching to the Jews and only then—and often after rejection—to the Gentiles. Second, the Roman proconsul does not persecute the Christians; just the reverse, he converts. Church and empire were not always enemies. Third, Luke parallels Saul with Peter, confuting a magician. Fourth, Luke knows the Mediterranean world well. As early as the nineteenth century scholars noticed that he has proconsuls where proconsuls should be and tribunes where tribunes should be. His gospel shows him to be occasionally unfamiliar with the Holy Land and with Jewish practices, but now he is at home. Fifth, Luke suddenly speaks of "Saul, whose other name is Paul" (13:9), thus introducing the name by which we know the great apostle. It was not uncommon for Diaspora Jews to have both Jewish and Gentile names, for example, John Mark, and, writing for Gentiles, Luke may have wanted to use the name Paul.

After success in Cyprus the missionaries leave for Asia Minor where, without explanation, John Mark suddenly decides to return to Jerusalem (13:13). Luke strengthens the Peter-Paul parallels. Paul gives a speech (13:17-43) reminiscent of Peter's (2:14-36), and he too cures a cripple (14:8-10, paralleling 3:1-10). Luke makes clear that Paul did not force the mission to the Gentiles but rather was carrying on a process done by Peter and by the deacon Philip. Jewish resistance frustrates the missionaries' work, but the Gentiles accept them so completely that they think Paul and Barnabas are gods. They bring them sacrifices ("oxen and garlands,"14:13), and the missionaries "scarcely restrained the crowds from offering sacrifice to them" (14:18)! Although Luke presents a breathless pace for Barnabas and Paul, he does acknowledge the apostles' concern for organization: ". . . they . . . appointed elders *(presbyteroi)* for them in each church [in Asia Minor]" (14:23). The elders' exact responsibilities are unknown; they certainly included preaching and liturgy.

Paul and Barnabas return to Antioch. Soon "certain individuals came down from Judea and were teaching the brothers, 'Unless you are circumcised according to the custom of Moses, you cannot be saved'" (15:1). The Antiochene church sends Paul and Barnabas to Jerusalem to settle matters. They find there that "some believers who belonged to the sect of the Pharisees stood up and said, 'It is necessary for them to be circumcised and ordered to keep the law of Moses'" (15:5). When we get over our surprise at converted Pharisees, we can see that these were good Jewish Christians who feared that the Law, God's great gift to Israel, would be disparaged if Gentiles did not have to observe it. The "apostles and elders" in Jerusalem discuss the matter. Making his final appearance in Acts, Peter defends the mission to the Gentiles.

Then James, the relative of Jesus, speaks. He acknowledges that the faith should go to the Gentiles, but they should not disregard the Law. Very tellingly, Luke reports that James said, "*I* have reached the decision . . . " (15:19) that the Gentiles observe a few important parts of the Law, such as avoiding food "polluted by idols," that is, offered in pagan temples, and from illicit marriages. As head of the conservative Jerusalem community James had taken a great step in welcoming the Gentiles. Although Paul will always be the hero of Acts, we should acknowledge the faith and generosity of these Jewish Christians who did not want the Law to stand in the way of the faith's reaching all people.

The matter now settled, the apostles and elders compose a letter about the council's conclusions that they entrusted to Paul and Barnabas, who take the letter to Antioch. This is a great moment for Paul, for even the Jewish Christians in the Holy City have acknowledged the rightness of his work.

Paul's Second and Third Missionary Journeys (15:36–20:16)

The second journey gets off to a poor start. Barnabas wants to bring John Mark along, but "Paul decided not to take with them one who had deserted them" (15:38), so the two courageous apostles split up. Barnabas and John Mark return to Cyprus, both disappearing from Acts. The church in Cyprus also disappears; not until the fourth century does it reappear in any historical text.

Paul chooses a new companion, Silas, and returns to the churches he founded in Asia Minor, where he acquires another helper, Timothy, son of a Jewish mother and Greek father. Then Luke suddenly has Paul at the western end of Asia Minor, where he has a vision of a man inviting him to Macedonia, that is, to Europe. Paul follows the vision and soon arrives in Philippi, where he founds a church to which he will one day write a letter. He also converts a businesswoman named Lydia, who is baptized with her whole household (16:6-16).

When Paul exorcises a slave girl who had made money for her masters by prophesying, these owners bring charges against him. The magistrates arrest Paul and Silas and then have them flogged and imprisoned. Luke parallels Paul with the apostles and Peter via yet another prison escape. But Paul refuses to leave, telling the jailer that Silas and he are Roman citizens, whom it was illegal to flog. The terrified magistrates apologize to Paul. This episode tells us that Paul probably came from a prosperous family that had either the status or money to get the citizenship.

The apostles next go to Thessalonica and found another church, this too a recipient of a letter, the earliest NT book. But Paul encounters much opposition from the local Jews, and the Thessalonian Christians send him to Beroea, where the Jews treat him better and some aristocratic Greek women and men convert. But the Thessalonian Jews stir up trouble, and Paul moves on to Athens (17:1-15).

Paul here enters the fountainhead of Greek culture. He debates with the local Jews but also in the marketplace "with those who happened to be there. . . . Also some Epicurean and Stoic philosophers . . ." (17:17-18). His speech differs from all the others in Acts because he addresses educated Gentiles who enjoy debate. "Now all the Athenians and the foreigners living there would spend their time in nothing but telling or hearing something new" (17:22). Paul gives a learned presentation and even quotes a pagan poet, but he does not sway many in his sophisticated audience. Some want to think about what he said, but others actually laugh at him when he speaks of the resurrection (17:32). This is the first of many encounters between the Christian faith and intellectuals who hold faith in contempt. But some Athenians listen; Luke mentions a woman named Damaris and a man named Dionysius.

But overall Athens disappointed Paul, and Luke says simply that he left and went to Corinth, a Roman-founded seaport. Luke tells us that there Paul met Aquila and Priscilla, who "had recently come from Italy . . . because Claudius had ordered all Jews to leave Rome" (18:2), an event that occurred in 49 C.E. "Paul went to see them, and, because he was of the same trade, he stayed with them, and they worked together—by trade they were tentmakers" (18:3), so we have some more information from Luke about the great apostle. Again Paul preaches to the local Jews, and again they reject him, but this time they charge him before the proconsul Gallio, who presided in Corinth between 51 and 52, so here we have the first definite date in the NT. Gallio shows the typical Roman approach to questions of religion: "If it were a matter of crime or serious villainy, I would be justified in accepting the complaint of you Jews; but since it is a matter of questions about words and names and your own law, see to it yourselves" (18:14). This was the classic Roman way of dealing with religious matters: if they did not threaten the state, then let the locals deal with them. After eighteen months in Corinth, Paul leaves for Ephesus, taking Priscilla and Aquila with him. He debates with the Jews of Ephesus in an apparently civil encounter because Luke says, "When they asked him to stay longer, he declined," saying "I will return to you, if God wills" (18:20). He then returned to his home base of Antioch, the second missionary journey now complete.

This was one of the most momentous journeys in history. Paul introduced Christianity to Europe, where it would grow and flourish for two millennia, and it was European Christianity that spread through much of the world, a world Paul could not even imagine. To be sure, modern Catholics do not equate Christianity with its European expression, and we want to be open to Third World expressions of faith, but this in no way lessens Paul's remarkable achievement.

Saying nothing about Paul's visit to Antioch, Luke has him again on the road, literally roaring through Asia Minor and arriving back at Ephesus. There he meets Apollos, an Alexandrian Jew who "knew only the baptism of John [the Baptizer]" (18:25), which suggests that some of John's disciples kept up his ministry after his death. "Priscilla and Aquila . . . explained the Way of God to him more accurately" (18:26). Contrary to what later NT writers would say, Luke shows Paul allowing women to teach.

Paul stays for three years in Ephesus, where he debates with the local Jews and makes converts, but the conversions cause people to purchase fewer silver statues of the city's patron, the goddess Artemis. The silversmiths riot in anger against Paul but do not hurt him. Yet this passage still holds some importance: religion never impacts only the spiritual life. Here Christianity affected the local economy. In the early second century a Roman governor in Asia Minor complained that when the local area went Christian, people purchased fewer animals for sacrifices and so farmers lost money. Paul had spiritual concerns, but as long as the church lives in the world, other forces will always interact with it.

Paul leaves Ephesus but arranges to meet with the elders of the Ephesus community at the nearby town of Miletus. In a moving farewell speech, he justifies his work at Ephesus and elsewhere, and he pleads with the elders to be good shepherds for their community. "When he had finished speaking, he knelt down with them all and prayed. There was much weeping among them all . . ." (20:36-37).

In one of the "we passages" Paul arrives at Caesarea where he meets the evangelist Philip and his four prophesying daughters. The prophet

Agabus then reappears and predicts that Paul will be "[handed] over to the Gentiles" (21:11) if he goes to Jerusalem, something Paul accepts: "The Lord's will be done" (21:14)

Jerusalem and Rome (21:17–28:31)

Paul returns to Jerusalem and to immediate conflict. The Christians welcome him (somewhat hesitantly), but some Jews, who think Timothy is a Gentile, accuse Paul of polluting the Temple by bringing Timothy into it. A riot breaks out, and a Roman tribune saves Paul by arresting him. But he permits Paul to speak to the people. Hoping to pacify his accusers, Paul recounts his conversion. Rather surprisingly, Luke slips up here. At 9:7, "The men who were traveling with [Saul] . . . heard the voice," but at 22:9 Paul tells the crowd, "Those who were with me . . . did not hear the voice." His speech fails to move the crowd, and the tribune, deciding Paul is a troublemaker, orders him to be flogged. But Paul reveals that not only is he a Roman citizen, who cannot be flogged, he was also born one. The tribune replies, "It cost me a large sum of money to get my citizenship" (22:28).

Hoping to stop the trouble, the tribune frees Paul the next day but also orders the Sanhedrin to meet with the apostle. Things go badly. Some Sanhedrin members stand up for Paul, but most do not. The tribune fears a riot and returns Paul to prison, where the Lord appears to him and says, "Keep up your courage! For just as you have testified for me in Jerusalem, so you must bear witness also in Rome" (23:11).

Some Jews plot his death, but Paul's nephew learns of the plot and informs the tribune, who has Paul transferred to the custody of the Roman governor, Felix, in Caesarea. The governor has a Jewish wife and knows a fair amount about Christianity, but he is torn between getting a bribe from Paul and pleasing the Jews. Felix gets no bribe, and so he leaves Paul in jail for two years.

The new governor, Festus, receives appeals from the Jews about Paul, who, fearing the results of a local trial, appeals to the emperor, that is, to a higher court in Rome. Festus replies laconically: "You have appealed to the emperor; to the emperor you will go" (25:12). In a scene reminiscent of Luke's Passion narrative, Festus has Paul meet a Jewish king named Herod, this time Herod Agrippa II, another Roman puppet. Paul defends himself in a speech so persuasively that Herod Agrippa says, "Are you so quickly persuading me to become a Christian?" (26:28). In a good touch, Luke has Herod say to Festus, "This man is doing nothing to deserve death or imprisonment" (26:31), just as another Herod found no guilt in Jesus (Luke 23:15). In an even better touch, the king says to Festus, "This man could have been set free if he had not appealed to the emperor" (26:32).

This last sentence takes the reader aback: if Paul had not appealed to the emperor, he would be freed. He blew it! He spoke too soon, and he blew it! Not exactly. Here we see a classic Lukan device: the ways of God differ from the ways of humans. The Lord told Paul (23:11) that he must bear witness for him in Rome, so Paul's journey to Rome is part of God's divine plan. What is important is not that Paul be free but that he serve the Lord. God is guiding his journey to Rome.

The voyage contains the last of the "we passages." The ship sets sail from Caesarea, follows the coasts of Syria and Asia Minor, then south to Crete, only to encounter a fierce storm that wrecks the ship off the coast of Malta. The prisoners and crew board a new ship at Malta, stop in Sicily, and then arrive in Italy. Luke says simply, "And so we came to Rome" (28:14). Representatives of the Roman community greet Paul, but Luke provides no names. True to form, "[Paul] called together the local leaders of the Jews" (28:17), and the debates begin. Ominously, the Roman Jews tell him, "We have received no letters from Judea about you" (28:21), indicating that the Roman and Jerusalem communities are in contact, and it will just be a matter of time before negative reports of Paul arrive. But they may not be necessary, because the Roman Jews say, ". . . with regard to this sect [Christianity] we know that everywhere it is spoken against" (28:22). But the Roman Jews do listen to Paul, "and some were convinced . . . while others refused to believe" (28:24), the pattern for most of Paul's dialogues with the Diaspora Jews.

Luke closes with his last summary: Paul spends two years in Rome "proclaiming the kingdom of God and teaching about the Lord Jesus Christ with all boldness and without hindrance" (28:31).

When does Acts end? Scholars date Paul's voyage around the year 60, which would get him to Rome in 61. As we noted earlier, Luke does not report on Paul's death. Thus Luke concludes around the year 63, the year before the Great Fire of Rome that Nero blamed on the Christians.

Luke's ideas were controversial in his day. Many Christians still believed in an imminent end, but Luke was correct that the church would go on for an indefinite time. This in turn means that he was correct that the church was more than just a group of believers awaiting the End together; rather, it is a continuation of Christ's ministry under the guidance of the Holy Spirit. He was also right that Christianity should be a religion for all people and not just for Jews, although the idea originated with Paul, not him. He did, however, make it clear that Paul was no isolated troublemaker but rather stood within a tradition: Peter and James and the apostles and disciples of the Jerusalem community supported Paul and, most importantly, so did the Lord. Finally, without this book our knowledge of the earliest Christians would be diminished by ninety percent. We would have to scrape it out of occasional references in letters and hints in the gospels. Luke did not write like a modern historian, but he did write like an ancient one and in so doing left behind a remarkably valuable book.

Chapter Thirteen

Letters in the Pauline Tradition *actually written by Paul*

Seven NT letters are certainly by Paul. Seven others are attributed to him, but the majority of scholars do not consider them Pauline, that is, written by the apostle himself. They do believe that the now anonymous authors tried to write in the Pauline tradition, which is why they used Paul's name. This chapter will look at the ones which a minority of scholars consider Pauline.

The Second Letter to the Thessalonians

    I. Greeting (1:1-2)

   II. Thanksgiving and prayer (1:3-12)

  III. Instruction about the Second Coming (2)

  IV. Request for prayers (3:1-5)

   V. Importance of labor (3:6-16)

  VI. Greeting and prayer (3:17-18)

Because of its brevity this letter should be read in its entirety.

This brief letter was traditionally thought to be Pauline, but the majority of modern scholars have concluded that it is not. They base this conclusion on several things, including the almost mechanical similarities to 1 Thessalonians, in the identical opening words and paired thanksgiving (1 Thess 1:2 = 2 Thess 1:3; 1 Thess 2:13 = 2 Thess 2:13). While we would expect Paul to use typical ideas and phrases, these parallels seem too close. This letter also lists a number of things that must occur before the end of the age (2:1-12), yet in 1 Thess 5:2 the true Paul says "the day of the Lord will come like a thief in the night," that is, with no signs or warnings at all. Finally, "Paul" says that he signed 2 Thessalonians in his own handwriting. "This is the mark in *every* letter of mine; it is the way I write" (3:17). Yet he alludes to only one letter, 1 Thessalonians (2:15), which the true Paul did *not* sign with his own hand, thus contradicting the assertion in 2 Thessalonians. Clearly the author knew of letters such as 1 Corinthians (16:21) and Galatians (6:11), written after 1 Thessalonians, in which Paul did use his own hand.

Denying Pauline authorship deprives scholars of a time or geographical setting. The references to false teachers and prophets parallel concerns of letters written in the late first century, and the vivid description of the end parallels letters like 2 Peter, written around 125, which try to prop up belief in the Parousia just as Lukan notions of an indefinite time before the end were catching on. Thus a date toward the end of the century seems feasible. The location could be anywhere Paul's name carried weight, such as Asia Minor or Greece, but by the end of the century the apostle's fame had spread to Syria and Italy as well. The place simply cannot be determined.

The letter starts with a greeting and a prayer for grace, followed by a thanksgiving to God for the Thessalonians' faith. But the author quickly adopts a triumphalist and harsh tone. "For it is indeed just of God to repay with affliction those who afflict you" (1:6). "These will suffer the punishment of eternal destruction" (1:9). They will suffer this "when the Lord Jesus is revealed from heaven with his mighty angels in flaming fire" (1:7-8). We look in vain for any note of mercy or even a chance for the evildoers to repent. (We will see this attitude repeated and magnified in the book of Revelation). Possibly the author and his readers have endured persecution and cannot yet bring themselves to forgiveness of the persecutors.

"Paul" next describes the Second Coming, concerned that his readers would be "quickly shaken in mind or alarmed either by spirit or by word or by letter, as though from us, to the effect that the day of the Lord is already here" (2:2). Since the world still existed, why would anyone think the day of the Lord had already arrived? Clearly some were interpreting it symbolically, another argument for non-Pauline authorship since a disbelief in a physical Parousia was unlikely in the 50s.

"Paul" now explains that "that day will not come unless the rebellion comes first and the lawless one is revealed" (2:3-4). He goes on: "And you know what is now restraining him, so that he may be revealed when his time comes. For the mystery of lawlessness is already at work, but only until the one who now restrains it is removed. And then the lawless one will be revealed" (2:6-8). When this man comes, Satan will also be at work in "all power, signs, lying wonders . . ." (2:9).

The author explains none of this, but rather assumes that his readers understand him. In the early and medieval church scholars identified the lawless one with the Antichrist, but in the NT only 1 and 2 John mention that title. Clearly this evil person is human, possibly a persecuting Roman emperor. The "rebellion" suggests a major apostasy because the author sees the revolt as something negative, so it must be a revolt against God or Jesus. And is "what is now restraining him" a reference to a person or a thing? To a natural or supernatural being? To a force that is good or evil? The text does not make any of these clear. And who is the person restraining the mystery of wickedness? As usual, apocalyptic speaks a language of its own.

Understandably the author urges his readers to "stand firm and hold fast to the traditions that you were taught by us, either by word of mouth or by our letter" (2:15). The Thessalonians must rely upon the Lord (3:3).

"Paul" closes by dealing with some disciplinary problems. He points out how hard he worked among the Thessalonians, and he repudiates those who are idle. (Did they quit working since the day of the Lord was so near?) But he finally introduces a positive attitude toward sinners. "Now such persons we command and exhort in the Lord Jesus Christ to do their work quietly and to earn their own living" (3:12). Next he gets angry with all who refuse "to obey what we say in this letter," and he actually tells his readers to "have nothing to do with them" (3:14), only to relent: "Do not regard them as enemies, but warn them as believers" (3:15)—the true Christian attitude to take and an encouraging change from the merciless tone found earlier in the letter.

The letter closes with prayers and the claim that Paul wrote this letter in his own hand.

The Letter to the Colossians

IV. Paul's struggles (2:1-3)

V. Warnings against false teachers (2:4-23)

VI. Christ's resurrection (3:1-4)

VII. Christian behavior (3:5–4:6)
- Avoiding vice and practicing virtue (3:5-17)
- Christian family life (3:18-21)
- Behavior of slaves and masters (3:22–4:1)
- General admonitions (4:2-6)

VIII. Personal notes and messages (4:7-18)

Because of its brevity this letter should be read in its entirety.

Of all the letters claiming Pauline authorship but not accepted as such today, Colossians remains the most controverted. Yet most scholars, and certainly the most prominent (Brown, Erhmann, *NJBC*), do not accept Pauline authorship. We will treat this as a post-Pauline letter.

Paul did not personally evangelize Colossae, a city in Asia Minor. This letter says that his disciple Epaphras, known from the authentic Pauline letter to Philemon (v. 24), founded the community at Colossae. An earthquake destroyed the city in 61. Originally, when scholars considered this letter to be Pauline, they dated the letter no later than that year. Scholars who reject Pauline authorship still date the letter relatively early, in the 80s. Since it mentions a second city in the area, Laodicea (4:15), which was also destroyed in the earthquake, possibly this letter was intended for those Christians still living in the general area. The place of writing was most likely another city in Asia Minor whose community knew the Colossae-Laodicea area, maybe Ephesus, where Paul had worked (1 Cor 16:8).

Why do scholars not accept it as Pauline? Mostly because of its theology, which includes a christology (theology of Christ) not known in the authentic letters and an ecclesiology (theology of the church) that treats the church as a supramundane mystical reality, whereas the historical Paul always wrote of local, earthly churches. Colossians 2:11 speaks of a spiritual circumcision, whereas the historical Paul wrestled with the problem of actual circumcision for Christian men. Many scholars insist that the Greek of the letter differs from Paul's; for example, Paul often wrote brief, direct sentences, whereas the author of Colossians wrote long, involved ones. (Col 1:3-8 is actually one sentence in Greek, something not evident from English translations.)

The letter starts in a Pauline way, with the author claiming to be Paul, "an apostle of Christ Jesus by the will of God." He also adds a second author—in this case Timothy—as the historical Paul often did (1 Cor 1:1; 2 Cor 1:1). He then thanks God for the faith of the Colossians and praises the work of Epaphras, founder of the community.

At 1:15 "Paul" starts quoting a christological hymn, presumably one known to the community. The hymn creates a picture of a cosmic Christ, "the image of the invisible God, the firstborn of all creation" (1:15), that is, to know Christ is to know the Father whom we cannot see. Indeed, ". . . things visible and invisible, whether thrones or dominions or rulers or powers—all things have been created through him and for him" (1:16). The thrones, ruling powers, and the like refer to angelic beings, which many ancient people thought ruled the world. "Paul" asserts Christ's superiority over them.

Importantly for Catholics, "[Christ] is the head of the body, the church" (1:18). The author presents the church as a cosmic entity, transcending time and space and headed by Christ himself. But let us make two notes about this verse. Many Catholics routinely say that the pope is the head of the church, a claim that *no* pope has *ever* made. Christ is the head of the church; the pope uses the title "Vicar of Christ." Second, no NT text refers to the church as the "mystical body" but rather as the "body," that is, the NT posits an *organic* relationship between head and members. The term "mystical body" was not used of the church until the twelfth century. This represents yet another good example of development of doctrine as well as another caution about reading Scripture backwards. Centuries after the NT, theologians created a new and deeper understanding of the church, but this was not the understanding in the first century.

The cosmic work of Christ extends well beyond the church: "For in him all the fullness of God was pleased to dwell, and through him God was pleased to reconcile to himself all things, whether on earth or in heaven, by making peace through the blood of his cross" (1:19-20). Working the authentic Pauline images of Christ as the new Adam (Rom 5:12-21) and the need for creation to be reconciled to God (Rom 8:19-23), "Paul" portrays Christ as the redeemer of humans but also the restorer of the whole of creation by his redemptive death. Pauline or not, this is brilliant christology.

In another attempt at conveying authenticity, "Paul" recounts his struggles on behalf of the faith (1:24-29), which allows him to use his struggles on behalf of the communities of Colossae and Laodicea against the threat of false teaching. Regrettably, "Paul" describes this false teaching in such an uncertain way that scholars have explained it by pagan traditions, Jewish traditions, philosophical challenges, and just simple misunderstanding of Christian teaching. Although no one can pinpoint the exact nature of the perceived threat, certainly it contained Jewish elements. "Paul" speaks of the Colossians' having been circumcised spiritually (2:11), which suggests the false teachers told them they needed to be circumcised. He says that Christ wiped out our debt to the Law (2:14), and he warns the Colossians about observing new moons and sabbaths (2:16)—the Jews had a lunar calendar and, of course, the Sabbath was a Jewish feast. "Paul" also warns his readers not to abase themselves to angels and worship them (2:18); Jews did not worship angels but had a strong belief in their existence and their participation in human life. But the Colossians lived in a heavily pagan area; no doubt pagan influences were there as well. "Paul's" solution to the problem is a positive one: the Colossians should always recall the superiority of Christ to all these other elements and beings.

"Paul" now turns to Christian living, centering moral behavior in the faith. The Colossians are "God's chosen ones" (3:12), and so they must practice compassion, generosity, humility, gentleness, and patience. They must forgive others as the Lord forgave them. "And let the peace of Christ rule in your hearts, to which indeed you were called in the one body" (3:15). The one body is the church.

Next "Paul" provides practical advice for daily life. The modern mind can accept "Husbands, love your wives" and "Children, obey your parents," but it recoils at "Wives, be subject to your husbands" (3:18-20). This teaching reflects the views of a patriarchal society. The modern mind recoils even more at "Slaves, obey your earthly masters in everything" (3:22). As we discussed in the chapter on the letter to Philemon, the early Christians simply accepted slavery as part of their world. But "Paul" seems to have an upper-class view here because he spends four verses recounting slaves' obligations to their masters but only one verse (4:1) on the masters' obligations to their slaves.

This passage (3:18–4:1) is the earliest example of what scholars call the "Household Code," that is, a code of behavior for daily living. Such a code also appears in Ephesians, Titus, 1 Timothy, and 1 Peter. It reflects not just the moral code of the day but also the new situation of the Christians. Jesus is now dead about fifty years, and the church is settling into the world. The days when church leaders had to worry about people speaking in tongues (1 Cor 14:1-25) are fading; now day-to-day issues dominate. We should not be surprised that the early Christians followed the general norms of ancient society. They agreed with most of them, and they wanted to fit into the world, now that the Second Coming was indefinitely delayed. Some Christians, then and now, would call this a sell-out to the larger society, whereas others—including me— would say that the Christians were effecting a religious revolution and did not wish to be seen as social revolutionaries. Whatever the cause, the Household Code was widely applied by ancient Christian leaders.

As in the authentic letters, "Paul" finishes up with encouragement to his readers to persevere and with personal news. He mentions several people known to be associates of the historical Paul: Tychicus (Acts 20:4), Archippus (Phlm 2), Onesimus (Phlm 10), and Aristarchus, Mark, Demas, and Luke, all known from Phlm 24. Two, Jesus Justus (4:11) and Nympha (4:15), are otherwise unknown; maybe they were known to be companions of the historical Paul. All but one of the authentic names appear in the letter to Philemon, which most scholars place in Ephesus, a short journey from Colossae. Clearly the Colossians could have known the letter to Philemon; the heavy references to that tiny letter make no sense if they did not.

Luke has the epithet "the beloved physician" (4:14), which is the source of that tradition about him. Although some scholars want to spiritualize him as a "physician of souls," there is no reason to doubt that Luke was indeed a physician.

The Letter to the Ephesians

   I. Greeting (1:1-2)

  II. The work of the Father, Son, and Holy Spirit (1:3-14)

  III. The Church as the Body of Christ (1:15-23)

  IV. Work of Christ unites and transforms Christians (2)

  V. Paul's ministry (3:1-13)

  VI. Prayer for his readers (3:14-21)

  VII. Unity of Body and diversity of gifts (4:1-24)
- Unity in the Body of Christ (4:1-6)
- Diversity of gifts (4:7-16)
- Christians not to live like pagans (4:17-24)

VIII. Christian behavior (4:25–6:9)
- New ways of living in Christ (4:25–5:20)
- Christian family life (5:21–6:4)
- Slaves and masters (6:5-9)

IX. Moral exhortations (6:10-20)

X. Conclusion and prayer (6:21-24)

Please read chapters 1, 3, and 4.

As with several other letters, scholars have focused much attention on whether Paul wrote this. The overwhelming consensus is that he did not. The reasons are two: style and content. Like the author of Colossians but even more so, the author of Ephesians uses long, complicated sentences, very different from those of the unquestioned Pauline letters. In 1:15 "Paul" writes, "I have heard of your faith in the Lord Jesus." In much of chapter 3 he explains his work and mission. But the historical Paul had worked and suffered in Ephesus (1 Cor 15:32; 16:8); he did not need to hear about the Ephesians' faith or to explain himself to them. Denying Pauline authorship to the letter, scholars date it sometime in the 80s of the first century.

The letter's name also presents some problems because some very early manuscripts do not contain the phrase "in Ephesus" in 1:1. In fact, a modern Catholic translation, *The Jerusalem Bible,* leaves the phrase out. The name of the city appears nowhere else in the text. Yet the letter has many similarities to Colossians, which many scholars think was written in Ephesus. Possibly a later scribe knew the intended recipients and added the phrase "in Ephesus." We will never know, and that does not seriously affect how we understand the letter.

The letter opens with a greeting by "Paul" but quickly switches to a theological topic, a magnificent portrayal of the cosmic Christ. God "chose us in Christ before the foundation of the world . . . [God] has made known to us the mystery of his will . . . to gather up all things in him, things in heaven and things on earth" (1:4, 9-10). Christ has triumphed over the power of darkness, the demons and evil spirits believed to have ruled the world before his coming (1:21). "[God] has put all things under his [Christ's] feet and has made him the head over all things for the church, which is his body . . ." (1:22-23).

"Paul" now switches from Christ to his readers, who had been dominated by evil spirits and giving in to lust, but God gave them salvation in Christ as a free gift (2:1-10). Continuing the cosmic theme, "Paul"

A street in Ephesus (Asia Minor), Turkey

next portrays the reconciliation of Jews and Gentiles being effected through Christ. "Paul's" readers have become "citizens with the saints and also members of the household of God" (2:19), that is, the Gentile readers of this letter have become one with Jews. The cosmic Christ of chapter 1 enables everyone to rise above ethnic divisions.

In chapter 3 "Paul" gives an account of his life because his readers have "heard" of what he did (3:2). He recounts what he has done, hoping his readers will see his life as an example, as he took his example from Christ. He returns, for the third time, to the evil spirits (3:10), but ends this section with a beautiful prayer (3:20-21).

Suddenly, in chapter 4, the tone changes; "Paul" speaks in the imperative, telling his readers how to live their lives. This puzzles us a bit. His injunctions are worthwhile, but he is writing to a community he says he does not know personally and uses a tone the historical Paul did not use in his letter to the Romans, a community he did not know. This suggests that, by the time this letter was written, the historical Paul had become an iconic figure whose authority could justify the imperious tone. Mostly he emphasizes the need for unity, a reflection of the cosmic Christ theme.

But that theme quickly gives way to warnings about immoral behavior and yet another admonition about the devil (4:27). The tone becomes momentarily positive as "Paul" urges his readers to imitate Christ (5:1), but he quickly returns to the warnings about immorality, this time sexual immorality. References to "those who rebel" and the conflict between the children of light and of darkness recall the Jews at Qumran but also the demons again, since they first rebelled against God.

The antidote to this immorality is the Household Code, a guide to daily morality. Inevitably the emphasis falls on obedient and submissive wives, children, and slaves. While that represents no surprise, in this letter "Paul" puts much stress on the obligation of husbands to love and care for their wives, including a famous image: "Husbands, love your wives just as Christ loved the church and gave himself up for her" (5:26). This verse has stirred controversy. Many people see a positive image here, relating human marriage to Christ and the church; others have pointed out that by identifying the husband as Christ this verse gives him an unshakable authority that no woman could ever challenge. Regardless of how we respond to this, we can see here how a biblical verse has modern resonance. As for slaveowners, "Paul" urges them to treat their slaves well and even points out that both master and slave have the same Master in heaven (6:9). Although modern Catholics will always wish "Paul" had urged manumission of the slaves, ancients would have considered his views on slavery quite lenient. Realistically, that was the best ancient slaves could have hoped for.

Again "Paul" turns to the devil, this time using a military image: "Therefore take up the full armor of God, so that you may be able to stand against the wiles of the devil. For our struggle is not against enemies of blood and flesh, but against the rulers, against the authorities, against the cosmic powers of this present darkness, against the spiritual forces of evil in the heavenly places" (6:11-12). The military address continues: "Stand therefore, and fasten the belt of truth around your waist, and put on the breastplate of righteousness. . . . Take the helmet of salvation, and the sword of the Spirit, which is the word of God" (6:14-17). This imagery did not originate with "Paul"; it also appears in several prophetic writings, in the Dead Sea Scrolls, and in some Greek philosophical texts. But his use of it here continues his obsession with demons, an obsession not found in any other Pauline writings, authentic or pseudepigraphal.

"Paul" ends with some personal notes, referring to his "dear brother Tychicus" (6:21), a name taken from Acts (20:4), a book that may not yet have been written. This suggests that Tychicus was indeed a historical coworker of Paul, which in turn explains why four post-Pauline letters cite him as a means of effecting authenticity (here and Col 4:7; Titus 3:12; and 2 Tim 4:12). The final verses contain a prayer for God's grace upon the community.

Chapter Fourteen

The Pastoral Letters

These are similar in character, and so reading any one will give you a sense of them. 1 Timothy is the longest and Titus is the shortest.

"Pastoral Letters" is the name traditionally given since the eighteenth century to three letters claiming to be written by Paul. These are 1 and 2 Timothy and Titus. They acquired the name "pastoral" because they deal with pastoral problems.

Into the twentieth century scholars debated whether Paul wrote these, but the debate has now ceased. Scholars acknowledge Pauline influence and a possible Pauline community from which the letters emerged, but almost no one accepts Pauline authorship. In the NT the letters appear according to their length, the longest being first, but we cannot be sure of the sequence in which they were written, although Titus seems to be an abbreviation of 1 Timothy. Most scholars date the three letters to 100–110 and believe that one person wrote all of them. The location of the writing cannot be determined beyond the general eastern Mediterranean area.

Scholars deny Pauline authorship to these letters for three reasons. First, one-fourth of the words used appear nowhere in genuine Pauline writings. Second, for Paul the word "faith" meant acceptance and commitment to Christ's calling, whereas in these letters "faith" means teachings about Christ. Third, whereas Paul speaks of charismatic ministries, these letters focus on formal offices, including those of presbyter and bishop *(epískopos)*, a word Paul uses only once (Phil 1:1). These letters emerged from a church that had settled down and had to get along with day-to-day problems.

These letters also emerged from a church or at least from an author who wants desperately for the Christians to fit into the larger world. Clearly "Paul" worried about what outsiders would think of the Christians and did not want anyone rocking the boat. This contrasts significantly with the real Paul, who not only rocked the boat but practically overturned it. It also shows that at the time these letters were written the eschatological attitude had faded. This author expects the church to be in the world and wants the Christians to get along in it.

First Letter to Timothy

I. Greeting (1:1-2)

II. Dangers of false teaching and Timothy's duty to fight it (1:3-20)

III. The life of the community (2:1–6:2)
- Importance of prayer (2:1-7)
- Obligations of women (2:8-15)
- Qualifications for ministers (3:1-13)
- God manifest in the world (3:14-16)
- False asceticism (4:1-5)
- Advice to Timothy in dealing with problems (4:6–5:2)
- Enrollment and duties of widows (5:3-16)
- Obligations of presbyters (5:17-25)
- Obligations for slaves (6:1-2)

IV. False teaching and the problem of wealth (6:3-19)

V. Final exhortation to Timothy and farewell (6:20-21)

This letter purports to be addressed to Timothy, a companion of Paul known to us from the Acts of the Apostles and from several references in Pauline letters (Romans, Philippians, 1–2 Corinthians). After a quick greeting to his "child in the faith," "Paul" starts attacking false teachers whom he urges Timothy to control. At a time when many doctrines were just coming into formation, much confusion reigned and some outrageous ideas were proposed. "Paul" wants people to stick to the basics of the faith and so warns about "speculations" (1:4), an attitude that may preserve the faith of simple believers but that, if abused, would crush any attempt at speculative theology, including the kind the real Paul engaged in. "Paul" criticizes the false teachers' interest in myths and genealogies, suggesting that these people may have been Gnostics, a group of second-century Christians who developed a number of these. Possibly these teachers were Jewish, because "Paul" accuses them of perverting the understanding of the Law (1:8). He truly loathes them and lumps them with criminals (1:9-11). More effectively, he distinguishes these teachers who flaunt their own views from himself who had been directly called by God. But so angry is he with these teachers that he singles out two by name, Hymenaeus and Alexander, "whom I have turned over to Satan" (1:20).

Chapter two takes a different tack as "Paul" turns to how Christians relate to outsiders. He insists that there is one God for all, thus emphasizing our bond with all people, and he uses an important phrase: ". . . there is . . . one mediator between God and humankind, Christ Jesus himself human" (2:5). Significantly, he does not distinguish between the historical and risen Jesus, so Jesus not only redeemed us with his life but he also, in his risen humanity, continues to mediate for us with God today. It is a brilliant insight, although one not developed here.

"Paul" also insists that Christians pray "for kings and all who are in high positions, so that we may lead a quiet and peaceable life . . ." (2:2). He wants the Christians to be known as loyal citizens and good neighbors. But "Paul's" concern for getting along with others leads to his inclusion and even expansion of the Household Code, which we saw in earlier letters. He tells women how to dress (2:9), tells them to "learn in silence with full submission" (2:11), and asserts, "I permit no woman to teach" (2:12), thus contradicting Luke, who shows Paul's woman friend Priscilla teaching Apollos (Acts 18:26). "Paul" blames woman for bringing sin into the world but says that "she will be saved through childbearing" (2:14-15), turning the joyous event of a birth into a counter to the sin of Eve. In the Roman world patriarchy reigned, and now he wants outsiders to see the Christians can be patriarchs too.

"Paul" now turns to those in charge, first dealing with the *epískopos* or bishop. He must be morally worthwhile, sensible, reliable, hospitable, and the husband of one wife. (As we noted in the Introduction, celibacy for clergy became mandatory centuries later.) Next come the deacons, a lesser category of clergy, and they must have many of the same qualities as the bishops—respectability, moderation, and sobriety. Verse 11 speaks of women who must also be respectable and reliable, and scholars have wondered if this refers to female deacons, but the next verse says that deacons must be "husbands of one wife," which suggests that all deacons are men. Given the sentiments expressed in the Household Code, it would be surprising if "Paul" permitted women deacons in his churches. This does not mean, of course, that there were none (cf. Rom 16:1).

In an effective change of pace, "Paul" presents a brief, poetic exposition on the "mystery of our religion," telling how Christ was "revealed in flesh, vindicated in spirit, seen by angels, proclaimed among Gentiles, believed in throughout the world, taken up in glory" (3:16). The references to Gentiles and "throughout the world" suggest a mostly Gentile audience.

But this brief interlude disappears, and "Paul" returns to the false teachers, accusing them of getting their ideas from devils. These teachers reject the material world, forbid marriage, and prohibit certain kinds of food (4:1-11), clearly ascetic extremists, although the reference to food suggests Jewish converts. We simply do not know and, as always, we must be careful not to judge those being criticized without knowing their point of view. A solid ministry provides the best antidote to false teachers, and "Paul" praises Timothy, whose youth should not be held against him.

"Paul" next discusses another church group, the widows. Actually he does not speak of all widows, but only those with no families to take care of them, those who "are really widows" (5:3). We cannot say that widows formed an actual order in the church this early, but they had to meet certain conditions to be enrolled in the group. One was chronological—"let a widow be put on the list if she is not less than sixty years old" (5:9)—but most conditions are moral, "good works" (4:10). Enrolled widows should not marry again, and "Paul" will not allow young widows to enroll because "when their sensual desires alienate them from Christ, they want to marry" (4:11), although he concedes, "I would have younger widows marry" (4:14), a departure from the view of the real Paul who wrote, "To the unmarried and the widows I say that it is well for them to remain unmarried as I am" (1 Cor 7:8).

Returning to authority, "Paul" now speaks of elders or *presbyteroi*. They must have the same moral qualities as the bishops and deacons. He does not specify the relations among the three orders. Clearly the deacons do not have the status of bishops, but we cannot be sure how elders relate to bishops. Raymond Brown observed, "In all likelihood those bishops were presbyters, but . . . not all presbyters were bishops" (*Introduction to the New Testament*, 657), a view held by many scholars. But "Paul" does not make it clear.

Reverting again to society's view of the Christians, Paul says, "Let all who are under the yoke of slavery regard their masters as worthy of all honor, so that the name of God and the teaching may not be blasphemed" (6:1), the concern for a good reputation outweighing the horrors of slavery. We have seen this before in the NT; the attitude is deplorable, but that is what it was.

"Paul" finishes up with what we would expect: a warning about false teachers (6:3-10) and an emphasis on Timothy's calling to buttress the church against this threat (6:11-16). After a brief warning to rich Christians—one more proof that the church did not consist solely of the poor and lower classes—"Paul" gives Timothy yet another warning and then wishes him, "Grace be with you."

We can only wish we knew more about the situation in which "Paul" wrote this letter. What church was this, who exactly were the false teachers, what were they teaching, and how much did the community interact with the local Gentiles that he worried so much about their public image?

Before departing from 1 Timothy let us note two particular verses. At 5:23 "Paul" advises Timothy to take "a little wine for the sake of your stomach," proof that the Bible does not, as some right-wing Christians claim, forbid any consumption of alcoholic beverages, including eucharistic wine. Most famous is verse 6:10: "The love of money is the root of all evil."

Second Letter to Timothy

I. Introduction and thanksgiving (1:1-5)

II. Exhortations to Timothy (1:6–2:13)

III. Dealing with false teachings (2:14-26)

IV. The Second Coming (3:1-9)

V. Follow Paul's example (3:10-17)

VI. Paul's charge to Timothy (4:1-5)

VII. Paul's present situation (4:6-18)

VIII. Greetings to members of the local church (4:19-22)

Although a sizeable majority of scholars think the same author wrote all three Pastorals, this letter differs considerably from 1 Timothy and Titus, referring often to the lives of Paul and Timothy.

"Paul" starts with greetings and mentions the names of Timothy's mother Eunice and grandmother Lois (1:3). Since the author wishes to be taken for Paul, these names are probably authentic and lend credence to the letter. "Paul" then urges Timothy to preach the faith fearlessly, which he himself cannot do because he is in prison (1:9, 12) in Rome (1:17). This probably means his house arrest (Acts 28:16). The author contrasts Timothy's loyalty to "Paul" with those who deserted him, and he wishes the best to the family of a man who stood by him (1:15-16). The names cited appear nowhere else in the NT. They may be authentic; the reference would have little value if they were not.

"Paul" urges Timothy to be like those who face hardships (soldiers, athletes, farmers), and he then briefly recounts his Gospel, a puzzling reference since the historical Timothy would certainly have known it. Timothy must stand firm because of threats from false teachers; like those in 1 Timothy, these teachers engage in foolish speculations. Although not mentioning a specific office like bishop or deacon, "Paul" lists the familiar qualities of a servant of Christ: kindness, patience, gentleness. He also mentions two false teachers by name (2:18); again, the names appear nowhere else. But he does mention at least part of their teaching, that the resurrection had already occurred. Since the two have Greek names, possibly they were converts who could not accept the resurrection of the body and so interpreted resurrection as a spiritual rebirth.

"Paul" now switches to the last days when his enemies will get their just due. He lists a catalogue of vices (3:1-9). If his enemies practiced even half of them, this unknown community must have made Corinth look like a kindergarten. "Paul" urges Timothy to follow his example and also to follow the Scriptures because "All scripture is inspired by God and is useful for teaching, for reproof, for correction, and for training in righteousness" (3:16). (However, the Greek is ambiguous, and the sentence may be "All scripture inspired by God is . . ."—which makes sense if the opponents were promoting "scriptures" of their own, as we know the Gnostics did.) No books that came to make up the NT had achieved scriptural status by this time, so "Paul" here refers to the OT as genuine "scripture." Belaboring a familiar point, "Paul" again tells Timothy to correct false teaching.

Trying to give more authenticity to the letter, the author portrays the historical Paul meditating on the end of his life in an immortal verse: "I have fought the good fight, I have finished the race, I have kept the faith" (4:7) The author may not have been the historical Paul, but he well and succinctly summed up the apostle's life.

"Paul" next cites eight names (4:10-14). Two, Demas and Luke, appear in the authentic letter to Philemon (v. 24); Luke, later thought to be an evangelist, appears in Colossians as well. Mark, also later to be thought an evangelist, appears in Philemon as well as in Acts, Colossians, and 1 Peter (5:13), where he is associated with Rome, the ostensible place of this letter. Titus appears in Galatians and 1 Corinthians and will be the recipient of the third Pastoral letter. Tychicus appears in Acts (20:4). Crescens and Carpus appear nowhere else. There is an Alexander, who gets a negative reference, and this is probably the Alexander of 1 Tim 1:20 rather than the Alexander mentioned in Mark 15:21. Five names (Demas, Luke, Mark, Tychicus, and Titus) all have either Acts or authentic Pauline letters behind them to give this letter the ring of authenticity, and most likely the other three are also authentic.

But "Paul" is not done. A few verses later (4:19-21) he conveys greetings to four people—Prisca and Aquila appear in Romans, 1 Corinthians, and Acts; Erastus is in Romans and Acts; Trophimus is in Acts. Again "Paul" strives for authenticity.

The letter's farewell includes greetings from four people (4:21), Eubulus, Pudens, Claudia (a woman), and Linus. None appears elsewhere in the NT, but the last catches our attention. Reliable historical tradition identifies a man named Linus as the first successor of Peter as head of the Roman church. Is this the same man? Almost certainly. "Paul" wants to give the impression that the great apostle wrote this letter from Rome. Associating the writer with the second head of the Roman church would surely have done that.

One final note. In his last book Raymond E. Brown, commenting on 2 Tim 4:3 (fear of false teachers with "itching" ears for novelties), wrote, "The fear has too often made ecclesiastical institutions constantly defensive against new ideas. In such an atmosphere there will come a moment when no ideas constitute a greater danger than new ideas, and when deaf ears are more prevalent than itching ears" (*Introduction to the New Testament*, 679–80).

Letter to Titus

I.   Greeting (1:1-4)

II. Qualifications for *epískopoi* (1:5-16)

III. Christian life in the community (2)

IV. Dealing with outsiders (3:1-7)

V.   Advice to Titus (3:8-11)

VI. Farewell and blessing (3:12-15)

This brief letter supposedly was sent to Titus, another of Paul's companions who appears in Galatians and 2 Corinthians. This reads much like an abbreviation of 1 Timothy because it contains so many similar themes, although it takes a more positive approach.

The letter opens with "Paul's" greetings and then sets its destination as Crete. No other NT book connects Titus with Crete, so this may have been a tradition known to the author and his readers. "Paul" then goes immediately into the appointment of worthy elders. Familiar requirements appear: the leader must be moral, hospitable, self-controlled, and the husband of one wife. And why are reliable presbyters necessary? Because false teachers plague the community with their speculations and myths. Here the myths are identified as Jewish, although with no specifics. "Paul" considers the teachers to be rebellious and threats to the community.

Titus has the pastoral care of the community and must provide good moral instruction. As befits a society that equated age with wisdom, older men and women should lead moral lives not just as Christians but as role models for younger men and women. Inevitably, "Paul" says that women must obey their husbands and, once again, slaves must obey their masters; he does not spell out any obligations on the part of husbands to wives or of masters to slaves (2:1-10).

"Paul" next insists that "the grace of God has appeared, bringing salvation to all" (2:11), which includes Jews, pagans, and presumably even false teachers, and Titus must teach this always. This is followed by the admonition to obey "rulers and authorities" but also to be kind and polite "to everyone" (3:1-2); that is, unlike 1 Timothy, here "Paul" worries less about appearances and more about Christian behavior.

He closes with another warning about false teachers, another encouragement to Titus to teach fearlessly in opposition, and several references to other figures from Paul's career (Apollos, Tychicus) to give the letter a ring of authenticity.

Chapter Fifteen

The Letters of James, Jude, and First Peter

The Letter of James

This letter is brief and usually unfamiliar to most people, so please read it in its entirety.

As so often happens with the non-Pauline letters, a central question focuses on the author. The NT mentions five men named James, two members of the Twelve (often called James the Greater and James the Less), one minor figure mentioned only once (Matt 27:56), and another mentioned twice (Luke 6:16; Jude 1), and James the brother of the Lord who figures in Acts and is mentioned by Paul in Galatians. This letter may be by another NT James unmentioned elsewhere, but most scholars who try to identify the author believe it to be James the brother of

221

A market scene in the old city of Jerusalem

the Lord (recall the Catholic church understands the word "brother" to mean relative in a general sense, such as cousin).

But the identification with James of Jerusalem has not caught on with the vast majority of scholars, first because the Greek of the letter is too good for a native Aramaic-speaking Galilean, and second because James makes no mention of his "brother" in order to promote authenticity, the opposite of what authors claiming to be Paul do, constantly referring to his coworkers. Scholars date the letter around the year 80; there is no way to give it a location since Christian communities from Rome to Antioch spoke Greek. As usual, this is not crucial. The letter has a place in the NT and thus deserves our attention.

But—and in modern exegesis there is always a "but"—is this a letter? Most scholars say "No" because it consists mostly of ethical exhortations, so that exegetes characterize it as a rhetorical address to a now unknown community.

Yet another problem arises. Is this work actually Christian? It mentions Jesus only twice (1:1; 2:1), greets the "twelve tribes in the Dispersion [= Diaspora]" (1:1), and all the author's examples of Christian behavior come from the OT, such as Abraham (2:21), Rahab (2:25), and Elijah (5:17). Furthermore, the community to which he writes meets in a synagogue (2:2), and the reference to Abraham identifies him as "our father." Some authors believe this to be a Jewish work used by a Christian writer to give advice to a community. Against this argument are the two mentions of Jesus as well as a closing discussion of the Lord's coming (5:7-11). Furthermore, 1 Peter also greets those in the Diaspora (1:1). Since many ancient Christians were converts from Judaism and since many Gentiles received instruction about the OT basis of Christianity, most scholars conclude that this is a Christian work but one sent to a community knowledgeable about Judaism.

The letter greets the recipients and then gets right into practical matters, although so quickly that none gets a real treatment. James refers to "trials" that came upon the community and says these will lead to perseverance. Apparently these trials were not persecutions. He next urges people to pray for divine wisdom in that situation. At 1:9 he starts on a major topic of the letter, the sad lot of rich people, who will wither like the grass. Then he turns to temptation, dismissing the notion that God sends temptations (1:13). Soon, however, James gives more attention and space to problems, after first advising his readers to listen to the Word of God and put it into practice, a theme he will return to again.

Chapter two holds the key to the letter. The first part deals with respect for the poor. James laments how congregations favor the rich over the poor, even though the rich "oppress you . . . [and] drag you into court" (2:6). James insists on the need to be rich in faith, a good contrast. This section also shoots down a familiar image, that the early Christians were all poor. James makes it clear that rich people belonged to the church. To be sure, we cannot say what percentage of Christians were rich or poor, but some rich people definitely had joined the Christian movement.

Now James turns to what became the most controversial part of his letter, the relation of faith and good works. Paul had written, "A person is justified by faith apart from the works prescribed by the Law" (Rom 3:28), but James writes, "faith without works is . . . dead" (2:26). For generations scholars saw an opposition between this author and Paul. But Paul never denigrated good works because of faith. His own unshakable faith manifested itself in his tireless working to spread the faith. Paul himself testified that his sayings could be misunderstood (1 Cor 6:12-20), and scholars believe this is what happened here. Some of Paul's disciples misunderstood him to mean that if one had faith, here understood as belief, good works were unnecessary. James does not attack Paul, but those who misunderstand him. And he does so quite effectively, using examples of charitable acts (2:15-16) as well as the sardonic observation that even the demons "have Faith," that is, they believe in God (2:19)!

Apparently vicious gossip had been rending the community, so James gives an effective disquisition on uncontrolled, abusive language, including a famous line: "How great a forest is set ablaze by a small fire! And the tongue is a fire. The tongue is placed among our members as a world of iniquity; it stains the whole body, sets on fire the cycle of nature, and is itself set on fire by hell" (3:5-6). Working from one source of disunity in the community, he turns to others (jealousy, ambition) and concludes, "The harvest of righteousness is sown in peace for those who make peace" (3:18).

But this quiet appeal for unity now becomes an invective against sinners, such as adulterers and slanderers; ultimately James returns to his favorite target, the rich, and in very bitter tones: "Come now, you rich people, weep and wail for the miseries that are coming to you. Your riches have rotted, and your clothes are moth-eaten. Your gold and silver have rusted, and their rust will be evidence against you, and it will eat your flesh like fire. You have laid up treasure for the last days. . . . You have condemned and murdered the righteous one . . ."

(5:1-5). We wish we knew what was happening in his community. God loves everyone, rich and poor, but James clearly loathes the rich. His attack on them sits between his warnings about disunity and his account of the coming of the Lord. The message cannot be missed. The rich cause disunity but will pay the price when the Lord comes.

Yet after he advises the community about how to prepare for the Lord's coming, he ends on a positive note, urging his readers to bring back sinners because "whoever brings back a sinner from wandering will save the sinner's soul from death and will cover a multitude of sins" (5:20). May we assume (hope?) that this also applied to the rich?

A final note: James 5:14-16 refers to an anointing of the sick by the presbyters. Later generations of Catholics claimed this referred to the sacrament of extreme unction, now usually called anointing of the sick. Since the NT never uses the word "sacrament," modern Catholic biblical exegetes would consider this passage to be the basis of the development of the doctrine that would result in extreme unction. As usual, Catholic teaching has a biblical base, but we should not read back into the NT a full-fledged development that only occurred centuries later.

The Letter of Jude

   I. Greeting (1-2)

  II. Purpose for writing (3-4)

 III. False teachers (5-16)

 IV. Exhortation to be faithful (17-23)

  V. Doxology (24-25)

Because of its brevity this letter should be read in its entirety.

This brief letter claims to be by Jude, the "brother of James" (v. 1), an allusion to Mark 6:3, which lists James and Jude among the brothers of Jesus. This claim would give the author credibility, especially since Jesus' relatives did maintain a place of honor in the early church. It is not out of the question that this Jude wrote the letter, but it is unlikely since this author knew his Greek and was probably not a native Aramaic speaker. Since he assumes that the name of James would carry weight for his readers, "Jude" probably wrote in a Palestinian environment where James was important and where members of Jesus' extended family would have lived. As for the time of composition, we will consider that in our discussion of the letter.

Jude wrote the letter to the unnamed recipients in order to preserve their faith because "certain intruders have stolen in among you . . . ungodly [people] who pervert the grace of our God into licentiousness and deny our only Master and Lord, Jesus Christ" (v. 4). "Licentiousness" implies sexual looseness; however, the epithet "ungodly" implies atheism, and it is difficult to believe that atheists could get any hearing in a Christian community. Jude's lack of specificity does not help.

But Jude's concern is for those who could be harmed by these intruders, and so he gives a catalogue of disasters inflicted on people who wandered from the truth. Jude compares the infiltrators to a variety of OT sinners, including the people Israel after the Exodus, the fallen angels, the residents of Sodom and Gomorrah, Cain, Balaam, and Korah. He emphasizes their instability and sterility: "They are waterless clouds carried along by the winds; autumn trees without fruit, twice dead, uprooted . . . wandering stars for whom the deepest darkness has been reserved forever" (vv. 12-13). They can still repent, but if not, the Lord will judge them harshly when he comes. This sentiment puts this letter in the company of many others, such as 1 John, that invoke the Second Coming as the time when Christ will hold sinners responsible for their deeds.

Jude ends this invective with a warning about such people, but, significantly, he says it comes from the apostles (vv. 17-18). He has invoked a relationship to James and thus to Jesus, but he still feels the need to cite the apostles. This also indicates that, by the time he wrote, the authority of the apostles had taken on great significance. This leads scholars to date this book toward the end of the first century when numerous people were interpreting the Christian message in various ways, and, in doctrinal disputes people would cite authorities. We should also note that this "apostolic citation" has no parallel in the NT; possibly Jude cites an oral tradition known in his community.

But for all the invective Jude ends in a positive way, encouraging his readers to have compassion on sinners and make an effort to save them (v. 25). He closes with a doxology or prayer of praise.

When you read this letter you may have some noticed some unfamiliar accounts in its catalogue of OT events. Jude cites several additions to the OT text, particularly from the *First Book of Enoch,* a Jewish work of the first century B.C.E., supposedly written by the ancient Hebrew patriarch Enoch (Gen 5:18-24). This is an apocryphal book. "Apocrypha" (a Greek plural) is the name scholars give to books that claim to be by or about biblical figures but are not in Scripture. They are noncanonical; that is, they are not in the accepted canon or list of books. Apocryphal status does not necessarily mean that a book teaches false doctrines. For example, some NT apocrypha tell of Jesus performing miracles that are not reported in the gospels. It is not heretical to say that Jesus performed miracles; on the other hand, fidelity to gospel accounts does not mean the book belongs in the canon.

Yet here we have a canonical book openly citing an apocryphal book, or rather books. God's locking the disobedient angels in a dark place (v. 6) is from *1 Enoch;* the archangel Michael's struggle with Satan for the body of Moses (v. 9) is from *The Assumption of Moses,* another Jewish apocryphal book; Jude later cites Enoch by name (v. 14). Even Jude's discussion of the biblical figure Balaam goes beyond the OT, drawing on Jewish traditions.

For many Christians this presents a serious problem: why is an inspired author citing Apocrypha and why is such a book in the NT? But this supposes that when Jude wrote, the canon of the OT had been settled for both Christians and Jews. There is no proof that it was. To be sure, the ancient Jews, including Jesus and his apostles, considered some books, such as those in the Torah as well as Psalms and great prophets like Isaiah (Luke 24:44) to be Scripture, but the exact contours of the canon remained undetermined. Possibly Jude did not consider these works apocryphal. There is no way to determine if he considered them actually canonical, but he would hardly have cited them in a letter trying to get people to change their ways if these books possessed no authority for his readers. Later generations would make sharp distinctions between apocryphal and canonical, but Jude simply did not, and we must respect his choice in his historical situation.

In 1 Cor 10:4 Paul writes about the rock Moses struck and from which water poured forth (Num 20:2-13). He says that the rock followed the people in the desert. The OT gives no account of that; Paul got it from a rabbinic legend, and now it is part of the NT. Jude was not the only NT writer to cite noncanonical sources.

The First Letter of Peter

I. Introduction: Greeting and thanksgiving (1:1-9)

II. Traits of a true Christian (1:10-25)

III. "A Chosen Race" (2:1-10)

IV. Christian life in the world (2:11–4:6)
- Good examples and good citizens (2:11-17)
- Slaves (2:18-25)
- Spouses (3:1-7)
- Dealing with those who are hostile (3:8–4:6)

V. Trials and the End (4:7-19)

VI. Christian duties (5:1-11)
- Presbyters (5:1-4)
- Community at large (5:5-11)

VII. Conclusion and farewell (5:12-14)

As with James, this letter is brief and unfamiliar, so please read it in its entirety.

As usual with the pseudonymous letters, the quality of the author's Greek raises a problem: a Galilean fisherman could not have written this letter because the author was a native Greek speaker and educated to boot. But in 5:12 the author says that he wrote "through Silvanus," allowing the possibility that Peter dictated the letter and Silvanus put it into Greek. Scholars identify Silvanus with the Silas of Acts 15–18 (Silvanus being a different form of the name) and with Paul's coworker in 2 Cor 1:10 and 1 Thess 1:1. Since the author says he is writing from Babylon (5:13), a code word for Rome in Jewish and Christian apocalyptic writings, the author would have known Silvanus if he had accompanied Paul to Rome.

Objections to Petrine authorship center partly on the remarkable freedom the supposed apostle gave to Silvanus to compose the writing, but mostly on the more structured church organization presumed in the letter as well as its destination. The letter addresses Christians living in Asia Minor (modern Turkey), including areas on the south shore of the Black Sea. We know that by the end of the century the Roman church sent a fraternal letter to the church in Corinth (known as the *First Letter of Clement to the Corinthians*), but few scholars think the Roman church in Peter's day, that is, the 60s of the first century, would have exercised any pastoral ministry as far away as the shore of the Black Sea. Brown (*Introduction to the New Testament*, 722) does not suggest a date for the letter's composition but rather a range of 70–90. Few scholars would date it later.

"Peter" greets those living in the Dispersion (1:1), the Jewish term for the area outside Palestine where Jews lived, often understood as a spiritual exile. But he makes it clear that he writes primarily to converted pagans (4:3), so by "exile" he means our exile from our true home with God. He also uses a well-nuanced Trinitarian reference (1:2), a small proof that a Trinitarian understanding of God was beginning to emerge among the ancient Christians.

"Peter" starts in a very positive way, speaking of "a new birth into a living hope" (1:3) and of faith "more precious than gold" (1:7), all of which had been foreseen by the prophets (1:12), but he does include a reference to suffering (1:6-7), which becomes a major theme later in the letter. He goes on to point out the great price Christ paid to redeem his readers, making them special but also imposing demands on them. "Peter" lists some of these demands (2:1), but he will return to them at length.

First Peter 2:4-10 contains a passage that became controversial over the centuries since it speaks of Christians as "a royal priesthood" (2:9), which led some to think that Christianity does not need a formal ministry since we are all priests. But that is not how "Peter" meant it since the words are not original to him. Here he quotes Exod 19:6, "you shall be for me [God] a priestly kingdom and a holy nation," that is, the passage applies to all the people of Israel, who quite obviously were not all priests. "Peter" is saying that the Christians have become as precious to God as the people of Israel.

The letter now turns to a major problem facing Christians in the late first century, how to get along in a largely pagan society. "Peter" takes the path favored by most Christian writers: "Conduct yourselves honorably among the Gentiles, so that . . . they may see your honorable deeds and glorify God when he comes to judge" (2:12). Reflecting the fear of many Christians that their religious movement would be misunderstood as a social revolution, "Peter" gives his support to existing institutions: "For the Lord's sake accept the authority of every human institution, whether of the emperor as supreme [recall that Nero had executed the historical Peter], or of governors, as sent by him . . . . For it is God's will that by doing right you should silence the ignorance of the foolish" (2:13-15). He then goes on to urge slaves to accept their lot, regardless of how their masters abuse them: "For to this *you have been called*, because Christ also suffered for you, leaving you an example, so that you should follow in his steps" (2:21). Yet Peter says nothing about the obligations of the master to the slave.

We have come a long way from Paul's urging Philemon to treat the slave Onesimus as a brother, and "Peter" has set a dangerous precedent for later Christian writers, who used this passage to justify even the most brutal slavery. "Peter" was not a slave himself, nor were the later writers who justified slavery. The only Christian writer of the first five centuries who actually had been a slave was Patrick, the apostle of Ireland, who was kidnapped from his home in Roman Britain and enslaved in Ireland for six years. Writing decades later as a bishop, Patrick did not go on about how Christianity would transform the lot of slaves into something virtuous, but he did write of vicious treatment, especially of women slaves. Significantly, the one ancient Christian writer who knew in tragic personal detail what a slave's life entailed saw nothing redeeming in that life.

"Peter" now turns to marriage and writes in the same vein: do nothing to challenge the status quo. "Wives, in the same way, accept the authority of your husbands" (3:1). He then tells women how to dress, even getting to the point of warning about braided hair (3:3), but his intent is that modest women will bring credit to the faith. If a woman is married to a pagan, her virtuous life may convert her husband. "Peter" encourages husbands to "show consideration for [their] wives in [their] life together," and to remember that even though "woman" is "the weaker sex," women "are also heirs of the gracious gift of life" (3:7), that is, the redeeming life given by Christ.

The author finishes this section by urging Christians to agree among themselves; that is, they are not to let the kind of strife that infected Corinth in Paul's day weaken the community and give a bad example to outsiders. On the other hand, this advice can help to build up the community internally and not just fend off external criticism.

Now "Peter" turns to attacks on the community. Because of the vivid reference to "testing by fire" in 1:7, for generations scholars thought these attacks were persecutions. But we know of only two persecutions in the first century, the one by Nero and a second one by the emperor Domitian *ca.* 95, both of which happened in Rome. Modern scholars now believe "Peter" refers to community resentment and ostracization. If people ask the Christians why they believe what they do, "Peter" advises that they answer "with gentleness and reverence. Keep your conscience clear, so that, when you are maligned, those who abuse you for your good conduct in Christ may be put to shame" (3:16). Courtesy and respect would not deter a formal persecution. We can assume the Christians of that day suffered the kind of questioning and prejudice and suspicion that so many Muslims in Western countries do today.

Next comes a very influential but confusing passage. "Peter" says that Christ, during the period between his death and resurrection, "went and made a proclamation to the spirits in prison" (3:19). For centuries Christians thought this referred to his visiting the souls of the great figures of the OT, such as Sarah and Abraham, who could not get into heaven until Christ had redeemed humanity from original sin. This visit to the dead became known as the Harrowing of Hell, and many medieval artists portrayed Jesus leading from the mouth of hell all the worthies of the OT, including Adam and Eve. But modern scholars note that the word "spirits" is an odd one to use of deceased humans, and the phrase "spirits in prison" refers better to evil spirits imprisoned in hell. In this interpretation, what Christ did was to inform the evil spirits that he had destroyed their reign over humanity. Supporting this are the following verses, which speak of how baptism, the entry into life in Christ, "now saves you," along with a reference to how the "angels, authorities, and powers [are] made subject to him [Christ]" (3:22). But the Harrowing of Hell has a long tradition behind it, and this verse will continue to puzzle scholars for some time to come.

Now "Peter" reminds his readers how they abandoned their old life of "drunkenness, revels, carousing, and lawless idolatry" (4:3). He warns them not to fall back into this life, and then uses another puzzling reference about how "the gospel was proclaimed even to the dead" (4:6). Earlier generations aligned this to the Harrowing of Hell, but then why is this verse not adjacent to 3:19? Modern scholars believe it means those Christians who had already died after having received the Gospel.

"Peter" now turns to suffering again, although he first includes what he would consider a positive note, assuring his readers that the end is imminent (4:7). Aligning the suffering of his readers with that of Christ, he sums up their duty nicely: ". . . if any of you suffers as a Christian, do not consider it a disgrace, but glorify God because you bear this name" (4:16).

Since he worries about his readers' behavior, "Peter" logically finishes with advice to the elders *(presbyteroi)* and the people. He admonishes the elders, "Do not lord it over those in your charge, but be examples to the flock" (5:3) because the "chief shepherd" is coming soon. He urges the people, especially the younger ones, to "accept the authority of the elders" (5:5). Further advice includes a very famous image: "Discipline yourselves, keep alert. Like a roaring lion your adversary the devil prowls around, looking for someone to devour" (5:8).

"Peter" says that he penned a few words himself—as Paul sometimes did—but then credits Silvanus with the writing of the letter. He sends greetings from the community in "Babylon," which symbolizes Rome, as well as greetings from "my son Mark" (5:13). He means a son in the faith. "Peter" finishes appropriately with wishes of love and peace.

Chapter Sixteen

The Letter to the Hebrews

I. Prologue (1:1-4)

II. Christ the Son (1:5–4:16)
- Christ superior to angels (1:5–2:18)
- Christ superior to Moses and Joshua (3:1–4:11)
- God's wisdom (4:12-16)

III. Christ the High Priest (5:1–10:39)
- Jesus as the high priest (5:1-10)
- Moral exhortation (5:11–6:20)
- Christ and Melchizedek (6:21–7:28)
- New covenant, Christ as sacrifice (8:1–10:39)

IV. Living the Faith (11:1–12:29)
- Old Testament examples of faith (11)
- Example of Jesus (12:1-12)
- Acceptance of grace (12:13-29)

V. Final exhortations, blessing and farewell (13)

Please read chapters 1–8.

Despite the title, this book has none of the characteristics of a letter other than its farewell. The author does not name himself, nor does he send greetings to anyone. Nothing identifies the community to which the "letter" was sent, nor does the author indicate any personal connection with the community. It consists largely of moral exhortations mixed with some fine christology.

As for the title and the author, by the year 200 a manuscript of this work included the title and mentioned Pauline authorship, the latter presumably derived from a reference to Timothy at the close (13:23). "Hebrews" is such a vague designation that no one can be sure where the name originated. As for Pauline authorship, no scholar accepts that today because of the massive difference between the style and language of Hebrews and the unquestioned Pauline letters; some doctrinal elements differ from Paul as well. Even in the ancient world scholars questioned Paul's authorship. The great Alexandrian biblical exegete Origen (d. *ca.* 254) observed, "As for who has written it, only God knows." Modern scholars agree.

The date of the work poses fewer problems since Clement of Rome, traditionally the third pope after Saint Peter, cited the work in a writing of his own, *ca.* 95. Most scholars date it to the 80s of the first century because the letter deals with a church that is shaking off the formal remnants of Judaism, a break most likely to have occurred by that decade. While no one can determine the place of writing, many scholars believe its intended readers lived in Rome, but that view results from the early knowledge of the book in that community. As is true for so many NT books, the value of the work does not rest on a certain knowledge of the author, the time and place of writing, or the identity of the recipients.

Hebrews shows considerable literary skill, and it contains the longest sustained single theological argument in the entire NT. Yet it is not well known. Why? Probably because of its theme, the superiority of Christ to the great figures of the OT and the parallel superiority of the Christian message to the teachings of the OT and Judaism. This has little relevance to modern Catholics since our spiritual ancestors made the choice between the two traditions some twenty centuries ago. More importantly, the church has worked hard to improve Catholic-Jewish ecumenical relations, and a letter that trumpets Christianity's superiority to Judaism simply seems unecumenical, if not downright rude. Furthermore, many NT books tell Christians that our way of life, not the proclamation of our superiority, will win others over.

Why does Hebrews do this? The answer lies in 6:4-6, verses that tell of how some people had converted to Christianity but had then returned to their old faith. The author wants them to know what a mistake they had made.

What kind of superiority are we talking about?

> Christ is superior to the Hebrew prophets (1:1-3).
> Christ is superior to the angels (1:4-11; 2:5-18).

Christ is superior to Moses (3:1-6).

Christ is superior to Joshua (4:1-11).

Christ as High Priest is superior to the Jewish high priests (4:14–5:10; 7:1-29).

The covenant Christ establishes is superior to the old one (8:1-13).

Christ ministers to a tabernacle superior to the Jewish one (9:1-28).

Christ's sacrifice is superior to those of the Old Testament (10:1-18).

This is not a subtle book.

Yet for all the emphasis on Christianity and Judaism, the author shows a knowledge of Greek culture. He uses a rhetorical device common to pagan authors, giving some important information and then exhorting readers to act on that information, and he does so right from the beginning, for example, linking 1:1-14 with 2:1-4. He also refers to the tabernacle of Israel and even the Law as but poor imitations of the spiritual experiences and the spiritual law known to and through Christ (8:5; 9:24; 10:1). This echoes the basic teachings of the Greek philosopher Plato, who believed that the real world was an ideal one and the world we experience is just a poor reflection of that real and ideal one. This does not mark a major importation of Greek philosophy into the NT, but it does demonstrate that some NT authors felt comfortable with the new culture into which the faith was moving.

The book starts right off with the theme of superiority, lacking the customary epistolary greeting. The author points to the superiority of Christ over the Israelite prophets (1:1-4). He then turns to Christ's superiority over the angels, which sounds strange to us, but the ancient Jews had a very strong belief in angels and their power to intervene in the world. Possibly some Christians erroneously considered angels superior to Christ; more likely the author just wants to illustrate another example of Christ's overall superiority (1:5-14). Using the Greek rhetorical device we just explained, the author says, "Therefore we must pay greater attention to what we have heard" (2:1), that is, since we know Christ is superior to the angels we should be faithful to such teaching. This also enables the author to show that Christ's taking on a human nature is not a sign of inferiority to the angels. Rather, he graciously chose to share our human nature in order to break the power of the devil (2:14-15).

Next (3:1-19) the author argues the superiority of Christ to Moses, the great lawgiver of Jewish tradition and a person important to Christ himself (recall that Moses appears next to Christ at the Transfiguration). Then the author shows Christ's superiority to Joshua (4:1-11), Moses' successor and the man who led the people Israel into the Promised Land. The author also uses some OT passages to justify his teaching, and this leads him to a very famous observation about the nature of the Bible: "The word of God is living and active, sharper than any two-edged sword" (4:12), the origin of the famous image of Scripture as a two-edged sword.

Although Jesus was a layman, the author treats him as a high priest, but one greater than any or all of the Jewish high priests (4:14–5:10). Because Jesus was and, in his risen state, remains fully human, he is a high priest who can understand our weaknesses and thus more effectively save us from them. Hebrews 4:15 includes the key and well-known saying that Jesus is like to us in all things except sin. Before going on, we must consider two important points about that statement.

First, since all of us sin, how can Jesus be fully human if he did not? It is because Christians believe sin to be a defect in our humanity, not an integral part of it. Indeed, Jesus is more fully human than we are.

Second, the verse says that only his sinlessness distinguishes Jesus from us. Too many people view Jesus as a god in disguise (which was actually a second-century heresy) who could, if he wanted, do absolutely anything: if he were alive today, he would be the world's greatest pianist, the world's smartest computer geek, the world's most prolific author. That is *not* what the Bible teaches. We may safely assume that, like all other humans, Jesus did some things well, other things less well. He is no less the savior of the world if he misspelled a word or forgot to pass on a message. "Like to us in all things *except sin*"—that is what the Scripture says and that is how we should understand Jesus.

After establishing Jesus' superior priesthood, the author exhorts his readers to understand their faith better, comparing their initial understanding to milk and a mature understanding to solid food (5:11-14).

Only in chapter 6 does the author explain his reason for this treatise: to win back those Christians who may be tempted to return to their old religion. He uses more than just claims of superiority here, offering the image of the faith as an anchor for our souls (6:19), which became a popular image in early Christian catacomb art.

Clearly concerned about the high-priesthood claim, the author returns to it (7:1-29) in a passage that deals heavily with the homage paid by Abraham, father of the Jewish people, to the priest Melchizedek, whom the author considers a foreshadowing of Christ. In the discussion the author cites Ps 110:4: "You are a priest forever, according to the order of Melchizedek," a verse familiar to Catholics from the ordination of Catholic priests. The notion of "forever" is central to the author's argument because Christ is the one true high priest. Jesus' priesthood is a perpetual one (7:24), whereas the Jewish priests cease to be so at their deaths. This is a well-constructed argument.

Having established the superiority of Christ as high priest, the author now shows that the sanctuary, the true tent (8:2) established by the Lord "and not any mortal" is superior to the Jewish Tabernacle. Next comes a startling development: Christ is the mediator of a new covenant (8:8), quoting the prophet Jeremiah (31:31). "In speaking of a new covenant," he continues, "he [Jeremiah] has made the first one obsolete. And what is obsolete and growing old will soon disappear" (8:13). Recall how strenuously Paul tried to reconcile the Mosaic covenant with the Christian revelation (Romans 9–11), but this writer—ironically, long thought to be Paul—simply dispenses with it. No matter how the author intended them, these words ran the risk of allowing if not encouraging Christians to take the earlier revelation lightly, a point often made by Catholic OT scholars who want Catholics to remember that the Christian Bible includes the OT as an integral part of God's revealed Scripture.

(We should also note here that in Greek the phrase "new covenant" is also the Greek title of the New Testament. The word "testament" comes from the Latin *testamentum* and has overtones of a legal witness to something, in this case to the life and work of Christ and to the early history of the church.)

The author goes on to justify his assertion. "Now even the first covenant had regulations for worship and an earthly sanctuary" (9:1). "But when Christ came, as a high priest of the good things that have come, then [he entered] through the greater and perfect tent (not made with hands) . . ." (9:11). Going on with Platonic imagery, the author says the "sanctuary made by human hands [was] a mere copy of the true one" (9:24), but he makes his most effective point by comparing the yearly bloody sacrifices of animals by the Jewish high priests to Jesus redeeming us with the once-and-for-all sacrifice of his body and blood, "to remove sin by the sacrifice of himself" (9:26). This brilliant argument provided the basis of much early Christian theology on the sacrifice of Christ, and Catholics can hear stirrings of a theology of sacrifice in the Eucharist.

In chapter 10 the author reiterates his major points: "And every priest stands day after day at his service, offering again and again the same sacrifices that can never take away sins. But when Christ had offered for all time a single sacrifice for sins . . ." (10:11), this one act has rendered the old sacrifices irrelevant (10:17).

The "letter" now turns from Christ to us. The author emphasizes what a wonderful opportunity Christ has given us, and we must respond to that with love and good work. He warns his readers against apostasy, and he cannot resist a severe comparison: "Anyone who has violated the law of Moses dies without mercy 'on the testimony of two or three witnesses,'" but anyone who tramples on the new covenant will be condemned to a far greater punishment (10:28-29). Yet the author understands how people might fall away. He speaks of the sufferings his readers had endured, including being "publicly exposed to abuse and persecution" (10:33), and so he urges them, "Do not, therefore, abandon that confidence of yours; it brings a great reward" (10:35).

In order to show his readers that they are not the first whose faith has been tested by trials he gives a wonderful list of people of the old covenant, both men and women, whose faith was put to the test (11:1-40): Abel, Enoch, Noah, Abraham, Sarah, Isaac, Jacob, Joseph, Moses, Rahab, Gideon, Barak, Samson, Jephthah, Samuel, and David. This impressive list alerts modern Christians to the benefits still to be gained by reading the OT. The author also steps outside the OT, citing Jewish traditions not found there (11:37).

Chapter 12 finds the author urging his readers to follow the example of Jesus, "the pioneer and perfecter of our faith . . . . Consider him who endured such hostility against himself from sinners, so that you may not grow weary or lose heart" (12:2-3). Those who lose faith and do not persevere will endure punishment, and he reminds his readers that "our God is a consuming fire" (12:29, echoing Deut 4:24). After this rigorous warning the author turns to the positive, recommending specific behaviors such as loving one another, remembering those in prison, keeping marriage pure, and avoiding avarice.

Returning to a prominent theme, he again urges faithfulness to what has been taught. They can rely on Jesus always. Why? Because "Jesus Christ is the same yesterday and today and forever" (13:8), a memorable phrase. Working from this, he again contrasts the durability of the Christian revelation with the transitory nature of others: "For here we have no lasting city, but we are looking for the city that is to come" (13:14).

As do many other NT writers, the author tells his readers to follow their leaders, who have the duty of watching over the souls of those in the community. He then adds a personal note, asking his readers to pray "so that I may be restored to you very soon" (13:19). Closing with a blessing, he mentions "our brother Timothy" (13:23), which some consider a half-hearted attempt to give the work a claim to Pauline authorship, but since there are so many other ways the author could have attempted that, we must allow the possibility that the author may have known Timothy himself. He also sends greetings from "those from Italy" (13:25), which suggest an Italian (Roman?) location for the writing, but the phrase could also mean that Christians from Italy were with the author when he wrote.

This is a document that did not have much appeal in the ancient world. It was the last book Western Christians admitted into the NT canon. As long ago as the sixteenth century scholars began to deny its Pauline authorship, which diminished its importance for many Christians. As we saw at the beginning of this chapter, its emphasis on the superiority of Christianity to Judaism makes ecumenical Catholics uncomfortable. But this well-constructed, well-argued work rewards careful reading, especially of its superb christology.

Chapter Seventeen

The Johannine Letters

Three small letters, 1, 2, and 3 John are collectively called the Johannine Letters, not because scholars believe the disciple John wrote them but because they are clearly related to the Gospel of John. The gospel definitely influenced 1 John, and the author of that letter apparently wrote the other two, so they are indeed connected. This means that they were written after the gospel and so date *ca.* 100 C.E.; the place of writing was most likely western Asia Minor.

As we saw in the gospel, it was produced by the community that looked to the Beloved Disciple, and we must look again to that community to understand the letters.

The three letters combined run to only ten pages in the average NT, so please read all of them in their entirety.

The First Letter of John

I. Prologue (1:1-4)

II. God and the community (1:5–3:10)
- God as light and love in the community (1:5–2:17)
- Antichrists (2:18-23)
- True children of God (2:24–3:10)

III. Community life (3:11–5:20)
- Love for others in the community (3:11-23)
- Testing spirits (4:1-6)
- Love and keeping the commandments (4:7–5:12)

IV. Postscript and farewell (5:13-21)

This NT book is misnamed, because it has none of the characteristics of a letter—no addressees, no salutation, no farewell from the writer—and scholars believe the author intended it as a general exhortation to the community. Nor does it contain effective literary devices. It is often repetitious, and some of its moral advice can only be called standard, for example, "This is his commandment, that we should believe in the name of his Son Jesus Christ and love one another, just as as he has commanded us" (3:23). On the other hand, the writer occasionally rises to superb prose, the famous example being, "God is love, and those who abide in love abide in God, and God abides in them" (4:16). This "letter" also raises some important historical questions.

Its relation to the gospel appears quickly, with references to light and darkness as well as with gospel terminology reworked, such as "in the beginning," here meaning the beginning of Jesus' ministry. We also see that some of the problems faced by Paul confronted this author, including a misunderstanding of the Christian message, but here that misunderstanding produced a sizeable party of dissidents. John characterizes their views: "If we say that we have no sin, we deceive ourselves . . . . If we say that we have not sinned, we make him [God] a liar, and his word is not in us" (1:8, 10). What would have led people to believe that they were sinless? Does this relate to the attitude of some of Paul's Corinthians, that they were above the Law? We do not know, but we get a glimpse of some of the difficulties early Christian leaders had to deal with.

In addition to that, this disunity leads to more than pride in a supposed sinlessness; it can yield hatred. "Whoever says, 'I am in the light,' while hating a brother or sister, is still in the darkness" (2:9). The author sees some help in specifying what needs to be done: "Now by this we may be sure that we know him, if we obey his commandments" (2:3), but no doubt those who so trouble the author thought they were keeping the commandments.

The "letter" now turns to what "John" believes is the real cause of the problem, as he congratulates his readers for overcoming the evil one (2:13-14). The author finds a problem with love of the world "for all that is in the world—the desire of the flesh, the desire of the eyes, the pride in riches—comes not from the Father but from the world" (2:15). Note here that "the world" now means an obsession with worldly things, a different meaning from the world God loved so much that he sent his only begotten Son to save it, as John's Gospel says (John 3:6).

Part of the author's concern is his eschatology: ". . . the world and its desire are passing away . . . it is the last hour" (2:17-18). Although this "letter" has connections to the Gospel of John, their eschatological views differ. The gospel only mentions the Second Coming twice, and neither reference is long (5:26-29; 14:1-3), favoring instead "realized eschatology," that is, the end of the age has begun with the coming of Christ. The "letter," on the other hand, makes the Second Coming a major concern, especially in discerning the negative signs of the end.

This was a common view and thus is no surprise here, but the author mentions, for the first time in Christian history, the figure of the Antichrist. Contrary to widespread belief, the Antichrist does not appear in the gospels or in the Book of Revelation, nor does the NT ever specify who this is.

The term literally means "one who is against Christ," and both Matthew and Mark speak of false or "pseudo-Christs" (Matt 24:23-25; Mark 13:21), while 2 Thessalonians speaks of the lawless one (2:3-12), but only in this letter and 2 John does the term Antichrist appear. And we cannot be sure what it meant.

The author says, "you have heard that antichrist is coming" (2:18), providing no explanation, which means this figure was well known to the readers. Furthermore, the appearance of the Antichrist would be one of the signs of the end of this world, which aligns the Antichrist with figures mentioned in Matthew, Mark, and 2 Thessalonians, but this author tells us nothing about this figure. Instead, he has more interest in "antichrists" (2:18). It is surprising to see that word in the plural, but the author means it that way. So, who are they? "They went out from us, but they did not belong to us; if they had belonged to us, they would have remained with us" (2:19). Now we know what has been troubling the author. His community experienced a secession, and apparently a major one since he considers the secessionists' departure a sign of the end of the world (2:18). In the long history of the Catholic Church many groups have left for a variety of reasons, but the church never considers their departure, no matter how unfortunate, to be a sign of the end.

Do we know anything about the secessionists, bearing in mind that our information comes from someone who considers them to be in league with the devil? The "letter" goes on to ask, "Who is the liar but the one who denies that Jesus is the Christ? This is the antichrist, the one who denies the Father and the Son" (2:22). These accusations are not easy to decipher, but it might be possible to link them with other verses. First John 1:7 tells us that "the blood of Jesus . . . cleanses us from all sin," that is, his physical suffering redeemed us. At 4:2-3 we

read that "every spirit that confesses that Jesus Christ has come in the flesh is from God, and every spirit that does not confess Jesus is not from God. And this is the spirit of the antichrist." In 2 John 7 we read that the Antichrist "do[es] not confess that Jesus Christ has come in the flesh" (v. 7).

We know from other ancient sources that at the turn of the century there were Christians who denied that Jesus had a genuine human body. They were not vicious heretics, out to destroy the faith, but Gentile converts coming from the Greek tradition that strongly separated the spiritual and physical. The philosopher Plato had once defined the body as "the prison of the soul," and very likely these Christians feared that a physical body would corrupt the image of a divine son of God. But people had seen Jesus. If he did not have a body, what did they see? A phantom. These Christians believed that Jesus only *seemed* to have a body. The Greek word for "seem" is *dokéo*, and so scholars call these Christians "docetists." If the Antichrists were docetists it would explain why the letter accuses them of denying the Son who had to become incarnate to redeem us and thus also of denying the Father who sent the Son. But we cannot be sure of this because 1 John does not provide enough detail.

The "letter" also castigates the secessionists for their moral failings, linking them again to the devil (3:8-10). Does this help to identify them? In warnings about the world the author mentions physical desires, but also pride of possession. At 3:17 he insists that those with worldly possessions should help those in need. Are the secessionists wealthy people who withdrew from the community and took their money with them, thus weakening the community's ability to do charitable works?

Whether or not we can solve the historical problems, we can appreciate the letter's moral teachings, especially its insistence on the need for love, just as Jesus loved us so much that he laid down his life for us (3:16). We already read the famous line about "God is love"; to this we can add "those who do not love a brother or sister whom they have seen, cannot love God whom they have not seen" (4:21). But even a meditation on love cannot wander too far from the community's problems. "By this we know that we love the children of God, when we love God and obey his commandments" (5:2), that is, the author stresses the need for order, which the secessionists had attacked.

At 5:6-8 the author uses a strange image, that water, blood, and the Spirit are the three witnesses of Christ. The water and blood almost certainly refer to John 19:34, where water and blood come from the pierced

The Church of All Nations, Jerusalem

side of the crucified Christ, a verse that hearkens back to John 7:38 about living water from the believer's heart being a sign of the Spirit. But this image also stresses the importance of the physical death of Jesus for the redemption of the human race.

The author finishes by wishing his readers well, and he then explains his purpose. "I write these things to you who believe in the name of the Son of God, so that you may know that you have eternal life" (5:13), but he still cannot get away from those troublesome themes: "We know that we are God's children, and that the whole world lies under the power of the evil one" (5:19). His very last words? "Little children, keep yourselves from idols" (5:20).

The Second Letter of John

    I. Greeting (1-3)

    II. The commandment to love (4-6)

    III. False teachers (7-11)

    IV. Farewell (12)

This brief letter was written by the same person who wrote 1 John, and it has similar themes. The author identifies himself as the Elder (*presbyteros* in Greek), an honorific title, and he writes to the Elect Lady, a symbol of the local church, which is unknown, although somewhere in Asia Minor. Possibly this church was founded from the local church of the Elder, who thus feels competent to give advice. He praises the community for its devotion to truth, a major Johannine theme, and then urges its members to live a life of love.

He turns immediately to a problem from 1 John, false teachers who refuse to honor Christ's human nature and deceive others. He refers to them as the Antichrist, used here in the singular, thus making this the second NT book along with 1 John to use that notorious title. Note that here too he refers not to a demonic being but to humans. The Elder treats these deceivers harshly. They do not deserve Christian hospitality (v. 10), and anyone who greets them shares in their wickedness (v. 11). As we saw in our look at 1 John, these false teachers may be docetists who seceded from the Elder's community.

The Elder seems worried about what moderns would call a "leak," since he says, "Although I have much to write to you, I would rather not use paper and ink" (v. 12), so he promises to make a visit. He closes with greetings from "the children of your elect sister," that is, the local church where he lives.

This letter contains no serious doctrinal content, merely repeating the warning of 1 John about those who deny Christ's full humanity, but it does give us a small insight into how the doctrinal difficulties at the end of the first century were being played out in local churches.

The Third Letter of John

I. Greeting (1-4)

II. Hospitality to strangers (5-8)

III. Criticism of Diotrephes (9-10)

IV. Exemplary character of Demetrius (11-12)

V. Farewell (13-15)

This little gem was also written by the Elder who wrote 1 and 2 John. We call it a little gem because it shows us how the earliest churches had to struggle with authority.

The Elder writes directly to an individual named Gaius, but he presumes his letter will be made known to the local church or at least to church members loyal to the Elder. He expresses his wishes for Gaius' welfare, both physical and spiritual, and commends Gaius for helping others, especially those on a journey for Christ's name, presumably missionaries who do not wish to depend on pagans for their sustenance.

Then he turns to Diotrephes, "who likes to put himself first" (v. 9), and who refuses to accept emissaries from the Elder. Diotrephes not only denies Christian hospitality to them but also "prevents those who want to do so and expels them from the church" (v. 10). The Elder says that he "will call attention to what he is doing" (v. 10), but, significantly, he has no power to remove him from office.

The Elder compliments someone named Demetrius; again he cryptically says that he cannot put everything in writing but hopes to visit soon. He finishes with greetings from friends to friends.

The key question revolves around the role of Diotrephes. The Elder considers him a petty tyrant, but we would like to hear Diotrephes' side. The Elder has an honorific position, but Diotrephes holds a juridical one:

he can refuse hospitality to the Elder's emissaries and expel from the local church those who extend it to them, and the Elder can do nothing about it. The letter gives Diotrephes no title. Was he an early bishop?

And was he really such a villain? Possibly he was a hardworking man who felt the need to organize the local church and resented that the Elder was interfering in his work. After all, how could he organize things when someone outside his church could simply send people to try to change things? Raymond Brown made the interesting suggestion that Diotrephes, like the Elder, feared the secessionists of 1 John, and, just to be safe, he did not want any missionaries of any kind coming to his church (*Introduction to the New Testament*, 404).

This letter shows that, as the early doctrinal disputes festered, the need for reliable, organized, formal authority began to grow. Informal reverence such as that given the Elder gave way to reverence for the office. In the second century this practice would grow extensively, not as a betrayal of the earlier way but as a simple consequence of a new historical situation. Few modern Catholics consider harsh authoritarianism to be a solution to dissent; instead they favor openness, discussion, and reconciliation. Yet at some point someone has to be able to speak authoritatively. Diotrephes may well have been one of the first Christians to recognize this. We can only hope he used his authority more justly than the Elder says he did.

Chapter Eighteen

The Book of Revelation
(the Apocalypse)

(This is an intensely complicated book with dozens of individual prophecies, so this outline is general.)

    I. Prologue (1:1-3)

   II. Letters to the seven churches (1:4–3:22)

  III. Heavenly worship of God (4)

  IV. The Lamb (5)

    V. Seven seals (6:1–8:1)

  VI. Seven trumpets (8:2–11:19)

 VII. The woman and the dragon (12)

VIII. The two beasts (13)

  IX. Visions (14)

   X. Seven plagues and seven bowls (15–16)

  XI. The Fall of Babylon (17–19)

 XII. The millennium (20)

XIII. New Heaven and New Earth (21:1-8)

XIV. New Jerusalem (21:9–22:5)

 XV. Epilogue (22:6-21)

This is a long and confusing book, but given its controversial nature and its constant misuse by people looking for the end of the world, please read this in its entirety. It may be long, but it is never dull.

Without doubt the strangest and most misunderstood work in the entire NT, this book has fascinated Christians for two millennia. *Apokalypsis* is the Greek word for "revelation," so the book can accurately go by either of its two names. Many people call it the "Book of Revelations," and while it does contain many revelations, that name is simply wrong. Martin Luther once said of this book, "Revelation? It does not reveal anything. It just confuses people." No scholar would disagree.

The main problem with the book is not the book itself but how people have used it. In spite of its proclaimed visionary nature, people insist that it provides a blueprint for the end of the world. But even a cursory reading proves that this cannot be so. For example, 6:14, recounting the effects of the opening of the sixth seal, says, "the sky disappeared," but 20:11 tells us that "the sky vanished." But how could the sky vanish twice? To this internal inconsistency can be added modern scientific knowledge. Revelation 8:10-11 tell us that a star named Wormwood fell to the earth, where it fell on the rivers. But we know that even the smallest star is many times the size of earth, so it cannot fall on the earth; it would engulf it totally. In some cases the passage is so vague that any interpretation is possible. "Its [the beast's] number is six hundred sixty-six" (13:18). Who might the beast be? Modern identifications have included Adolf Hitler, Joseph Stalin, Pope Paul VI (a right-wing fundamentalist interpretation), and Ronald Wilson Reagan (count the letters in his name). Finally, recall that in 2000 (Y2K), people predicted the end of the world because it marked the end of the second millennium, when Satan would be free to roam about the world (based on Rev 20:2), the second millennium being the 2000th anniversary of Jesus' birth. But as we saw in our discussion of the gospels, Jesus was born no later than 4 B.C.E., so the 2000th anniversary of his birth occurred no later than 1996!

Enough is enough. We cannot use visions to do history. This book is very important but not as a predictor of the future. Historically it gives an insight into a mentality prevalent among many early Christians. Spiritually, it reminds us that there are forces that transcend history and are controlled by God. And it really is fascinating to read.

So, who wrote it? where? to whom? and when? The first three questions are linked and are answered in the first two chapters of the book.

Earlier in the book we looked at apocalypticism, and we saw that the Jews who wrote apocalyptic books usually set them in a distant historical period and claimed they were written by ancient holy men like Enoch and Daniel. The author of this book does not use a pseudonym, but identifies himself as John (1:4). Many Christians identified him with John the apostle, who was also identified as the author of the Fourth Gospel. But even in the ancient world scholars questioned this. In the third century an Alexandrian bishop named Dionysius analyzed the Greek of the gospel and of Revelation, and he had little difficulty proving the same person could not have written both. "John" was not an uncommon name in the ancient Jewish world, and scholars have concluded that this man is known to us only as the author of this book.

Can we determine anything about him from the book? We know he was Jewish by birth and upbringing, partly because he used a Jewish literary genre to convey his ideas and partly because his Greek indicates that this was not his native tongue, which was probably a Semitic dialect like Aramaic. Since his place of writing, Patmos, was a prison island in the Aegean Sea, and since he says he was there "because of the word of God and the testimony of Jesus" (1:9), the Romans had exiled him there, possibly during a persecution. Finally, John was a man of some influence in the churches of western Asia Minor (modern Turkey) since he wrote with authority to seven of them, including important ones with Pauline connections like Ephesus and Laodicea.

When did John write from Patmos to the seven western Asian churches? The book gives no specific clues except for the references to persecution and to some heresies, specifically of the Nicolaitans, in the Asian churches. Scholars eliminate Nero's persecution as a possibility because that occurred after the Great Fire of Rome in 64. Paul and his associates had founded some of those seven churches, yet none of the pseudo-Pauline letters mentions any troubles in Asia similar to those in Revelation and certainly no state persecution in the area. Around the year 95 another emperor, Domitian (81–96), persecuted the Christians in Rome; possibly the persecution was taken up by some provincial governors. About 115 a Roman governor in Asia Minor named Pliny the Younger wrote of a persecution that occurred there twenty years before, that is, about the time of Domitian's persecution. That emperor's reign provides the circumstances under which a book like this would have been written. Like the Jewish apocalypses, it was written to encourage the faithful to bear up during the scourge and to assure them of God's ultimate and imminent victory over their enemies.

Because this book contains personal visions we can never be sure of their interpretations. Even in detailed commentaries, as long as or longer than this whole book, you will find phrases like "it seems that the author meant" or "it appears most likely." But if we cannot pin down every specific vision we can see some larger themes. For example, this book harks back to Genesis, which begins with God creating the heavens and the earth, while Revelation ends with a new heaven and a new earth. John has read the prophets and borrowed from them; his four living creatures (man, lion, ox, eagle) come from the book of Ezekiel (1:10). John uses liturgical themes, with references to golden lampstands that were found in the Jerusalem Temple. And, of course, he uses traditional apocalyptic themes of combat, God versus monsters and demons, and the suffering and eventual triumph of the good.

Here we simply cannot consider every interpretation for every verse, so we will concentrate on the more important and better known passages in order to understand what John was conveying to his readers.

But before we venture into such a strange kind of literature, let me just note that the Apocalypse is the most visual of NT works and a perennial favorite of artists, especially in the Middle Ages. Here we list some of its most famous images and the verses in which they appear. The literature may be unfamiliar, but the images are not.

- Alpha and Omega (1:8)
- Word of God as a Two-edged Sword (1:16)
- Sea of Glass (4:6)
- Seven Seals (5:1–8:1)
- Four Living Creatures (4:7-8)
- Four Horsemen (6:1-7)
- Wormwood (8:1)
- Army of Locusts (9:7)
- Bottomless Pit (9:11)
- Woman Clothed with the Sun (12:1)
- Great Red Dragon (12:3)
- Beast from the Sea (13:1)
- Mark of the Beast (13:6)
- 666 (13:18)
- Armageddon (16:8)
- Whore of Babylon (17:4)
- Scarlet Woman (17:4)
- Rider (Faithful and True) on White Horse (19:11)
- Millennium (20:2)
- Gog and Magog (20:8)
- Book of Life (20:12)
- New Heaven and New Earth (21:1)

- New Jerusalem (21:2)
- Pearly Gates (21:21)
- Streets of Gold (21:21)

The book starts with the word *apokálypsis* or revelation, which the author claims came from Jesus Christ, thus giving the book divine authority. The author identifies himself, warns his readers that the end is approaching, and then turns to the Asian churches. He offers the churches "grace . . . and peace from him who is and who was and who is to come . . . the Alpha and the Omega" (1:4, 8). Alpha (A) and (Ω) are the first and last letters of the Greek alphabet and thus symbols of the beginning and end.

The author identifies himself to his readers as "your brother who shares with you in Jesus the persecution and the kingdom and the patient endurance" (1:9) and tells them he was on Patmos when he heard a voice like thunder telling him, "Write in a book what you see and send it to the seven churches, to Ephesus, to Smyrna, to Pergamum, to Thyatira, to Sardis, to Philadelphia, and to Laodicea." When the seer "turned to see whose voice it was that spoke to me," he saw "one like the Son of Man," a figure known to Jews from the apocalyptic book of Daniel (7:13), thus placing John in the apocalyptic tradition, which would have been comprehensible to his readers in Asia. He also uses liturgical imagery since the Son of Man stands in the midst of "seven golden lampstands" (1:9-16).

Obeying the vision, John sends his book to the seven churches but includes cover letters with it. Since the end is near, the letters either urge the readers to change their behavior if it is evil or to persevere in it if it is good. John twice (to Ephesus and Pergamum) criticizes a group he calls the Nicolaitans (2:6, 15) but does not specify their teachings. He also warns the Ephesians about self-styled apostles, recalling Paul's tribulations with Christians who perverted or challenged his teachings. Smyrna apparently had many Jews, some of whom "say that they are Jews and are not, but are a synagogue of Satan" (2:9) because they slandered the local Christians. He also refers to the Jews at Philadelphia in the same terms (3:9). Many scholars have wondered about the identity of "that woman Jezebel, who calls herself a prophet" (2:20). Jezebel (1 Kings 16–22; 2 Kings 9) was the OT evil woman par excellence. John accuses her of eating food sacrificed to idols and also of adultery (2:22), and he utters terrible prophecies about her, but he apparently cannot force her out of office. We only know of her what John says, but clearly we see a woman dominating a local church. After alternately berating and praising churches, John finishes his mini-letters by accusing the Christians at Laodicea of being only "lukewarm. . . . I am about to spit you out of my mouth" (3:16). A book that treats of absolute good and absolute evil has no room for those who try to balance between the two.

We must be careful not to accept too completely John's portrait of these churches. He wrote as a visionary, and we cannot evaluate how his recipients accepted his letters.

The letters over, John turns to his long prediction of the end, starting with the court of the "one seated on the throne" (4:2) and including a variety of beings around the throne, such as the twenty-four elders (equals the twelve tribes and the twelve apostles?) and four living creatures, six-winged creatures with multiple eyes, "the first living creature like a lion, the second living creature like an ox, the third living creature with a face like a human face, and the fourth living creature like a flying eagle" (4:7). These images originated in the book of Ezekiel and in the Middle Ages they came to symbolize the four evangelists: the man for Matthew, the lion for Mark, the ox for Luke, and the eagle for John.

The one on the throne has a scroll sealed with seven seals that no one can open. Then appears the figure of the seven-horned, seven-eyed Lamb, who symbolizes Christ, another sacrificial victim. The Lamb can open the seals. As the first four seals are opened, out come four horses and riders (6:1-8), the famous Four Horsemen of the Apocalypse. The first represents triumph, probably a symbol of the Romans; the second represents war; the third represents famine; and the fourth, with pale horse and pale rider, represents death. Famous as they are, the four horsemen do not detain John, who goes on with the next two seals, which effect the destruction of the stars and the sky (6:12-14).

John now turns to the earth, to the survivors who will number only one hundred forty-four thousand "out of every tribe of the people of Israel" (7:4), a symbolic number of people who will receive seals on their foreheads to mark them off as among the blessed, a reversal of the mark of Cain in Genesis (4:15). The white-robed blessed call out their veneration of the Lamb. When the seer asks an angel who they are, he learns they are "they who have come out of the great ordeal; they have washed their robes and made them white in the blood of the Lamb" (7:14-15), a startling image, the pure white color being achieved by the red blood of the Lamb's sacrifice.

When "the Lamb opened the seventh seal, there was silence in heaven for about half an hour" (8:1), an image derived from the prophetic tradition of silence in the presence of God (Zeph 1:7) and a symbol that more dramatic events were about to occur.

And they do. Seven angels appear and blow seven trumpets, all of which are followed by disasters—the earth is burned up, balls of fire fall from the sky, the earth becomes darkened—and an eagle, a pagan symbol of a divine messenger, flies about announcing, "Woe, woe, woe to the inhabitants of the earth, at the blasts of the other trumpets" (8:13). When the angels blow these trumpets, the disasters now involve actions on earth. An angel uses a key to unlock the bottomless pit, and out comes an army of locusts who were "told . . . to damage . . . only those people who do not have the seal of God on their foreheads" (9:5). "On their [the locusts'] heads were what looked like crowns of gold; their faces were like human faces, their hair like women's hair, and their teeth like lions' teeth . . . . They have as king over them the angel of the bottomless pit; his name in Hebrew is Abaddon, and in Greek he is called Apollyon" (9:7-11).

When the sixth trumpet sounds, a voice from heaven orders the release of "the four angels who are bound at the great river Euphrates" (9:14). These four angels lead an army of two hundred million cavalry wearing "breastplates the color of fire and of sapphire and of sulfur; the heads of the horses were like lions' heads, and fire and smoke and sulfur came out of their mouths" (9:16-17). They destroy many people, but those lucky enough to escape do not change their ways, continuing to worship devils, here identified with "the idols of gold and silver and bronze and stone and wood" (9:20), an early identification of the pagan gods with demons.

As with the seventh seal, John interrupts his account before getting to the seventh trumpet. A gigantic angel appears to him amid seven claps of thunder and announces the end is near. He gives John a scroll to eat, sweet to the taste but bitter in the stomach. This derives from Ezekiel 2:8-10, where eating a scroll signifies a prophetic commission from God. The sweet and bitter represent the differing fates of the good and evil.

John switches now to two unnamed prophetic witnesses who suffer martyrdom in a great city, which may combine both Jerusalem, the city "where also their [the witnesses'] Lord was crucified" (11:8), with Rome since "members of the peoples and tribes and languages and nations will gaze their dead bodies" (11:9), the many races suggesting Rome. Most importantly, the martyred prophets rise from the dead: "Then they heard a loud voice from heaven saying to them, 'Come up here!' And they went up to heaven in a cloud while their enemies watched them," (11:12), paralleling Jesus' ascension (Acts 1:9). Now the seventh angel can sound his trumpet. When he does, heavenly voices announce, "The kingdom of the world has become the kingdom of our Lord and of his Messiah [Christ]" (11:15), words well known from Handel's *Messiah*. The irruption of this kingdom into this world will cause the judgment of nations and retribution on sinners. It also leads to some of the most famous passages in Revelation.

At 12:1 we meet "a woman clothed with the sun, with the moon under her feet, and on her head a crown of twelve stars." Ancient exegetes saw her as representing the church, but medieval tradition and many artists interpreted this woman to be the Virgin Mary. Modern Catholic scholars have returned to the interpretation of her as the church. The medieval tradition was somewhat self-contradictory, after all. Verse 2 says she "was crying out in birthpangs," but medieval tradition, working from the doctrine of the Immaculate Conception, said that Mary had no labor pains since she was free of original sin and thus of its consequence, such as labor pains (Gen 3:16). Furthermore, 12:17 says that the woman had other children, which contradicts Catholic belief that Mary was perpetually a virgin. As is so often the case, Raymond Brown well summed the modern Catholic view: "Yet sometimes the symbols are polyvalent, e.g., the woman in Rev 12 may symbolize Israel giving birth to the Messiah as well as the church and her children in the wilderness under Satanic attack after the Messiah has been taken up to heaven. She could also be the same as the bride of the Lamb, the New Jerusalem, who comes down from heaven in 21:2, but there is less agreement on that" (*Introduction to the New Testament*, 779).

"Then another portent appeared in heaven: a great red dragon, with seven heads . . ." (12:3) The dragon represents the demonic forces, and John calls it "that ancient serpent, who is called the Devil and Satan, the deceiver of the whole world" (2:9), an identification he repeats at 20:2. The book of Genesis speaks only of a serpent and does not identify it as Satan. The Jewish book of Wisdom said that "through the devil's envy death entered the world" (2:24), strongly implying the serpent was the devil, but this passage in Revelation became decisive for that identification.

Both the woman and the serpent appear in the sky, telling the reader that this is a cosmic struggle. Given all that has happened so far we would expect no less, but John wants to establish that the church's difficulties in the world stem from more than just Roman opposition or human weakness. The church transcends the values and forces of this world, and so does the church's opposition. The real struggle is between the dragon and the Lamb, not between the Christians and Rome.

The dragon stations himself in front of the woman so as to devour the child the woman is delivering (frightening imagery), but "her child was snatched away and taken to God and to his throne; and the woman fled into the wilderness" (12:5-6). God will protect his church and her children, particularly her son the Messiah.

"And war broke out in heaven; Michael and his angels fought against the dragon. The dragon and his angels fought back, but they were defeated, and there was no longer any place for them in heaven" (12:7-8). Christian tradition has portrayed Satan and other evil angels as sinning in heaven, then being driven out of there by the good angels led by Michael, ending up in hell, and then taking their revenge on God by tempting Adam and Eve to sin. But we can see the difficulty here: the struggle between Satan's angels and Michael's angels occurs at the end of time, not the beginning. This represents no problem for ancient believers but only for modern ones who try to impose a logical structure on a collection of visions. The tradition of Satan's fall is an old one, appearing in the OT (Isa 14:12), although without Michael. Jewish apocryphal literature expanded Satan's role considerably, and we should look there for some antecedents of John's view. But the key point remains: this visionary book wants to establish that the struggle between good and evil is a cosmic one and not one carried out only in this world.

"So when the dragon saw that he had been thrown down to the earth, he pursued the woman . . . . But the woman was given the two wings of the great eagle, so that she could fly from the serpent into the wilderness . . . . Then the dragon was angry with the woman, and went off to make war on the rest of her children, those who keep the commandments of God and hold the testimony of Jesus" (12:13-17). The dragon cannot attack the Messiah, nor can he attack the church (the woman), but he can attack her other children. This view comes straight from Jewish apocalyptic literature: individuals may suffer, but the People of God will ultimately triumph.

Now suddenly a beast rises from the sea, likewise with seven heads and ten horns. The beast does not act independently: ". . . the dragon gave it his power and his throne and great authority" (13:2), that is, the beast's power derives from that of the dragon. John makes it clear to his readers that the beast symbolizes the Roman empire: "it [the beast] was allowed to make war on the saints and to conquer them. It was given authority over every tribe and people and language and nation" (13:7). Scholars debate the meaning of the wound the beast suffered, and I recommend that the interested reader consult a full-scale commentary on Revelation. As for the image of the beast, the sea monster (Leviathan, Behemoth) had a long history in the imagery of the OT.

Next arises yet another beast, this time from the earth (13:11), an allusion that has escaped easy interpretation. This beast gets people to worship the first beast, partly by doing miracles that impress people, but this new beast also persecutes people who do not have the mark of the first beast on their foreheads—a reversal and parody of the mark the blessed received (7:3-4). At a later point in the book John calls this beast a false prophet (19:20), suggesting that he may have been a Jew or Christian who apostasized. We will never know.

Then comes the most famous verse in the book (13:18): the author reveals the identity of the first beast, not by giving a name but a number to be interpreted. The number, of course, is 666. John does not consider this much of a puzzle. He says: "let anyone with understanding calculate the number of the beast." Maybe this was easy in the first century, but not now. Let me explain how this works.

The numbers we use are called Arabic numerals because we got them from Arab mathematicians. Ancient Jews, Greeks, and Romans used letters for numbers; that is, a letter had numerical value. Roman numerals are best known, for example, Pope Benedict XVI means Pope Benedict the 16th. The letter "X" has the value of ten, "V" has the value of five, and "I" has the value of one. What scholars do with 666 is to start with the number and work backward, trying out names of people who could fit the description of the beast and seeing if the letters in their names could add up to 666. But it is not that simple. For example, what is the value of "XIV"? Naturally we think it is 14, because "X" can represent 10 and "IV" can represent 4. But if we add up the value of the individual letters, that is, "X" (10) plus "I" (1) plus "V" (5), we get not 14 but 16.

Another difficulty is determining the name. For example, the leading candidate for 666 is Nero because the name "Nero Caesar" in Hebrew letters adds up to 666. But his name was not just Nero Caesar. He was also called Nero Claudius Tiberius Drusus Germanicus. A colleague of mine once said the best way to interpret 666 is to decide in advance whom you wish it to signify and then arrange his name in letters that add up to 666!

Why is Nero the leading candidate? As just noted, his name in Hebrew can add up to 666. John wrote in Greek, but apocalyptic is a Jewish literary genre, so using Hebrew letters can work. Also, he wrote in the eastern Mediterranean where there was a widespread belief that Nero would return from the dead (the beast is seriously wounded and recovers in 13:14), and he would revenge himself on his enemies, which included the Christians. This is a logical but not conclusive interpretation.

Another possible interpretation is a different understanding of the number six. In the OT seven is the perfect number, and some scholars think that a triple six means triple incompleteness. But could so general an interpretation really be "the number of the beast"? Most scholars accept the identification with Nero.

As so many other NT writers do after a particularly negative passage, John turns to the positive, focusing on those blessed who stood by the Lamb (14:1-5). But he returns quickly to the warnings. This time the angels announce the fall of Babylon, which symbolizes Rome. John got this from the OT. Isaiah (ch. 23) uses Tyre, a Phoenician city, as a symbol of evil, and Nahum (ch. 3) does likewise with Nineveh, the capital of Assyria. The "one like the Son of Man" returns, but now he wears a crown and carries a sickle: "the hour to reap has come" (14:14-15), that is, the final stage has begun.

The newest number seven applies to bowls that carry plagues. Since this apparition tells of seven angels singing a hymn of Moses (15:3), John wants us to recall the plagues God unleashed on Egypt. John even uses direct parallels: the angel turns water to blood (16:4; Exod 7:14-25), frogs overrun the land (16:13; Exod 8:1-15). But the frogs are evil spirits who call together the kings of the world for a war against God at a place called Armageddon (16:16).

When the plagues end, Babylon's time has come. John starts with a famous image, the whore of Babylon. She dresses in scarlet, thus providing another famous image, the scarlet woman. She is drunk, but not with wine: ". . . drunk with the blood of the saints and the blood of the witnesses to Jesus" (17:6), a striking image. Chapter 18 keeps up the pressure on Babylon as an angel announces its fall (18:1). The people of God flee from the coming disaster, but the people of the world mourn the passing of the great city whose sins they had shared. All this deals with the end of the world, and the seer, who has suffered Roman exile, becomes fiercer and fiercer. "Then a mighty angel took up a stone like a great millstone and threw it into the sea, saying, 'With such violence Babylon the great city will be thrown down, and will be found no more'" (18:21).

John switches the scene to heaven where abundant joy greets the imminent marriage of the Lamb to the New Jerusalem, although the seer does not say that here. Babylon may be gone, but the demonic forces still exist. The angels leave heaven temporarily to battle against them. Symbolizing Christ, the rider named Faithful and True mounts his white horse for battle. The forces of good capture the beast and the false prophet (= the second beast). "These two were thrown alive into the lake of fire that burns with sulfur" (19:20).

Another famous and troublesome image appears. "Then I saw an angel coming down from heaven, holding in his hand the key to the bottomless pit and a great chain. He seized the dragon . . . and bound him for a thousand years . . . . When the thousand years are ended, Satan will be released from his prison and will come out to deceive the nations at the four corners of the earth . . ." (20:1-8). This, of course, is the millennium, the belief in the return of Satan to earth after a thousand years. Contrary to common opinion, this phrase did not always mean a literal thousand years. Ancient Christian scholars interpreted the phrase allegorically as a long, even undetermined time, but modern fundamentalists have taken it literally. Catholics have traditionally sided with the ancient scholars, who, as the years 1000 and 2000 have proved, were right. As we noted earlier, eschatological visions should not be turned into clear-sighted predictions of the future.

The forces of good prevail again, Satan joins the beast and the false prophet in the fiery lake of sulfur, and God now initiates the Last Judgment. John introduces yet another famous image: ". . . the book of life. And the dead were judged according to their works, as recorded in the books" (20:12).

Now John returns to Genesis: "I saw a new heaven and a new earth; for the first heaven and the first earth had passed away . . . . I saw the holy city, the New Jerusalem, coming down out of heaven . . . prepared as a bride adorned for her husband" (21:1-2). After enduring so many terrifying visions, John now enjoys blessed ones. An angel says to him, "Come, I will show you the bride, the wife of the Lamb . . . and showed me the holy city Jerusalem" (21:9-10), a powerful contrast: from the whore of Babylon to the bride of the Lamb. Just as wedding guests praise the beauty of the bride, so John praises this celestial bride with famous images such as the pearly gates and the streets of gold (21:21). Again linking the beginning and the end, John tells that the New Jerusalem has trees of life (22:2), recalling the one in the Garden of Eden (Gen 2:9).

John the seer has said some amazing and troubling things in this book, and so he closes it by assuring his readers of his calling. "The angel said to me, 'These words are trustworthy and true' . . . 'Do not seal up the words of the prophecy of this book, for the time is near' . . . 'It is I, Jesus, who sent my angel to you with this testimony for the churches'" (22:6, 10, 16). Thus John claims that both Jesus and the angels have given him this revelation, so who can question it? Since this revelation has such authority, "if anyone adds to them [the prophecies in this book], God will add to that person the plagues described in this book . . . " (22:18). (Some extremist Christians haul out this verse when publishers dare to print abridged Bibles.) Interestingly, this makes Revelation the only NT book whose author claims direct divine inspiration. Other writers, such as Paul and the evangelists, claim to speak the truth and to be faithful to Christ's teaching and example, but they never openly claim divine inspiration.

John's final words remind his readers that Christ is coming soon, and "The grace of the Lord Jesus be with all the saints. Amen."

This is a strange, difficult, and sometimes frightening book. For some Christians, taking away a literal forecasting of the end reduces the book's value. While we can sympathize with their disappointment, misinterpretation does not give a book value. Modern Catholic biblical exegetes, along with other mainstream Christian scholars, insist that we must read Revelation as a first-century book, and we must try to understand what it meant to its intended readers. We may never interpret all that John meant, but we can certainly grasp his central idea: God may seem absent, as in a time of persecution, but he never deserts his people. Human history is not a series of random events but rather a theater of divine activity. God worked through the tumultuous history of Israel, God worked through the suffering history of the first-century church, and God works in the world today. We must join John in recognizing another dimension to human life and history.

Chapter Nineteen

The Second Letter of Peter

I. Greeting (1:1-2)

II. Christian life as the End is near (1:3-21)

III. Condemnation of false teachers (2)

IV. The Second Coming (3:1-16)
   • Reality of the Second Coming (3:1-10)
   • Preparations for the Second Coming (3:11-16)

V. Closing exhortation and doxology (3:17-18)

Because of its brevity and importance this letter should be read in its entirety.

Although a brief, pseudonymous writing, 2 Peter has great historical importance as the last book of the NT to be written. It is usually dated between 120 and 130. Why do scholars date it so late? Since no other document even mentions the book before 220, we must look for evidence within the letter itself.

First, the quality of the Greek makes it clear that an uneducated, Aramaic-speaking fisherman cannot be the author, so there is no need to try to fit it into Peter's life, which ended in Rome in the 60s. Second, the writer alludes to 1 Peter (3:1), so it obviously comes later than that. Third, it also paraphrases Jude, so it also comes later than that. Fourth, when it paraphrases Jude it deletes all the apocryphal references (as we shall see in some detail). This suggests that the author wrote when Christians had become more organized and had reservations about books that quoted apocryphal sources, which could only be true if the Jews or the Christians themselves were forming a canon of the OT. Fifth, "Peter" refers to "all" of Paul's letters, thus showing that he knew of a collection of them, and he also compares them to "the rest of scripture" (we shall also look at this in more detail). It is highly unlikely that Paul's letters would be known in a collection and considered to be scriptural much before the early second century. Sixth, belief in an imminent Parousia is dying out (3:3-10), a sure sign of a later book.

Putting all this together, scholars conclude that a date of 120–130 is the most reasonable. As for the place of writing, we can only guess. The name "Peter" always has us looking toward Rome, and obviously a letter claiming Petrine authorship would be popular there. On the other hand, a community that knew Peter well would be skeptical about an "authentic" letter that suddenly appeared sixty years after the apostle's death. Furthermore, given Peter's prominence, a letter believed to be Petrine would have authority anywhere in the church. There is just no way to prove a place of writing. As for the recipients, the same is true: presumably they were located someplace in the eastern Mediterranean where apocalyptic views maintained popularity into the second century.

The author identifies himself as *Simeon* Peter, a title otherwise used only in Acts 15:14; he insists on his presence at the Transfiguration (2:16-18). Why did the author want so badly to be thought of as Peter? This would give the letter apostolic authority, but why not use James or John? The result would not be same, probably because by 120 Peter's name had become associated with ecclesiastical authority, and this author puts much emphasis on authority.

"Peter" starts with an exhortation to virtue as a proper response to all that God has given his readers (1:3-11). The virtues recommended are typical Christian ones: faith, goodness, understanding, and self-control. This section sounds more like a homily than a letter.

At 1:13-15 "Peter" says that his end is approaching, and he wishes that his readers will persevere after his death. He worries that they might misinterpret prophecy, which is itself a good. Here he first indicates his concern with order: "no prophecy is a matter of one's own interpretation" (1:20). "Peter" believes the interpretation of Scripture belongs to the community.

Next the author turns to another concern, false teachers. He takes over much of Jude's letter to make the point, sometimes using almost the same words: Jude 4: "people . . . who pervert the grace of our God into licentiousness and deny our only Master and Lord, Jesus Christ"; 2 Peter 2:1-2: "They will even deny the Master who bought them . . . many will follow their licentious ways." More importantly, he deletes Jude's apocryphal references. Gone are the angels fighting over the body of Moses (Jude 8-9); gone also is the book of Enoch (Jude 14-15). But "Peter" keeps the authentic OT references to Sodom and Gomorrah (2:6) and to Balaam (2:15). We see that he follows his own concern for order in the community by warning against false teachers but also by eliminating reference to any book whose orthodoxy might be suspect. According to Jewish tradition, a few years before "Peter" wrote, a group of rabbis met to outline for Jews what books belonged in the Hebrew Bible (Christian Old Testament), so the desire for order extended beyond Christian circles.

Next "Peter" turns to the day of the Lord, acknowledging that belief in it has begun to fade. He tries to prop it up by denouncing "scoffers" (3:3) and seeks support in the prophets and the "commandment of the Lord," which has been transmitted by the apostles, again invoking authority for his position. He also uses a weak argument, that "with the Lord one day is like a thousand years, and a thousand years are like one day" (3:8), the second half of that verse being a citation of Ps 90:4. "Peter" does not seem to realize that making God's time so indefinite could be used to posit a long-delayed Parousia as well as an imminent one.

Seeking more authority, he turns to Paul and "all his letters" (3:16), an explicit acknowledgment of a Pauline collection, but since this letter does not cite any Pauline verses we cannot know what letters "Peter" speaks of. He goes on to point out that parts of Paul's letters can be difficult to understand (no argument here!), and that these "the ignorant and unstable twist to their own destruction," thus providing another argument for need of authority. Then Peter drops a bombshell: "as they do *the other scriptures*," here using the Greek word commonly used of the Bible. We cannot be sure exactly how he means the term "scripture," but this strongly suggests that in the author's community Christians had begun to recognize that some of their books were equal in stature and sacredness to the books of the OT. Yet we have no idea how developed this idea was or, as with the reference to Paul's letters, what books "Peter" was talking about, or, as noted above, what community Peter was writing from. Clearly some sense of a canon was growing. What a shame we do not know more.

"Peter" was, of course, wrong about the day of the Lord, as our existence proves. Yet this letter points to the future of the church, a future that would include a new set of Scriptures and the continued growth of ecclesiastical authority.

Some Final Thoughts

This book has introduced you to the books of the New Testament, so what do you do now? Let me make a few suggestions.

An introduction is just that. By definition it cannot do a great deal. I hope this book has helped you to get a general grasp of the NT, but if you wish to know more about it there are several things you can do.

First, and most importantly, read the NT frequently. In this book I suggested that you read portions of various NT books, but try to read them all in their entirety, preferably on some reasonable schedule, e.g., ten pages per day. And consult books like those listed in the bibliography. Today few people can read the NT without some assistance, and many modern scholars have written works accessible to the general reader.

It is absolutely essential to read the Old Testament because every page of the New Testament presumes it. When NT people, Jesus included, speak of Scripture, they mean the OT. This was their Bible. It shaped their religious attitudes, they lived by it, and, as we saw so often, they had to reconcile their own teachings to it. Some parts of the OT are interminably dull, but try the narrative books like Genesis, Exodus, Judges, Joshua, Ruth, the books of Samuel and of Kings. To these add readings in the prophets, especially Isaiah, who figures so prominently in the NT. Also look into the Psalms for some beautiful religious poetry. Books like Proverbs and Job play little role in the NT, but reading them gives you a sense of how OT figures dealt with everyday problems. There are many good introductions to the OT, and some titles in the bibliography can get you off to a good start.

Throughout the book I have tried to separate what the NT actually says from the many traditions that grew up about it and occasionally from misleading media portrayals. Let me be clear. I enjoy many of these traditions, especially at Christmas, and I am not criticizing them. Furthermore, traditions like the names of Mary's parents (Joachim and Anna) and Peter's being crucified upside down may be historically true, but they are not in the New Testament and thus not part of inspired Scripture. Likewise, films about Jesus usually conflate the four gospel stories, which is fine for movies, but they can mislead believers about the NT. As we have seen, to understand the gospels it is important to know why Luke included Jesus' words, "Father, forgive them; for they do not know what they are doing" and "Truly I tell you, today you will be with me in Paradise," and the other evangelists do not, the kind of subtle understanding that films simply cannot provide. So enjoy the traditions, enjoy the movies, but never let what is outside the NT substitute for knowing what is inside it. As you become familiar with the NT, this will become easier to do.

If you are active in your parish, take part in a Scripture reading group. If your parish does not have one, speak with the religious education coordinator about establishing one. The NT authors wrote for communities, and what better way to read the Scriptures than in a community?

The Bible also makes good spiritual reading. There are many fine spiritual writers, both historical (Augustine of Hippo, Bernard of Clairvaux, Teresa of Ávila) and modern (you choose from the multitude!), but you cannot go wrong with your spiritual reading when you read the book inspired by the Holy Spirit. Granted, parts of both the Old and New Testaments, such as genealogies, are hardly spiritually edifying, but many parts of the Bible are and contain superb spiritual insights.

Something else you should do is attend a Jewish Sabbath service. You will be welcomed, you will get a sense of a tradition that extends back to 2000 B.C.E., and you will experience the kind of worship that Jesus himself observed. And if Jewish friends invite you to a Passover *seder*, go and be part of a ritual practiced by Jesus and his disciples. The popes have made Jewish-Catholic ecumenism a central focus, and what better way to practice it?

And, as I said in the Introduction about reading the NT, enjoy it!

For Further Reading

No one book can do the New Testament justice, and you may want to do some more reading. I have listed some titles here, but before getting to them I want to say a few words about choosing books on the Bible. In 1965, Richard Cardinal Cushing of Boston gave his *imprimatur* to *The Oxford Annotated Bible*, an edition of a new Protestant translation called the Revised Standard Version. This action was universally praised by Catholics and mainline Protestants as a great step in the ecumenical understanding of the Bible. This edition had footnotes that explained where Protestants and Catholics differed on the interpretation, such as the virginal conception of Jesus, so that it recognized differences while celebrating commonalities.

When you are choosing a book to read about the Bible, please understand that Catholic and mainline Protestant exegetes will often take the same approach, and they will differ from fundamentalists or extreme evangelicals. This may not be evident when you are looking at the book. A good way to judge is to look at the publisher: is it a mainstream, respectable publisher? Look at the author: does she or he teach at an accredited college or seminary? You can also look to see if the author teaches at a Catholic institution although, in an ecumenical age, the author may be a Protestant or Orthodox Christian. But affiliation with a Catholic institution will assure the reader that the author understands and is sympathetic to Catholic concerns.

The best way to understand the New Testament is to read it, and for that you need a Bible. You can buy a volume that has only the NT, but you should get a complete Bible with the Old and New Testaments. Since Catholics and Protestants disagree on the contents of the Old Testament, Protestant bibles will often include the Apocrypha, which is the name given to the books that Catholics accept as part of the OT and Protestants do not.

Get an annotated Bible, that is, a Bible that will have notes at the bottom of the page to explain some of the verses. These notes were prepared by scholars in order to help the reader understand the text. There is no need to consult them on every verse, but they will be helpful when you come across puzzling references, for example in the OT prophetic books.

There are many good annotated Bibles. A good Catholic one is *The Jerusalem Bible*, which has a modern, often matter-of-fact translation; the NT edition of this is *The New Testament of the Jerusalem Bible* (New York: Doubleday, 1986). Another good one is *The HarperCollins Study Bible: New Revised Standard Version with the Apocryphal Books* (New York: HarperCollins Publishers, 1993). This edition was prepared by the Society of Bible Literature, an ecumenical American scholarly group. The contributing editors are Catholics, Protestants, and Jews. This is not surprising. Today many Bibles are edited ecumenically. And although these are the two versions I used in preparing this book, let me emphasize that many good editions are available.

Once you have a Bible, try to read it on a regular basis. As this book has shown, the "plain text" is nonsense. Most biblical books are sophisticated theological works. On the other hand, the more you read and become familiar with the books, the easier they will become to understand because you will have a sense of the author, his style, and his goals in writing the book.

Books used frequently for preparing this book:

Paul Achtemeier, Daniel Harrington, Robert Karris, George MacRae, and Donald Senior, *Invitation to the Gospels* (Mahwah, NJ: Paulist Press, 2002). An introduction to the gospels for a general audience. I made particular use of MacRae's contribution, which is quoted in the discussion of John's Gospel.

Raymond E. Brown, s.s., *An Introduction to the New Testament* (New York: Doubleday, 1997). The late Father Raymond Brown was America's foremost Catholic exegete, and I relied heavily upon his work—and not just this book—for many passages in my book. This introduction is scholarly, but those who have read this book should be able to use it.

The New Jerome Biblical Commentary, edited by Fathers Raymond Brown, Joseph Fitzmyer, and Roland Murphy (Englewood Cliffs, NJ: Prentice-Hall, 1990). This is a one-volume commentary on all the biblical books, with all the articles by Catholic scholars. It also contains many valuable topical articles on such subjects as Jewish history.

Bart D. Ehrman, *The New Testament: A Historical Introduction to the Early Christian Writings* (2d ed. New York: Oxford University Press, 2000). Ehrman focuses much on how the books came into being in their historical context; unlike Brown, he does not deal much with their theology, but this is a very good introduction to modern approaches to the NT.

Howard Clark Kee, Eric Meyers, John Rogerson, and Anthony Saldarini, *The Cambridge Companion to the Bible* (New York: Cambridge University Press, 1997). This is an ecumenical introduction to the entire Bible and a very good introduction to the Old Testament. It has many useful sidebars explaining difficult terms or historical questions, and it has helpful photographs of the biblical places.

These are not the only works I consulted for this book, but my intent here is to keep the bibliography brief.

Other Resources

Bible dictionaries are very handy. These are usually one-volume works that are mini-encyclopedias that enable you to look up a topic. For example, you are reading about the Pharisees, who had become a well-established group during Jesus' ministry. But you want to know how the Pharisees came into being and what happened to them after the NT. You would consult a biblical dictionary article on "Pharisees," and there would be all the information. Of course, the larger and more detailed the dictionary, the more extensive the information would be.

Another useful tool is a biblical atlas, such as *The Collegeville Atlas of the Bible*, edited by James Harpur and Marcus Barybrooke and published by Liturgical Press. Here you can consult maps that show things such as Paul's missionary travels or the spread of Christianity, and you can look at illustrations, including reconstructions of sites now in ruins such as the Jerusalem Temple. Some atlases are very expensive; *The Collegeville Atlas* is reasonably priced.

Since many passages in the Bible can be confusing, most readers like to have commentaries handy. These come in two forms. There are one-volume commentaries that discuss all the biblical books and also contain topical articles, all in one large volume. There are many of these. The best-known Catholic one-volume commentary, noted above, is *The*

New Jerome Biblical Commentary. It was published in 1990 as a successor to and updating of the 1968 *Jerome Biblical Commentary.* This is a work largely for scholars, although as you get to know the Bible you may find it helpful. Of more use to the general reader is *The Collegeville Bible Commentary,* edited by Diane Bergant, c.s.a., and published by the Liturgical Press and available in one hard-cover volume or two paperback volumes, one for the OT and one for the NT, with Robert Karris as editor of the NT volume. Other one-volume works are often ecumenical in character.

But suppose you don't want to get a commentary for the entire Bible? Many publishers offer commentaries in series so that you can choose to study just the book(s) that interest you. The Liturgical Press offers *The Collegeville Bible Commentary: Old Testament Series* and *The Collegeville Bible Commentary: New Testament Series.* The commentaries run from 64 to 144 pages. The NT series has books on each Synoptic gospel, Acts, Hebrews, Revelation, along with volumes covering more than one book, e.g., John's gospel and the Johannine epistles, or Galatians and Romans. These are inexpensive paperbacks.

A great way to find things in the Bible is a concordance, which is a guide to words used in the Bible, although not extremely common ones like "the" or "in." For example, you know that Jesus cursed a fig tree, but you do not know where that passage can be found. You could consult a concordance. Since it is likely that the word "tree" appears far more often than the word "fig," you would look up "fig," and you find that Jesus' cursing of the fig tree appears in Matthew 21 and Mark 11. So, a concordance sounds like a worthwhile book to have, right? Right, but . . . .

There are two important considerations. First, a book that contains all the words in the Bible is bound to be very large and thus very expensive. This might be a purchase that the parish or school or religious educator's office should make.

Second, the scholarly concordances are to the Greek and Hebrew texts, since those are the actual words of the Bible, but you will be using one for an English translation. Before you get a concordance it is essential that you see what translation the concordance is for. For example, if you are using *The New American Bible,* then a concordance to *The Jerusalem Bible* may not be helpful. To be sure, some words will always be translated the same way, for example, "mother" or "father." But not all words will since, obviously, these are different translations. As we saw in the beginning of this book, the Greek word *episkopos* was translated by two different English words in the same translation (*The Jerusalem*

Bible). So be sure to get a concordance that goes along with the translation you or your group are using.

All the books mentioned already will guide you to further reading, but I want to single out just one valuable text: *Gospel Parallels: A Synopsis of the First Three Gospels*, edited by Burton Throckmorton and published by Thomas Nelson Publishers. This book has the synoptic gospels printed in parallel columns so that you can see how they agree or how they differ. This is a great help in understanding the gospels as theological documents because you can see the evangelists' emphases. For example, in Matt 8:19 a scribe said to Jesus, "Teacher, I will follow you wherever you go," but Luke just says "a man" spoke to Jesus and he does not call him "Teacher." Matthew's audience would be impressed that a scribe, a Jewish religious scholar, had chosen to follow Jesus and used a term of honor to address him. Luke's overwhelmingly Gentile audience would not likely have known what a scribe was or why he would call Jesus "Teacher." As I said earlier in the book, modern Catholic exegetes go through the gospels, noticing a little clue here and a little clue there, and these cumulatively help them to understand how the evangelists understood Jesus and his mission.

There are two other useful sources. Some publishers have periodicals intended for a popular audience. The best-known is probably *The Bible Today*, which is published by Liturgical Press and accessible to a non-professional audience. It has many helpful articles, and it will alert you to new books in the field. It is an essentially popular work, but its contributors are all scholars.

The other useful source is your local Catholic college or university, which will have a theology or religion department whose scholars spend their lives working with general audiences—their undergraduate students. Many professors would be happy to help parishes with adult education programs, and the parishes get people who can offer the most up-to-date understanding of the Bible and who know how to present it to a general audience. Too often this resource is underutilized.

I hope you have enjoyed this book and that it will help you get started on a journey into the joys and insights of the New Testament. All the best!

Index

Judea in the Time of Jesus

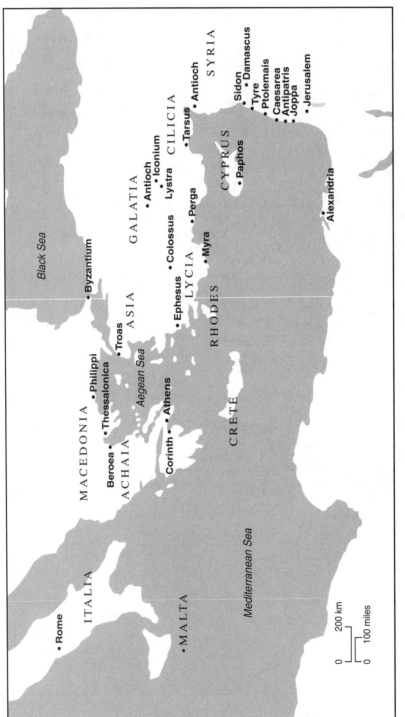

The Roman Empire